Once A Saint

AN ACTOR'S MEMOIR

IAN OGILVY

Constable • London

CONSTABLE

Some names and details have been changed to protect the privacy of others.

First published in Great Britain in 2016 by Constable
This paperback edition published in 2017

1 3 5 7 9 10 8 6 4 2

A CIP catalogue record for this book
is available from the British Library.

ISBN 978-1-47212-202-5

Typeset in Adobe Garamond by Hewer Text UK Ltd, Edinburgh
Printed and bound in Great Britain by CPI Group (UK) Ltd, Croydon CR0 4YY

Papers used by Constable are from well-managed forests and other responsible sources.

Constable
An imprint of
Little, Brown Book Group
Carmelite House
50 Victoria Embankment
London EC4Y 0DZ

An Hachette UK Company
www.hachette.co.uk

www.littlebrown.co.uk

Ian Ogilvy was born in Woking, Surrey and educated at Eton College. After two years at the Royal Academy of Dramatic Art, he went on to a long, successful and continuing career as an actor, and is best known for taking over the part of Simon Templar – the Saint – from Roger Moore. He also appeared in *Upstairs Downstairs*, *I, Claudius*, and many other television productions. He has performed in the West End many times and has appeared in a number of films. His play *A Slight Hangover* was staged in the UK, and he has published two novels – *Loose Chippings* and *The Polkerton Giant*. His series of five children's books about his hero, Measle Stubbs, has been translated into over twenty languages.

Ian Ogilvy lives in California with his wife Kitty, and if you want to know any more about him you really should read this book.

This book is dedicated to those women whom I have loved but whose names I have omitted. When it comes to old lovers, I think linen-laundering should be mostly a private business. Particularly when children are involved. Of course, being left out can be as hurtful as being put in – so, to those who are grateful to have been excluded, you're welcome – and to those offended that I've made no mention of you, I'm very sorry. Just know that our time together was a joy and that, in my cold and heartless way, I love you still.

Acknowledgements

Thanks to my agent, Robert Kirby, at United Agents, for finding me such a prestigious publisher.

Thanks to Andreas Campomar and all at Little, Brown, for being that prestigious publisher.

To Kenneth Roman, author of *The King of Madison Avenue*, the definitive biography of my uncle, David Ogilvy. I found in its pages information about my family I never knew.

To Bill Mcdonald, author of *The True Intrepid*, which has a chapter devoted to the wartime exploits of my aunt, Betty Raymond.

To my wife Kitty, who read the manuscript – something of a chore for her I feel, since she's heard me tell every story contained in it, some of them many times over.

To my children Emma and Titus, who made helpful suggestions, some of which I listened to.

Chapter 1

When I was fifteen years old my father decided that it was high time I had sex with somebody other than myself. 'Come for a drive,' he said.

Going for a drive with Francis Ogilvy meant that you sat in the back seat with him and he told the chauffeur where he wanted to go. My father had never learned to drive. He said he'd tried it once, during the war. He'd been put into a jeep in the middle of an empty parade ground and within half a minute had managed to crash into a wall. It was the first, last and only time he ever got behind the wheel of anything, which was one of two reasons why we had a chauffeur. The other reason was because Francis Ogilvy was the chairman of a large advertising company and it was thought by his fellow executives that a man in his position, who couldn't drive, ought to have a nice car and a chauffeur, which is why the company paid for both of them – a bit of additional good fortune for the Ogilvy family, who could spend the money on something else.

The car we had when I was fifteen was a black and angular monstrosity called the Austin Princess. It was a poor imitation of a Rolls-Royce, built presumably for customers who couldn't

1

afford the real thing – but it did have the required head height in the back seat that my father liked (he measured this by putting on a top hat and insisting on at least two inches' clearance between it and the car ceiling) and the all-important sliding glass partition that separated the passengers – audibly at least – from the chauffeur.

We'd driven in companionable silence for some time, with the partition down, so that my father could tell the chauffeur not to go so fast. Thirty miles an hour was the maximum speed Francis would stand for. Traffic would back up behind us for miles and there was always a lot of horn honking coming from the rear, which the chauffeur was instructed to ignore. At a moment of his choosing, my father pushed the button to raise the partition. Once it had slid into place, he said – in the tone of voice one might use when discussing which pub to visit next – 'Now look here, old boy. Have you ever been to bed with a woman?'

My father had asked me some difficult questions over the years. One of his favourites was, 'Why is a mouse when it spins?' (The proper answer is 'The higher the fewer', but my father preferred his own, which was 'Rhododendron'). But this latest question was an easy one to answer and, to my adolescent mind, a ridiculously superfluous one to ask in the first place. This was 1958. I was a stupid, skinny, incompetent, girlish, bespectacled public schoolboy, entirely lacking in any self-confidence, something of a mother's boy, whose only contact with women had been limited to the mother-whose-boy-I-was, my sister, my nanny and some assorted aunts. Other women – the ones who might at a pinch be prepared to notice me at all – were thin on the ground. The girl who might be prepared to have sex with me was yet to be conceived.

'Not as such,' I said, hedging my bets.

My father turned his head and stared at me, one sandy eyebrow raised. He didn't have to say anything. The eyebrow was enough.

'No,' I muttered.

The head swung back, the pale blue eyes scanning the road ahead for any hazards the chauffeur might have missed. A small cough. A long pause.

'Would you like to?'

'Yes, please.'

'All right. I'll see what can be arranged. Don't tell your mother.'

He pressed the button that lowered the glass partition. 'We can go home now, Bismuth.'

'Very good, sir.'

'Slowly, Bismuth.'

Several weeks went by and I was beginning to think that either my father was all talk and no action, or that he had quite forgotten to do whatever it was he had once intended to do. Then, one evening, when my mother was out of the house, he leaned his massive frame into my bedroom and said, 'I thought we might go out tonight. Wear a suit.'

A suit? I only had one. I put it on. But why? Could this be the moment? I could feel the first tendrils of nervousness crawling about in my stomach.

In the back of the Austin Princess, my father lowered the partition an inch. 'The Embassy please, Bismuth.' (I don't, in fact, know what the chauffeur's name was in 1958. They were inclined to come and go quite frequently. This might have had something to do their collective frustration at the thirty-miles-an-hour restriction).

Ian Ogilvy

'The Embassy. Yes, sir.'

Embassy? Obviously this was some sort of diplomatic evening, to which I was being dragged for some reason or other . . . of course, Francis had been an RAF intelligence officer during the war . . . but how would I be involved? Was this some sort of mission we were on, some sort of Bulldog Drummond adventure involving the Russians – it had to be the Russians, or perhaps the Chinese . . .

The partition slid upwards, cutting us off from the current Bismuth. 'This club – the Embassy Club – I expect you're wondering how I know about it?'

Club? Oh.

My father took my silence as an invitation to explain. 'In advertising, there are lots of clients. We like to keep them happy. Some of them are fairly ordinary sorts of chaps, up from the country for a couple of days. Farmers, some of them. Milk Marketing Board. Egg ditto. You know?' (I did. At one time or another, my father's company handled the advertising for both British milk and British eggs. The slogans were famous. *Drinka Pinta Milka Day! Go To Work On An Egg!*) 'Well, anyway, these chaps like to be entertained when they're in town. We take them to theatres, nice restaurants, and sometimes to nightclubs. The Embassy is a nightclub. There are girls there. Jolly nice girls. They're called hostesses. Their job is to be nice to the clients. They dance with them and talk to them and listen to their boring stories. In return, the clients buy them overpriced champagne and even more overpriced teddy bears. The girls pretend to drink the champagne and they give the teddy bears back to the club when the clients leave. I know most of them quite well. The girls, I mean, not the teddy bears. Don't tell

4

your mother. Now, I don't want you to think I spend any time *alone* with these girls, because I don't. This is just business. Clients and business. Let's be clear about that, all right? But – I like them enormously. The girls. All of them. Great fun. Very pretty. And jolly *nice* girls, I want you to understand that.'

I nodded solemnly. They sounded jolly nice.

'You know what a prostitute is?'

'Yes.'

'These are *not* prostitutes.'

I shook my head. They didn't sound like prostitutes. They sounded like jolly nice girls.

'One of them, in particular, I think you might like to get to know. A jolly nice, jolly pretty girl, called Jasmine. She's twenty-four. I've told her all about you and she's looking forward to meeting you. Would you like to meet her?'

Any nice, pretty, 24-year-old girl who was looking forward to meeting me was a phenomenon only previously encountered in some of my damper dreams.

'Meet her? Oh. Very much. Gosh. Thanks.'

'I think you'll like her.'

I didn't doubt it.

'Of course she's black, you know.'

It was about nine o'clock in the evening. Outside the cocoon of the Austin Princess, London was in darkness. It was darker in the back of the car – but from the lights of passing shop windows I could see that my father's eyes were locked on my face – waiting with a degree of poorly concealed amusement for my reaction.

Looking back at my young self, I like to think that I hadn't even a particle of prejudice inside me and most likely I didn't, considering the liberal way I'd been brought up; but racial bigotry was commonplace at that time, which makes my father's choice of partner for me just that little bit more extraordinary – more extraordinary than if he'd picked, say, a friendly blonde girl from Essex. But any uncertainties I might have felt at hearing that Jasmine was *not* a friendly blonde girl from Essex were submerged that evening beneath the exoticism of the adventure. Nothing this exciting had ever happened to me before and, at that moment, the absolutely least important aspect about pretty twenty four year old Jasmine, who was *looking forward to meeting me*, was the fact that she was black.

'That's all right, is it?'

'Oh – absolutely. Smashing.'

'Glad to hear it.'

I think at that moment that I passed some sort of test of my father's devising. It remained to be seen if I could pass the next one.

The Embassy Club was in Soho. Inside, it was dim and discreet. The walls and ceiling were dark red. A small band played beside a diminutive dance floor. The theme tune, repeated several times in the course of the evening, was 'Luck be a Lady Tonight'. I was rather hoping that luck would have nothing to do with it because, if I was going to have to rely on luck, the night was sure to be a bust.

An obsequious waiter showed us to our booth. He insisted on calling my father 'Sir Francis'. My father, who never in his life got within shouting distance of the New Year's honours list, smiled graciously and ordered a whisky and soda.

'And you, young sir?'

I can't remember what I ordered. It was probably a gin and lime. Alcohol for the underage wasn't really such a very big deal in 1958. Ever since we were quite small, my sister Kerry and I had been encouraged now and then to drink small amounts of wine mixed with water, and early drinking was considered part of growing up. My own boarding school even boasted its own pub, called Tap. It was open to boys of sixteen and up, where – if you worked really hard at it – you could get quite drunk on the weak beer they served. So the only disapproval my father might have felt at my ordering hard liquor, in a nightclub, at the age of fifteen, would have been at my effeminate choice of cocktail. As for the club – well, if it was all right for the Valued Customer's fifteen-year-old son to be ordering a girly wartime drink right under the Valued Customer's nose – and the Valued Customer not appearing to be offering any objection – then it was all right by them.

With the drinks came the girls. Three girls. Two of them hurled themselves at my father, nuzzling his ears and ruffling his hair. 'Francis! Darling! How lovely to see you! Ooh, gorgeous as ever! We missed you! Where have you *been*, you naughty man?'

I was only vaguely aware of all this professional affection going on next to me, because the third girl was standing quietly aloof, gazing at me from a pair of beautiful brown eyes. 'Hello,' she said. 'I'm Jasmine.'

My father was a genius. He couldn't have done it better. Everything about Jasmine was perfect. Perfect, that is, from the point of view of a timid schoolboy who looked like a girl but who was tongue-tied in the presence of a real one. Jasmine was exceptionally pretty, but not overwhelmingly so. The sort of girl-next-door type you yearned for and could conceivably hook up with – rather than say a Brigitte Bardot type, with whom you obviously couldn't.

Jasmine was demure and quiet and only came up to my shoulder. She was dressed youthfully, in a little form-fitting, flowery, shoulder-baring dress. Her skin was the colour of a Starbucks latte. She laughed at everything I said. She smelled wonderful. She sat very close to me. She didn't take her eyes off me. And she liked me *immediately*. Of course, even then, with all my painful naivety, I knew that she was being paid to like me. But she did it so well, so charmingly, that it became easy to pretend to believe it. So I did.

We had dinner. Jasmine and I danced. The band played 'La Cucaracha'. I prided myself on a pretty cool cha-cha-cha and tried it out on Jasmine. She was having none of that Latin separation. She pulled me close to her and we shuffled round the tiny dance floor, locked together like two halves of a clam. My right hand was resting, in the approved fashion, lightly on the small of her back. With her left hand, she moved my right hand down onto her unapproved left buttock. My heart thumped.

The band played several other slow and smoochy numbers, but I only remember 'La Cucaracha'. Later, we went back to the table. My father, surrounded by two girls, three teddy bears and several empty champagne bottles, was getting sleepy. I had another gin and lime. Jasmine snuggled close to me. My arm draped itself accidentally-on-purpose across her shoulders, in the way teenage boys have been managing these things since time and the back row of the cinema began. In the darkness, Jasmine took my hand and pulled it down to cover one small breast. I couldn't breathe.

My father struggled to his feet, dislodging girls and teddy bears.

'Well, I'm tired. I'm going to bed.'

'Noooo! Franciiiiisssss! Pleeeease! Staaaayyyy!'

'No. Bloody exhausted. I'm off. Have fun you two. Don't tell your mother. G'night.'

He started towards the door, which was callous of him, since he'd omitted to tell me what happened next.

'Erm . . .' I squeaked, managing to get halfway out of my seat before Jasmine pulled me firmly back down again.

My father waved and was gone.

Jasmine gave it five more minutes and then whispered in my ear. 'Let's go back to my place.'

We took a taxi, to somewhere in Paddington. Jasmine paid, which was a relief, because I appeared to have come out without my wallet.

Her flat was tiny – not much more than a bedsitter. She disappeared into the bathroom and I stood uncertainly at the foot of the small bed, wondering what I was supposed to do next. Perhaps Jasmine sensed my indecision, because she poked her head out of the bathroom door and said, 'Why don't you take your clothes off?'

Why not indeed? This was going terribly well because Jasmine was doing all the work. If she'd left it to me, nothing would have happened at all.

When I got down to my underwear – which I presumed one kept on until the last minute – I realised to my horror that I was wearing a pair of my Chilprufe underpants. They were hideous, childish things, woollen and baggy, extending from the waist to the knees, the colour of dingy cream, and designed exclusively to keep horny schoolboys chaste – but I couldn't take them off, not until I'd got some sort of green light from Jasmine, who was the undisputed director of this drama. I stood there, shivering slightly and trying to flex my sad little pectorals. Then Jasmine came out of the bathroom, with nothing on at all.

This was as good as any green light. I quickly yanked off the Chilprufes – but Jasmine had seen them. She must have seen them, because she was laughing. Perhaps she was laughing at something else. I didn't know and I didn't care.

Everything went off very satisfactorily. Perhaps because of the gin and limes it lasted marginally longer than might be expected. Then we went to sleep. In the morning, both still squashed together in her small bed, Jasmine said the five most flattering words any woman who didn't love me has ever said to me in the course of my life. 'Shall we do it again?' So we did. Then she drove me home in her smart little car and I sat there next to her, grinning like a chimp, all the way back to our flat in Ovington Square.

When the holidays ended and I went back to my boarding school, I made the mistake of telling my friends the story. Nobody believed a word of it. Why would they? Fathers simply didn't do that sort of thing for their sons. Understandably, I was labelled a lying braggart.

Somehow my mother found out. She was furious. Not with me, with her husband. I think my mother was upset at the idea that I had actually met some of these girls – all of whom she was convinced Francis was bedding – and that the very act of meeting them and then sleeping with one (the whole sordid business arranged by her feckless husband) had somehow put me into the position of siding with him against her.

Also, I've always had a sneaking suspicion that my mother would have quite liked me to be gay.

When I was about four years old, the kindergarten school I went to held a fancy dress competition. I could have gone dressed as a pirate, or a soldier, or a Corsican bandit – anything but what my mother dressed me up as, which was a little girl, in a blonde wig and a party dress and buckled patent leather shoes, in which adorable get-up she blithely sent me off to school. When it was my turn to go up on the platform and tell everybody what I was supposed to be, I said what I'd been told to say. I announced – with excellent diction and enough voice projection to reach the back row – that I was 'a little girl'.

I must have been very convincing, because the kindergarten teacher in charge of the parade (she obviously hadn't penetrated my disguise) bent down to my level and said, 'I know you are, dear – but what have you *come* as?'

Later, when I was about seven, a friend of my mother visited. Mary O'Reilly had a new 8mm cine camera, which was a novelty at the time. My mother decided we should make a film. The plot was simple: adorable little girl (me again) in a pink organdy dress wanders in the rose garden, smelling the flowers. She smiles winsomely at the camera. She skips prettily round the flowerbeds. She plucks a single red rose and looks soulfully at the sky. Then, quite suddenly, she frowns and stamps her foot and shakes a fist at the camera – and then pulls off wig and dress and throws away the rose and stands there in her Chilprufe underwear, revealing herself to be not a pretty little girl at all – but a rude and obstreperous *boy*!

By the time the idea for this film was being bandied about, I was old enough to realise that something was not quite right about it. I put forward my objections, but my mother overruled them all by saying that Mary would be *dreadfully* upset if we didn't do the film the way she planned it – and she'd come *all* the way from Manchester – and she was our *guest* after all – and it wouldn't take very *long* – and it would be really *funny*.

I suggested that it wouldn't be in the least bit funny, that it wasn't Mary O'Reilly's idea in the first place, and that my sister could do it better than me.

'But Kerry *is* a girl, darling. That sort of destroys the joke, do you see?'

I did the film. But my shame all the way through the skipping and the smelling and the plucking was palpable, and my rage at the end was real and not acted. When I finally ripped the dress off, I think I managed to tear it in half, and the wig was never useable again.

Whether it was these small efforts on my mother's part to nudge me ever closer to my feminine side – or whether my father simply thought I was a bit of a sissy who needed a hearty shove in the opposite direction – I don't know. All I do know is that, at the age of fifteen, my father got me laid, a gift from him for which I am eternally grateful. What he (and Jasmine of course) achieved in a single night was to make me much more confident, much less nervous, and much fonder of him than I ever thought possible – and it broke forever the fragile hold my mother had over me when it came to matters of the heart.

Chapter 2

The first place I remember living was in London. It was a large flat in Hanover House, in St John's Wood, close to Lord's cricket ground and London Zoo. The number of our flat was 74. There was a 74 bus which took us everywhere. Later, at my prep school, my number was 74. There were 74 boys there. I'm not superstitious but I like the number 74 and, if I come across it during my day, I feel just that little bit better about things.

Hanover House was (and still is) a red brick mansion block of flats, overlooking a small park. In front of the park there was (and still is) a bronze statue of St George killing the dragon, which was the first statue I ever saw. To my childish eyes – and to my grown-up ones as well – the battle between saint and serpent looked very one-sided. Dragons were supposed to be big – much bigger than, say, a horse. Tenniel's illustration of the Jabberwocky (undoubtedly a species of dragon) in Carroll's *Through the Looking-Glass* showed an enormous and grotesquely scary creature, with bulging eyes and scaly skin and hideous leathery wings. As a child, the picture unsettled me – although some of the dread it inspired was offset by the fact that the

13

Jabberwocky had teeth exactly like Bugs Bunny and was sporting a jaunty white waistcoat with three buttons on it.

But this dragon in St John's Wood was a puny thing, not much larger than a golden retriever – and I remember thinking that it couldn't have been all that difficult for bullyboy George to trot his enormous horse up to the little reptile, give it a bit of a trample, and then in a casual sort of way lean over the side of his steed, as the statue depicts him doing, and leisurely stick the point of his lance into the poor creature. Not difficult at all and certainly not very dangerous. It was the sort of thing that even Nanny could have done.

There was a railway bridge near the statue and Nanny would let me lean over the parapet and watch the trains go by underneath. They were all steam trains in those days – not an electric or a diesel engine to be seen. They passed by underneath quite slowly, making a tremendous amount of noise and smoke and steam – those arriving at nearby Marylebone station slowing down, those departing gathering momentum. I remember enjoying being enveloped in all this noise and smoke and steam as the trains chuffed by beneath me – the enveloping being the whole point of leaning over the parapet in the first place – and now of course I wonder just how many carcinogenic particles I was inhaling into my young lungs while dear Nanny – who, like everybody else, probably thought coal smoke was fairly harmless stuff – looked fondly on.

Very little was considered dangerous back then, possibly because, after suffering first the Blitz and later the flying bombs, there was nothing Londoners were scared of any more. There were no seatbelts for cars, no helmets for cyclists – or for motorcyclists either – no flu shots, no emissions controls, no speed limits outside of urban areas, just one available antibiotic, our first refrigerator had a lock on it, there were no vitamin pills and nobody had ever heard of cholesterol, or dyslexia, or chemotherapy – and the only radiation you might receive were the amusing X-rays that bombarded your feet when you bought a new pair of shoes.

When it was time to buy new shoes, my sister Kerry and I would be taken to Selfridges children's department. There was a wonderful machine there called a shoe fitting fluoroscope. It consisted of a vertical wooden cabinet with an opening near the bottom into which you put your feet. When you looked through one of the three viewing ports on the top of the cabinet (one for you, one for your mother and one for the sales lady) you could see a fluorescent image of the bones of your feet contained in the outline of your new shoes. There you were, looking down at your own feet – that weren't ordinary feet any more, they were *skeleton* feet, and you were looking right through the shoes and the skin and the muscles, and everything glowed a beautiful emerald green, just like Superman's kryptonite and no doubt just as damaging – and you could see exactly how your feet fitted inside your new shoes, and you could wiggle your toes and see the bones moving, which was very exciting – and never mind the X-rays that were sizzling through your young tissues and doing heaven knows what damage, or the fact that on one occasion involving the operation of these machines it was reported that a shoe model received such a serious radiation burn that her leg had to be amputated.

Cigarettes were everywhere. My father smoked two packs of unfiltered Players a day. Cocktail parties were popular and my parents gave lots of them. Kerry and I were given the job of passing round the canapés. Everybody drank hard liquor – martinis, whisky and soda, gin and french – and everybody, almost without exception, smoked cigarettes. Kerry and I, two adorable little waiters, spent much of our childhood wreathed in nicotine smoke.

In 1947, when I was four years old, Francis decided we should have a vacation. While everybody else in bleak, poverty-stricken, post-war Britain was going to Margate, or Brighton or Westcliffe-on-Sea for their summer holidays (or, just as likely, staying at home) Francis decided we should go to Corsica.

Getting to Corsica was no picnic. A train to Dover. A rusty ferry across the English Channel. A slow train to Paris. A slower train all the way down to the south of France. Another primitive ferry to Corsica. No taxis. A dusty, rattling old bus to our final destination, which I think was Calvi – at that time little more than a sleepy village. I remember almost nothing about this holiday, other than it was very hot – and then there was the part when, shortly after we got home, I developed a high fever that put me into a coma and nearly killed me. A number of doctors were called to the bedside and they all retreated, baffled. Nobody knew what was wrong with me. In desperation, my mother contacted a woman called Mrs Barraclough, who claimed to be able to diagnose any disease using her own distinctive method. She collected some of my saliva on a piece of pink blotting paper. Then, from her handbag, she took a small silver ball on the end of a thin silver chain and swung the ball over the blotting paper. She watched the ball's gyrations closely for a couple of minutes. Then Mrs Barraclough stuffed the contraption back into her handbag. 'Malaria,' she announced. And she was right.

I've never put any sort of trust in alternative medicine, but I can't deny that Mrs Barraclough got right what a score of doctors got wrong.

Years later I was going through some old books in my late father's library. A sheet of thin, flimsy paper fell out of one of them. It was headed *Top Secret – For Your Eyes Only*. It was a short wartime report on the island of Corsica and its suitability – or otherwise – for the establishment of military bases for service in the Mediterranean. Its conclusion was that Corsica was not a suitable place for a military base – and not really suitable for anything in fact – as its many marshes were infested with the *Anopheles mosquito*, the primary carrier of malaria. Obviously this was a report that my father had either read and forgotten all about, or had never bothered to read in the first place. Or perhaps he'd got as far as 'Corsica – an island in the Mediterranean sea . . .' and had then given up reading the report because something more interesting had come along. That's the alternative I like best – the idea that, at some point during the war, the germ of an idea for a future holiday destination had been planted in his head. Of course, had he bothered to read any further, he might have discovered all about the multitude of germs that would later be planted in me.

Beneath us in Hanover House, in the flat directly below number 74, there lived an ogre called Mr Archibald. When Kerry and I made too much noise, he would bang on his ceiling with a broom. I never saw Mr Archibald and I never wanted to. Fearsome tales were told of him by my father, about his cannibalism and his pointed teeth and his special fondness for the meat of young children. Just walking past his door scared me silly. When I was older and less gullible, it occurred to me that (A) Mr Archibald was in all likelihood not a cannibal at all and (B) there was a distinct possibility that Mr Archibald didn't even exist, and that all the banging we'd heard had been my father thumping on our own floor whenever Kerry and I got too boisterous. It wouldn't have been the first of his impersonations. After all, wasn't the Easter Bunny my father all along? He'd sneak out of our front door, put the cardboard Easter eggs (sugar rationing dictated that it would be many years before cardboard would convert to chocolate) on the doormat, ring the bell – and then dart back inside before Kerry and I could catch him at it. After a few years – I was probably no older than five or six – he got bored of this trick and admitted that it had been him all along. And, if he was going to come clean about being the Easter Bunny, he might as well go the whole hog and admit he was also the Tooth Fairy *and* Father Christmas to boot.

'Right, now look here you two. The Easter Bunny? Me. The Tooth Fairy? Me again. Father Christmas? Do you see a pattern emerging?'

Kerry and I didn't mind at all about him being the Easter Bunny and the Tooth Fairy and, after he'd finished explaining about Father Christmas – how all these presents we were receiving (and would *continue* to receive) were bloody expensive and he was damned if a fat man in a red suit who didn't exist in the first place should get all the credit for them – then we didn't mind about him being Father Christmas either. In fact, it was a great relief, even at that early age, not having to believe in something so improbable. The whole letter to Santa business, for instance – you scribbled down what presents you wanted, then you set the note on fire and watched the ashes float up the chimney . . . how, I wanted to know, could Father Christmas possibly read a cinder? And then there were the flying reindeer, and the fact that I'd once heard Santa, blundering about in the darkened bedroom where I was trying to fall asleep, snarl, 'Oh Jesus Christ God almighty where the buggering hell is the bloody thing?' It was a comfort to know the truth, and it was comforting to know that all you had to do was ask for it. And you always got the truth from Francis Ogilvy. Or at least *his* truth, which nearly always made more sense than anybody else's truth. To this day I can't help feeling slightly appalled at – and embarrassed for – a child of eight, or nine, or ten, who still believes in Santa Claus.

Francis felt the same way about God and Jesus and the Holy Ghost as he did about the Tooth Fairy, the Easter Bunny and Father Christmas. 'Arrant nonsense,' he would say. 'But believe what you like. Just don't ask me to believe it.' He hated going round the great art galleries of the world – the Louvre, the Prado, the National Gallery – and would usually refuse to do it. 'I cannot stand looking at endless pictures of that bloody family.'

Music left him cold. 'I know only two tunes. One is 'God Save The King' and the other one isn't.' He loved language and words. He sent a memo to the copywriters at his firm – 'Read ten pages of the Bible or Robert Louis Stevenson every morning before you get up. And thank God on your knees every night that you are not a Frenchman with the thinnest vocabulary in the world.' (An interesting exhortation that, from a committed atheist). With the benefit of his Latin scholarship, he also sent them this linguistic caveat: 'I know we're all very proud of our classical educations, but I won't tolerate 'per capita'. It should either be 'per caput' or 'a head.' (In the long run he seems to have lost that battle – everybody now uses the grammatically incorrect version).

An early memory was a scarlet steel racing car, which I got for Christmas one year, a present from my parents and not from the fat man in red. It was the sort of car you could sit in and pedal along the pavement. Unfortunately the thing was so heavy I never managed to pedal it at all, but it looked terrific, so it and me and Kerry were taken regularly to the small park across the road to play. I quickly abandoned the racing car and tried to impress Kerry's small girlfriends instead. I would spin round and round, trying to go as fast as I could. Then, dizzy, I'd fall over. 'That's what Scotch people do,' I said, improvisation being my forte. Since I was terminally cute, the little girls would giggle and clap and kiss me, giving me an early taste for the limelight.

I remember a lamplighter coming round the neighbourhood at dusk. He rode a bicycle and carried his long lamp-lighting pole over one shoulder. He'd stop at each street lamp, extend his pole, flip open the glass door and apply the flame to the gas jet. I remember the coal wagons, pulled by a pair of huge and dusty carthorses, which made weekly deliveries up and down our street. The coal men wore leather caps with long leather flaps that extended down their backs to protect them from the filthy coal sacks. They would hoist sacks onto their backs, and carry them to a round manhole cover set in the pavement. A special hooked tool pulled up the iron cover – then, with a rattle and a roar, the coal men would upend their sacks, sending the contents rumbling down into the coal cellar below.

Not surprisingly, impenetrable and toxic fogs were common. They were caused by the millions of London chimneys belching dense coal smoke day and night. The smoke mixed with the harmless winter mists, forming life-threatening smog. Some of these smogs were so thick that you could see only a few feet in front of you. The problem culminated in the great smog of December 1952. The effects of this phenomenon were horrible: it was thought that about twelve thousand Londoners died in the immediate aftermath, and a further eight thousand died in the following weeks and months.

We went to the theatre. Both parents having been actors, we went to a lot of theatre. We went to a pantomime every year at Christmas, musicals throughout the year, and anything else that they thought might be remotely suitable for children. I walked out of *Peter Pan* because the clock-swallowing crocodile, with its built-in tick-tocking warning device, scared me silly. We saw John Mills in *Charley's Aunt* and we went backstage afterwards to meet him. I remember thinking how small he was. We saw Annette Mills, who was John Mills' sister. Annette Mills had an early TV show for small children called *Muffin the Mule*, and she also did a live show in the theatre. All I remember of that act was her sitting at the piano and singing to Muffin, who was a large wooden string puppet. His hooves clicked and clacked as he danced on top of the piano, almost drowning out Annette's song, which went, 'We want Muffin, Muffin the Mule, dear old Muffin, playing the fool, We want Muffin, ev'rybody sing, we want Muffin the Mule!' There was a lot more to the show but that's all I can remember – apart from going backstage at the end and meeting Annette Mills and looking at Muffin, who was a tremendous disappointment because he was lying dead in one corner of her dressing room, in a heap of painted wood and tangled string.

When Kerry and I were both in our teens, Francis took us to see a brand new and sensational show called *West Side Story*. My father knew nothing about music but, if forced to listen to it, he quite liked simple bouncy tunes from shows like *Oklahoma,* or his favourite, *My Fair Lady.* Within moments of the orchestra striking up the jazzy, syncopated overture of Leonard Bernstein's masterpiece, my father struggled to his feet.

'Right. Come on. This is frightful. We're going home now.' Kerry and I dragged him back down into his seat, but he left at the interval and we had to make our own way home. After that, he became suspicious of the theatre and hardy went at all. It didn't help that some of the enjoyment he'd experienced in the past was no longer there because he was becoming deaf. 'I'm being punished,' he announced, with gloomy satisfaction. 'When I was an actor, everybody said I was very good, but they could never hear a bloody word I said.'

One of the last times Francis went to the theatre was when he took a number of important business clients to the brand new hit West End show, *The Sound Of Music.* Nobody had warned him about it. Five minutes after the curtain went up, Francis had seen enough. He struggled from his seat, turned and addressed the Very Important Clients – and, indeed, the entire audience, since he and the clients were sitting in the front row of the stalls. 'Jesus *Christ!*' he roared. 'Nuns and *fucking* children! I'm off!'

We went often to the London Zoo, which was just down the road. It was a bad zoo then – but I suppose they all were in those days. Most of the animals were confined in small, bare cages, reduced to pacing endlessly up and down all day long on patches of urine-soaked concrete. The smell in the lion house was noxious. Guy, the famous silverback gorilla, sat lethargically in his narrow enclosure, motionless apart from his eyes, which gazed with scorn at the gaping crowds. You could ride on the elephants and the camels, you could feed most of the animals with anything you happened to have on you – the white rhino was very fond of buns – and at four o'clock in the afternoon, the chimpanzees had a riotously funny tea party whether they wanted one or not.

I saw old Queen Mary – the widow of George V and the grandmother of Queen Elizabeth II – gliding by in her car. The old lady looked neither to the right nor the left, and she certainly didn't lower herself to acknowledge the group of patriotic, flag-waving little kindergarteners gathered on the school steps to watch her stately passage.

Rationing was still in full force. Ice cream was a luxury, as was anything made with sugar. A big treat was an orange with a hole cut in the top. A cube of white sugar was stuck in the hole and you squeezed and sucked the juice through the sugar lump until the thing went dry. Food at home was limited to a few things like Spam or corned beef, so sometimes we went out to lunch. There weren't so many places to eat out in London then, so you went more often to the restaurants of the great hotels – the Ritz, the Savoy, the Berkeley – where my father seemed to be very well known because the head waiters were always asking him if he would like the usual. I developed a taste for potted shrimps and also for steak Diane, a spectacular dish cooked at your table in flaming brandy. I ordered that so often that eventually my father told me to stop and have something else. Injured, I asked why I couldn't have what I wanted?

'The potted shrimps are all right, I suppose.'

'Dreadfully common,' said my mother who, since she'd retired from acting and was with a man who had a proper job, had become a snob – and yet, as the daughter of a perfectly nice but quite ordinary country doctor, had not the slightest reason to be one.

'I don't give a damn about that,' said Francis. 'That bloody steak though – it's appallingly vulgar to have all that fire and smoke right beside the table.'

Being quite common myself, I've had potted shrimps several times since then, but I never ordered steak Diane again.

Chapter 3

In the nineteen months between my birth (in September 1943) and the death of Adolf Hitler, the Führer sent 9,500 V1 flying bombs across the English Channel. He also launched the even more destructive V2 rockets, about 1,400 of them – all of which missed me, but hit a lot of other people instead.

We were fairly safe in Surrey, of course, which is why my father had evacuated us to the country instead of keeping us in London with him. He was relatively protected during these aerial attacks, since he was stationed in the underground War Rooms, serving as one of many RAF intelligence officers to Winston Churchill. Churchill defined one of the requirements for his staff as the ability to write well – '. . . like that man who's writing the bombing reports.' It was my father who'd been writing them.

Francis rose through the ranks of the Royal Air Force, ending up as a wing commander. The rank had nothing to do with flying. As far as I know, he never once got into an aeroplane during the war, instead doing his specialist job in the basement of the New Public Offices, at the corner of Horse Guards Road and Great George Street. There, under a five-foot-thick layer of bombproof concrete called The Slab, he spent the entire war (according to him) advising Winston on how to run things. The War Rooms are open to the public and his name can still be seen, as one member of a duty roster, on a yellowing sheet of paper in a glass frame on one of the doors down there.

Meanwhile, my mother Aileen, my sister Kerry and I cowered in Surrey. Shortly after I was born, my mother – who had a hard enough time coping with one baby and was finding it intolerable coping with two – advertised for a nanny to help her out. An Estonian refugee called Aime Domberg came to the door. She took one look at my eighteen-month-old sister Kerry, who was clinging to my mother's skirts and squalling about something or other, then a second look at newborn me in my mother's arms (also probably squalling) and tried to retreat. My mother claimed that she went down on her knees and, with tears streaming theatrically down her cheeks, begged the woman to stay for just a few weeks. When Miss Domberg hesitated, my mother thrust me into her arms and said, 'Here, this one's quite small – just help me with this one.'

Aime Domberg – (whose real name was Nanny) – stayed and looked after us all for the next sixteen years.

When the war ended, Wing Commander Francis Ogilvy took off his uniform and went back to work for his pre-war employers, the advertising firm of Mather & Crowther.

My father had several jobs before becoming an ad man. Born in 1903, he'd enjoyed stellar scholastic careers at Fettes and Cambridge. After university, he'd been a schoolmaster (until he discovered he disliked poverty and mobs of small boys), an oil salesman in Calcutta (until he became deathly ill and had to be sent home), an actor (until he discovered he hated poverty and actors), a theatrical producer (again with the poverty and the actors) and a waiter (only because he discovered that being a vagrant and sleeping on the Embankment was marginally worse) – until finally in 1929 he answered an advertisement in *The Times* placed there by Mather & Crowther, in search of a copy writer.

My father wrote them a short letter: 'I have no idea what a copy writer does, but I'm your man.' They took him on and, by the time he returned to his old job after the war, he was their managing director. Times were different then. Try that tactic now and see how far you get.

Francis wasn't my only relative to help Churchill win the war. There were two others. One was my father's younger brother, David Ogilvy. The other was my mother's younger sister, Betty Raymond.

Both, at one time or another, worked under the leadership of Sir William Stephenson – the 'Quiet Canadian' – whose wartime code name was 'Intrepid'. Stephenson – a Canadian millionaire – created and funded a shadowy, semi-secret organisation called the British Security Coordination. He was the central figure in covert operations between the United Kingdom and the United States in the years leading up to (and during) the war. The BSC was initially headquartered in a nondescript room – number 3603 – in Rockefeller Center in New York, and Stephenson's title there was 'British Passport Control Officer'.

Stephenson was a small man, of few words and even fewer bodily movements. This strange stillness, combined with his piercing eyes and his disconcerting silences, struck terror into many of his staff – a response magnified by his almost super-natural ability to disappear into a crowd and then reappear at a spot several miles away in just a few minutes. People remarked that you could be having a conversation with a couple of colleagues and Bill would suddenly be there – and they'd never seen him arrive; and then, quite suddenly, Bill wouldn't be there any more – and they'd never seen him leave.

Ian Fleming partly modelled his James Bond character on Stephenson, even down to the Canadian's favourite drink, a martini shaken not stirred.

This was the extraordinary man for whom both my Uncle David and my Aunt Betty worked during the war.

Among other talents, Betty Raymond was a professional forger.

When the war started in 1939, my aunt was working as a bookkeeper in a small country hotel. My father and mother were together by this time, although not yet married. Francis was already working for the intelligence services and he recruited his future sister-in-law because she fitted the descrip-tion of what his superiors were looking for at that time – 'Two or three women of education, whom they could trust, and who would be good with their hands.'

Betty started training in the spy business, where it was discov-ered that her manual dexterity was of a very high order. She was a tiny woman, only just over five foot tall – a pretty, fluffy little blonde with a sharp brain, an even sharper tongue and small, delicate hands. She was taught a number of extraordinary skills by an expert craftsman in the business of skullduggery, a veteran of World War I called William 'Steam Kettle' Webb. Once the training period was over, Betty and another woman called

Dorothy Hyde joined the ranks of the British Security Coordination and were sent to a mail interception centre on the island of Bermuda – which I can't help suspecting must have been rather a treat, if only to get away from the German bombs, English weather and Spam.

Suspect letters and documents were routed to this mail interception centre, and it was Betty's and Dorothy's job to examine them. But not just examine – they had to be able to put everything back together again, eradicating any evidence that the papers had ever been tampered with. The work was detailed, painstaking and nerve-wracking. A neatly sliced-open letter would have to be repaired using a technique of 'chamfering' the two edges of the paper, so that they could be then glued together without trace. Roughly torn-open documents would have to be repaired using undetectable glues, like the whites of eggs. Betty learned how to use a glass rod with a hook at one end to remove a letter without disturbing the envelope at all – and then replace it using the same technique. Once, by mistake, a letter to a member of the British royal family was intercepted and ripped open; extra special care had to be exercised putting that one back together.

Sometimes Betty had to travel to the documents, rather than having the papers come to her. Often on these occasions, she had only a limited number of hours or even minutes to complete the job, while the courier from whom the documents had been stolen was distracted for as long as possible. One package she had to open and then close up again consisted of a single sheet of very soft, very porous paper, folded in half, stuck all the round the edges with some sort of brown glue and then sewn together with thread – and there was a wax seal to cope with too. She had twenty-four hours to handle this. When she finally got the package open it was in shreds. She handed it over to her boss and he went white with terror – but Betty managed to reassure him that everything would be all right. She took a short nap while the contents of the document were being examined. Then, when the tattered paper was returned to her, she asked only to be left strictly alone with it for as long as possible. Somehow or other, she managed to repair the damage and the document was replaced in the unsuspecting courier's bag, intact and unblemished, by noon the following day.

She was also one of a handful of people who could forge signatures. They could take hours to perfect. Betty would practise two or three hundred times. Some signatures were harder than others and sometimes, if copies of the document weren't available, she would be given only one attempt. As Betty later explained, once begun, a signature had to be finished in one smooth movement – any break in the pen strokes would be instantly detectable by an expert in forgery. On one occasion, working with her co-forger Dorothy, the signature proved so complicated as to be almost impossible to reproduce; *almost* impossible – but, ingeniously, they got it done in the end.

The story was this: a fake letter had been produced by British intelligence, purportedly from a real Major Elias Belmonte, of the Bolivian legation, who was stationed in Germany. The letter was addressed to Ernst Wendler, the German minister to Bolivia. It was known that Major Belmonte was rabidly pro-Nazi, and the British authorities were concerned that, with his backing, some right-wing military figures in Bolivia might attempt a coup against their own government – a coup that would be supported by the Nazis. German influence could then spread, from that source, all over South America.

So a letter from Belmonte to Ernst Wendler was concocted in Canada, on stolen Bolivian legation notepaper, filled with damning evidence of Belmonte's ties to Germany. The text was riddled with Belmonte's fervent hopes that Bolivia and the rest of South America be soon saved from all North American influence – to be replaced of course with good, strong, commonsense National Socialism, in an exact copy of the good, strong, commonsense German pattern.

The letter was a perfect piece of counter-espionage. But Major Belmonte's signature was a problem. It was proving impossible to do at all. First Betty would try to do it, then Dorothy would have a go – but neither woman was satisfied with the results. Then, in a flash of inspiration, they decided to break the rule about a signature being completed in a single, flowing stroke of the pen. Dorothy wrote the first half of the name, and then Betty completed it. It looked good. They practised for hours, perfecting the forgery. Finally, they wrote it together, at the foot of the fake letter.

They voiced their concerns about the signature to their boss, William Stephenson. Stephenson sent the letter to Canada, to be examined by handwriting experts from the Royal Canadian Mounted Police. The Canadians were told that the signature was suspected of being a forgery – could they confirm BSC's misgivings? The experts examined examples of Belmonte's real signature and compared them, under a microscope, to Betty's and Dorothy's forgery – and declared the thing to be genuine. The letter was dispatched, then conveniently 'stolen' from the courier in Buenos Aires, where an FBI agent reported the theft to Washington. The letter was handed over to J. Edgar Hoover. British and American authorities – themselves under the impression that the letter was a real one, actually written by Major Belmonte – pressed for its release to the Bolivians. Soon its contents were all over South America. The *New York Times* reported, 'Photostat copies of the letter, whose signature was authenticated by the chief of the Bolivian general staff, were published in all morning papers.'

The forged letter resulted in a seismic shift in the attitudes of most South Americans towards the Axis powers. The immediate result was the expulsion of the German minister in Bolivia, the closing of the German mission in La Paz, the arrest of Nazi sympathisers and a general cold-shouldering of German officialdom all over South America.

Six months later, most Central and South American countries broke off all relations with Germany – a decision that (according to US Under Secretary of State Sumner Welles) – '. . . saved New World unity'.

Betty was once asked to forge the signature of Lord Halifax, Britain's ambassador to the USA. She had no idea what she was signing – the top half of the paper was covered over. It could have been something important, like a discussion of troop availabilities – or it could have been a request from the ambassador for a fresh pot of Cooper's Oxford marmalade. My aunt never did find out which.

Betty and Dorothy were moved around, sometimes to Washington, sometimes to New York. In a corridor in some nameless building, she ran into David Ogilvy. Neither was aware that the other was working for the same boss. They knew each other slightly – they had met once or twice because of the developing relationship between my father and mother. Betty greeted David warmly, but he cut her dead. He stormed off to his superiors and complained that he had just been accosted by somebody from the UK, whom he knew slightly but who had no business behaving towards him as an equal since she was, no doubt, some sort of junior cipher clerk. David's immediate boss checked out Betty's status – and then told him not to jump to conclusions, since Miss Raymond not only had a much higher security clearance than David, but she also officially outranked him by several degrees.

The only thing about this story that redeems my Uncle David somewhat is that he told it to me himself.

Betty even had a close call with violent death. Returning from a covert operation somewhere in the Caribbean, she was on board a passenger-carrying banana boat sailing to New York. The shabby little ship was infested with Nazi sympathisers. One night, out on the open deck, she was approached by a young man with a German accent. He had a hypodermic syringe in one hand. He tried to stab the needle into her thigh. She ran, with her would-be attacker close behind her. Frantically searching for somewhere safe, she ended up bursting into the cabin of an attractive young American civilian and spent the rest of the voyage hiding with him in his bed.

After that adventure, Bill Stephenson gave her a gas gun for protection. It was in the form of an ordinary-looking fountain pen, but when you pressed the metal clip, it fired a burst of concentrated tear gas into the face of your attacker. Stephenson had a pen of his own and had actually used it once to save his life – something Betty never had to do but, as she said, it was nice to know you could.

I have this pen, along with some of her letter-opening tools: a thin piece of ivory, a pair of scalpels and her glass rod with a hook at one end.

Betty sailed back to England in 1942, on a merchant ship that was part of a large convoy. Halfway across the Atlantic her ship broke down. German U-boats were operating in the North Atlantic and were decimating the convoys that were bringing sorely needed materials to England – so they stopped for nothing and nobody; Betty's armada steamed away, leaving them alone and horribly exposed. A powerless ship wallowing helplessly in the Atlantic swells was an easy target for a torpedo. For a day and a half the crew worked feverishly to repair the damage, while everybody else on board sat waiting for the explosion – which never came. They were lucky that time, and the ship eventually made it to friendly waters.

Betty was given a job in London by the new American spy agency, the OSS. (The Office of Strategic Service; it was the forerunner of the CIA). They gave her a flat near the American embassy in Grosvenor Square and £80 a month – an enormous sum in those days. But she never did a day's work for them, because they never once called on her services.

Bill Stephenson did, though. In the United States – in Bermuda and Washington and New York – he had been her remote and rather frightening boss; but, on his frequent visits to England, Intrepid became her lover.

Not much is known about this affair. In later years, when talking about these events, Aunt Betty was understandably coy; Stephenson was a married man, after all, and this was wartime and there were secrets that needed to be kept. But she did tell one story that demonstrates their relative closeness. When the

V1 rockets first appeared over London – the dreaded doodle-bugs with their put-put-puttering pulse engines emitting hell-ish crimson flames – Betty saw and heard one from her flat in North Audley Street. She had no idea what it was, and the sudden silence when its engine was automatically shut down, followed by the whistle of the doodlebug's descent and the subsequent *crump!* of the explosion, terrified her. Betty grabbed the telephone and called Stephenson where he was staying at Claridge's hotel a couple of blocks away. 'Bill, I'm frightened! What is this? What do I do?'

'Nothing serious, dear. Put the phone down and put your head under the pillow,' was the less-than-helpful reply.

It was a clandestine wartime romance, nothing more. And after 1945, Betty never saw him again.

In the late 1950s and into the 1960s, Betty worked for Hughie Green and his long-running television show, *Opportunity Knocks*. The programme was the forerunner of all contemporary talent shows, and was wildly popular. Betty's job, which she did alone, was spotting and booking the acts. It meant long hours in the cold and echoing ballrooms of station hotels, in places like Sheffield and Cardiff and Southend-on-Sea, auditioning one interminable act after another and trying to sort the ludicrous from the bad and the passable from the good.

Hughie Green was an Englishman who had spent time in Canada as a child and who later, at the outbreak of the war, joined the Canadian Air Force, ferrying aircraft across the Atlantic. He spoke with a strange, mid-Atlantic accent that always sounded fake to me, as did his used-car-salesman smile, which rarely left his face – or rather, being one of those leering, lopsided sorts of smiles, rarely left one half of his face. He had a beautiful daughter called Linda and, when we were both about sixteen, I fell in love with her. She only *liked* me back. She was the first of my cardiac disappointments.

Hughie's catchphrase was, 'And I mean that most sincerely' – and he used it whenever he praised an act on the show, which he did with most of the acts, no matter how awful they were. And some of them were pretty awful, although a few discoveries were made and some subsequent careers blossomed. Freddie Starr, Su Pollard, Paul Daniels, Bonnie Langford, David Whitfield, Les Dawson, Little and Large, Frank Carson, Pam Ayres, Pete the Plate Spinning Dog – they all owe a debt of gratitude to Hughie Green.

The oddest act Aunt Betty ever booked was Tony Holland. Tony was a handsome young bodybuilder. His performance consisted of him putting a record on the turntable – (it was a catchy little number called 'Wheels', recorded by a group with the happy-sounding name of The String-A-Longs) – and then, stripped down to a pair of brief Speedos, Tony would twitch his muscles in time to the music.

And that was all he did.

First his biceps, then his pectorals – he got an appreciative laugh from the old ladies when he turned around and rhythmically tensed his glutei maximi – turning back, he could ripple his abdominal muscles from side to side, which was talented to perform but disconcerting to watch because it looked like he'd swallowed an indecisive weasel – next came the thighs and knees and then the big muscles on his broad back – in fact, I think the only muscles he neglected to use were the ones at the corners of his mouth, because Tony Holland was a dedicated bodybuilder and, while the audience could laugh if they must, he was presenting a genuine exhibition of the Maxalding technique of muscle control, which, as far as Tony Holland was concerned, was not a laughing matter.

Tony won the most votes on his first appearance, so they brought him back the following week – and again the week after that, and again for the next three weeks – every week for six weeks he won performing the identical act, twitching away to 'Wheels'. He was a huge success. He made a career out of this odd performance, appearing in clubs and cabarets all over the country – and it all started with my Aunt Betty.

I once asked her about Tony Holland and why on earth had she booked him?

'Oh, Jesus Christ, dear. Look. You're sitting in some fucking awful draughty hotel ballroom, in somewhere dreadful like Bollocks-on-the-Weir, suffering for hour after fucking hour through one godawful pop group after another – nothing to break the monotony – you're deafened in both ears, you've got a raging migraine in one side of your head and thoughts of suicide in the other – when all of a sudden this nice-looking young man appears with practically nothing on and stands there twitching his muscles in time to a catchy little piece of what passes for music these days – well, what do you think? Of *course* I was going to fucking book him.'

David Ogilvy, my father's younger brother, was a Scot who founded an advertising agency in New York and who turned himself into the most celebrated ad man in the world. Talk to anybody involved in the advertising world and the name David Ogilvy is usually greeted with the kind of reverence more often associated with the Buddha. Somebody once said that the product that David sold best was himself – his trademark pipe jutting from one corner of his mouth, his scarlet braces, his crinkly-eyed good looks – they were all as much trademarks of the product as the famous black eyepatch on the Hathaway shirt man, or the flying lady mascot on a Rolls-Royce.

As a young man, very much in the shadow of his more brilliant brother, David decided to take himself off to the USA – both to learn the American ways of advertising and to get out from under the influence of Francis. He started working for Doctor Gallup, in Hollywood, doing the first ever Gallup polls – and the first ever market research – that the film industry had ever attempted.

He discovered a number of interesting facts – fairly obvious to us now, but at that time news to the studio bosses: boys liked films starring boys, girls liked films starring girls, and old people liked films starring old people. Most Americans didn't have the money to go to the racetrack, so they preferred films about baseball or football to movies about horse racing. The majority of film goers were young people, under the age of thirty, buying at that time 65 per cent of all the tickets – and people under twenty accounted for half of that number. Therefore, Hollywood should stop making so many movies for older audiences and concentrate more on the teen market – and this was in 1939, long before the shift to a fully youth-oriented industry became the norm. David discovered who was popular and who wasn't – contrary to her producers' fond belief, Marlene Dietrich was (at that time at least) box office poison with American audiences. He produced charts and diagrams and graphs, showing who liked what and why and who and when. No survey of this sort had ever been done in

Hollywood before and it is generally considered that David Ogilvy's work there altered the attitudes of the motion picture industry forever.

His talent as a researcher led him into the wartime intelligence services. Asthma and some deafness in one ear prevented him from joining the armed forces in the UK, so it was thought he would be of more use if he stayed where he was, in New York.

David was recruited to join the BSC. Under the leadership of William Stephenson, BSC's directives included investigating enemy activities, instituting security measures against sabotage to British property, and organising American public opinion in favour of aid to Britain. One of David Ogilvy's jobs, along with colleagues Ian Fleming, Roald Dahl, Leslie Howard, David Niven, Cary Grant, Noël Coward – and others less well known – was to disseminate information in the American press – information both true and false – that might influence the so-far reluctant USA into joining the war.

Reports that might discourage the public from that view were to be downplayed; tales of Nazi atrocities were to be emphasised – and anything of dubious veracity they could think up, which made the Germans look rotten and the British look heroic, was to be planted in every newspaper that would take the story.

Attitudes among ordinary Americans were slowly changing – and then the Japanese attacked Pearl Harbor, rendering much of BSC's work suddenly superfluous. Yet it was the BSC team that helped the USA set up a foreign intelligence service of its own. There was none before the Stephenson-inspired Office of Strategic Services (OSS) – which morphed over time into today's CIA. General Bill Donovan of the OSS wrote that, 'Bill Stephenson taught us everything we ever knew about foreign intelligence operations'. And, by war's end, BSC represented the British intelligence agencies MI5, MI6, SOE (Special Operations Executive) and PWE (Political Warfare Executive) throughout North America, South America and the Caribbean.

After the war, David stayed in the United States and founded, with the help of my father, the advertising giant called Ogilvy Benson & Mather. The 'Benson' (which was later dropped) and the 'Mather' were both distinguished names borrowed from English ad agencies but no man of either name ever served on the board of David's company – yet they must have lent a certain gravitas to the fledgling firm, giving David early successes with the Hathaway shirt company, with Rolls-Royce, and with the promotion of Puerto Rico – the campaign my uncle was most proud of. Quickly, he became the wunderkind of Madison Avenue, and later, from the late 1960s until his death in 1999, the owner of a spectacularly beautiful castle in central France, called Château de Touffou, which I would visit every summer holiday with my own young family.

David married three times. First to an American called Melinda Street, the mother of my cousin David Fairfield Ogilvy, now a successful and charming real estate magnate who lives in Connecticut.

David's second marriage was to another American – Anne, a member of the old, rich and influential Cabot family, who were considered so select that they were featured in a short but famous ditty that pretty much summed up their position in American society:

And this is good old Boston,
The home of the bean and the cod.
Where the Lowells talk only to Cabots,
And the Cabots talk only to God.

David's third and last marriage was to Herta Lans, whom I knew best because of our frequent trips to the château. Herta held nicely realistic views of her husband's many achievements in advertising, some of them a little scornful. 'They make him into a tin god,' she would say, 'because he writes some clever copy. But what they should really remember him for is what he has done to preserve Touffou.'

What David did for the château, parts of which date from the eleventh century, was remarkable. It was in disrepair when he bought it, but not for long. The largest project he undertook was to replace the roof, which took seven years and cost more than the amount he'd originally paid for the whole property. Every slate tile had to be hand-cut to match the original. Every massive, newly carved oak beam had to be fastened with matching oak pegs – no bolts or screws allowed. For seven years Touffou wore an exoskeleton of steel scaffolding; David said it looked like the castle had its hair in curlers. He renovated the inside, he removed all traces of Victorian vandalism, he shored up one of the tottering eleventh-century towers, and he created exquisite gardens where vicious games of croquet would be played under David's House Rules, which could be changed at will and at any time, depending on how badly David's game was going.

When Anne Cabot was the mistress of the house, breakfast would be brought to the guests in their beds. An old female retainer, long past retirement age, would carry a heavy tray across the broad central courtyard to the guest apartments in the separate Tour St Jean. She would stagger up the long stone spiral staircase, knock gently on the bedroom door and, when admitted by a guest (who was all too often appalled at the age and the infirmity of the old lady, not to mention the burden, often silver and always heavy, that the old lady was being asked to carry) would deposit the tray on a bedside table and then, gasping audibly, would make her way back to the kitchen to pick up the next tray for delivery to another distant bedroom.

When Herta came to Touffou, she sensibly dispensed with this feudalism. 'Everybody is quite capable of getting their own breakfasts!' she said, and that was the end of eating croissants in bed.

David once made the mistake of telling me that, technically, I was the head of this branch of the Ogilvy clan, since I was the oldest son of the oldest son. From that moment on, I exercised my seniority by treating his fake croquet rules with the contempt they deserved. He was amused at my sudden fame when I played Simon Templar in the television series, *Return of the Saint* – he would wonder aloud about which one of us was the more famous. Once, while staying there – and at the height of my short-lived fame – I had a phone call from my agent, with a job offer that meant cutting my Touffou holiday short. I went to David and said I was going to have to leave in order to get myself to Benidorm of all places, where I was to shoot a commercial for the Woolwich building society. David asked me for the name of the advertising agency that was depriving him of my company.

'Well, oddly enough, it's yours, David. Ogilvy & Mather.'

'Oh. And am I paying you a lot of money to do this commercial?'

'Quite a lot, yes.'

'I don't approve.'

David's disapproval had nothing to do with nepotism. He had a theory that using a well-known personality in a commercial didn't actually succeed in selling the product but only served to sell the well-known personality. On the other hand, he was pleased to be instrumental in giving me some money because he never believed I had any.

Once, in a fit of generosity, while strolling together round the gardens, he offered to give me the Touffou aumônerie. The word 'Aumônerie' translates to the office of Chaplaincy, but at Touffou it was the name for what had once been the resident priest's house in the grounds of the château. It was a small, but beautifully proportioned, square building, with several floors – all open plan, all presently unoccupied, other than by small flocks of dysenteric pigeons – and all connected to each other by the ubiquitous Touffou stone spiral staircases. At the time when David suggested it might be mine if I wanted it, only a corner of the ground floor was in use – to house his croquet equipment.

I didn't say, 'You're barking mad.' What I said was, 'That's incredibly generous, Uncle David. Oh wow – I'm just imagining our future summers here – me and the family of course – and lots of my lovely actor friends who naturally I shall invite to stay in my beautiful French house – just imagine what fun that'll be for us all – hordes of English thespians shrieking at the tops of their voices as they splash about in your swimming pool – later perhaps sitting in deckchairs in the middle of your

Cour d'Honneur, swapping theatre stories – having first beaten you hollow at croquet, which, by the way, they will all play with theatrical flair and matching brilliance – I bet you just can't wait, can you?'

'I take it back, I take it back,' David muttered.

Later in the day, probably out of gratitude, he pressed a cheque for a thousand pounds into my hand.

Chapter 4

When I was six, I was sent away to boarding school in order to prepare myself for when I would be sent away to a different boarding school when I was seven.

To my parents, this was a perfectly rational thing to do. The school was small, in Kent, and Kerry was already there, so I'd have somebody to talk to. Besides, they wanted a trip to New York, and while leaving me with Nanny would have been fine, they deluded themselves into thinking that boarding school would be better. It wasn't. Kerry had her own circle of friends and refused to talk to me at all. I was miserable, a nuisance, and embarrassingly incontinent – so much so, in fact, that on one horrible day my underpants were held up, for all the school to see, as an example of how not to behave inside one's trousers. To my relief, I was there only for one term. Then, in 1950, when I was seven, I went to my proper boarding school, the one for which I'd been prepared – Sunningdale school, in Berkshire.

Sunningdale was – and is – a very nice school, even if it does cater, almost exclusively, to the immensely privileged and the impossibly high-born. Two thirds of the boys who went to

Sunningdale were destined to go on to Eton. I was one of the poorest and least aristocratic children in the place. There were hordes of little lords at Sunningdale. One was called the Earl of Aboyne. I came up with a terrific joke. I asked him what a boyne was, and why was he the earl of it? I don't think he got it because he didn't laugh at all.

For all this wealth and privilege, Sunningdale remained a cultured, friendly place, with jolly teachers – (apart from Miss Patterson, who was a witch, and Mr Spears, who was something else entirely) – with no idiotic rules, where everybody was treated equally, where corporal punishment was almost unknown, with fine grounds covered in great banks of rhododendrons, and where a wonderful and far-ranging game called Malta was played on summer Sunday afternoons. The entire school was divided into two opposing navies, with some of the younger masters delegated to be referees. You could be a battleship, or a destroyer, or a submarine – I liked being a motor torpedo boat because motor torpedo boats were allowed to hide in the rhododendron bushes, and battleships and cruisers and destroyers weren't. If I met an enemy submarine, I could sink it with my torpedoes, but a battleship or a destroyer or a cruiser would be the swift death of me. I spent a lot of time hiding in the rhododendron bushes avoiding the big ships and only jumping out when an enemy U-boat trotted by.

We were all boys of course, ranging in age from seven to twelve, learning Latin, Greek, French, English, history, geography, maths – some sciences – and something called scripture, which was a study of the Bible, although not in any great religious sense, but rather as an introduction to all the sacred stories, so that we would at least *know* them, and not be embarrassed by our ignorance in later life. There were a couple of personal consequences to this policy towards the Bible. One was to enable me, quite recently, to correct an American Born-Again-Fundamentalist-Evangelical-Pentecostal-Snake-handling-Tongue-speaking-Charismatic (and all the rest of it) Christian as to whether the Book of Revelation was just that, or if it was the plural Book Of *Revelations*, which was what he insisted it was called. It's always satisfying to correct the expert. It also puzzles some of my more religious American friends when I do quite well on TV quiz shows when they feature a Bible category. My faithful friends can't understand how I, a faithless atheist, could possibly know so much more than they do, about a book they all believe in and yet – because of their constitutional separation of church and state – they often know so little about.

The other benefit to my Bible studies – with some sly help from my father – was to convince me that the entire thing was a bald and clumsy fabrication from start to finish and that I didn't have to believe a word of it if I didn't want to. Mark Twain sums it up: 'The best cure for Christianity is reading the Bible.'

All the same, even with this civilised approach to religion, we still had compulsory morning prayers every day and two full church services on Sundays, in the little wooden chapel at the edge of the pine wood, with its tarpaper walls and its corrugated tin roof. At the end of every Sunday evening service we droned out the most depressing hymn ever written in the English language, 'Abide With Me'. It was composed by Henry Francis Lyte, in 1847, while he lay dying from tuberculosis – so it's not surprising he was a bit down in the mouth. But what business did we little boys have, singing such gloomy guff as –

> *Swift to its close ebbs out life's little day;*
> *Earth's joys grow dim; its glories pass away;*
> *Change and decay in all around I see;*
> *O Thou who changest not, abide with me.*

Good stuff if you're dying of tuberculosis, but not if you're eight years old and wondering if Matron was going to give you back the torch she'd found in your bed that morning.

We were all called by – and addressed each other by – our surnames. You didn't want to be a Smith. At one time during my stay at Sunningdale, there were four Smiths. They were called Smith Maximus, Smith Major, Smith Minor and Smith Minimus – which, for those of us without the Latin, might be translated roughly into Smith-the-Greatest, Smith-the-Greater, Smith-the-Lesser, and Smith-the-Least. Being Smith-the-Greatest was terrific. Nobody messed with Smith-the-Greatest. Being Smith-The-Least was awful. The name invited scorn. The only hope for poor little Smith Minimus would be that the great and glorious Smith Maximus would soon leave Sunningdale, which would result in a promotion for him – from Smith Minimus to Smith Minor, which was bearable. But that was all he could hope for, because when the *new* Smith Maximus also left, the new Smith Minor would remain Smith Minor and never achieve Smith Major at all, because there already was a freshly promoted one of those. And, when the freshly promoted Smith Major also left the school, all that would remain would be our single unfortunate Smith, who'd started out as Minimus, struggled up to Minor and who could now go no further because, being the only Smith left, he wouldn't need any Latin tags at all – unless, by some stroke of good fortune, a new little Smith boy would arrive at the school – then, and only then, could our victim achieve the rank of Smith Major. And the possibility of *three* new Smiths arriving at Sunningdale, thus shooting our unfortunate up to the giddy heights of being Smith Maximus, well that was beyond all bounds of hope.

Prince Michael of Kent was a contemporary of mine. We called him Kent. He was a grandson of George V. Nicholas II, the last of the Russian tsars, was a first cousin to three of Michael's grandparents. When the remains of the tsar and his family were discovered in 1979, it was Prince Michael's blood that confirmed the matching DNA. When we were both middle-aged men, I met him again at a private dinner party.

'Bet you can't do this,' he said. He then recited from memory a long roll call of Sunningdale boys' names, mystically remembered from our distant past, that somehow had become stuck in his head. I don't know how accurate the roll call was, but I remembered many of the names and they were certainly in the right alphabetical order – but, as a feat of mental prowess, it couldn't have been all that rewarding for Prince Michael to perform, since it could impress only a limited number of Old Sunningdalians. I like to think he'd been waiting all his adult life to run into one of us again, if only to be able to say, 'Bet you can't do this.'

Carey Harrison was another schoolfriend. He was the son of Rex Harrison and Lilli Palmer and, when they came to take him out on visiting days, the excitement at seeing real film stars, in the flesh, was huge.

We slept in dormitories. About twelve beds ranged round the walls, with a row of wooden washstands in a line in the centre of the room. No hot or cold running water in the dorms, just big enamel jugs full of icy water, placed there the night before, ready for use the next morning. A flannel, a toothbrush, a tube of toothpaste. A small side table by your narrow iron bed, on which you could have a couple of photos of your family and just *one* stuffed toy. My friends were Leschallas, and Fishburn, and the Cecil twins, and an amusing but dangerously bad boy called Tritton, who got himself into terrible trouble all the time because he was a rebel. The trouble was, if he was being a rebel when I was with him, that meant I got into the same trouble. Tritton and I spent a lot of time in detention, improving our handwriting from a copying book. I must have written '*Attar of roses is an ingredient in perfume*' at least a hundred times.

We played cricket in the summer, soccer in the winter and rugger in the spring. I was hopeless at all three. I was so bad at cricket they made me the scorer – for the *Second* Eleven. When Sports Day came around, I ran in the Consolation races, which were for all the unathletic (and consequently unrewarded) boys without even a paper rosette to their names. I'd trail in last. Once by some fluke, I came in third; I won a plastic pencil sharpener in the shape of a dog.

The teachers were a mixed bag, mostly very good. Mr Fox was the headmaster. I once was called into his study because I'd been heard using the word 'bloody', which was positively the worst word you could say back then. 'You don't hear that sort of language at home, do you Ogilvy?'

'No, sir.' This was the correct answer, so I was let off with a caution. (It was the correct answer but not the accurate one. 'Bloody' was my father's fifth favourite word, after, 'Jesus', 'Christ', 'God', and 'Almighty' – but I knew better than to tell Mr Fox that).

There was young Mr Latham, straight out of university, who started the new boys on Latin. He'd made his own translation of Caesar's *Gallic Wars* and, when he wasn't telling us what *mensa* meant, he would read aloud from his unpublished manuscript. Mr Tupholme was an old teddy bear of a man, who taught classics to older boys and who was the school bank. He was in charge of the boys' pocket money, and was the person you went to when you needed to spend some of it. He'd write your request in a little notebook – ('No Sykes, you can't have a catapult, they're absolutely against the rules, as well you know. Silly little boy. Have a Dinky Spitfire instead.') – and once a week he would go off to Ascot or Windsor and buy all the stuff we'd asked for and bring it back to us and we liked Mr Tupholme very much.

We hated Miss Patterson, who taught maths. She was a tweedy, acid-tongued, middle-aged spinster, with hair like a Brillo pad, who would whack your knuckles with her ruler if you got something wrong. I never got anything right in her class. Miss Patterson and her ruler made me afraid of mathematics.

Mr Ling taught French and was slightly scary, but we were very intrigued by his crippled right hand because it was rumoured that he'd taken a bullet through the palm during the war. He wrote on the blackboard with his uncrippled left hand and his writing was illegible.

Mr Burroughs was scary too but he genuinely liked boys and kept a tin of goodies under his desk and, if you got something right, he'd call you up to the front of the class and solemnly present you with a sweet. Sugar rationing was still very much in force, and Mr Burroughs must have gone without his fair share in order to supply us boys with our rewards.

Mr Squarey taught history and cultivated his own eccentricities. He'd been at Cambridge with my father. Every day, on coming across me in a corridor, he'd bellow, 'How's your father, Ogilvy?'

'Very well, sir. Thank you sir.'

'Don't thank me, boy. Nothing to do with me.'

If you asked Mr Squarey a question, the reply was usually, 'Depends on the weather.' If you did something to irritate him – 'I don't know what your name is, Ogilvy – but you really are a dreadful little waste of time, aren't you?'

'Yes, sir.'

'What are you?'

'A dreadful little waste of time, sir.'

'I like your attitude, boy. Go away.'

And then there was Mr Spears, who was married to Mrs Spears. Mrs Spears was young and pretty and taught geography. Mr Spears was tall and handsome in a Nordic sort of way – and I can't remember what Mr Spears taught because, in my memory of him, his subject is secondary to what he liked to do to you. If you performed poorly in his class that day – and if you were a little bit adorable – Mr Spears would tell you to stay behind at the end of the lesson. You had to stand in front of him while he listed your shortcomings. Then he would put you over his knee and give you a gentle spanking with his bare hand – a hand that, once it had descended, seemed to linger on your bottom for a little longer than necessary before lifting off again for the next blow. It was almost as if its owner was exhausted by the effort of smacking you and was giving his poor old hand a well-deserved rest on your buttocks; but of course it wasn't that at all. The spanking was unsanctioned and illegal, but it didn't hurt, was merely mildly embarrassing and that was all Mr Spears ever did to me, although it's possible he did something worse to somebody else – perhaps the case, because someone must have blabbed. One day, in geography, we boys watched with cruel interest while poor, pretty little Mrs Spears struggled, sniffling and red-eyed, through the lesson – and occasionally (and thrillingly) bursting into a flood of uncontrolled tears. The next day, with no explanation whatsoever, Mr and Mrs Spears disappeared from Sunningdale and were never seen again.

There were school concerts – interminable affairs, produced principally to confirm in the minds of the parents just how adorable their offspring were. The first half was all music, with choral performances by the school choir, with squeaky demonstrations of violin playing, and hesitant piano renderings of the easy parts of 'Clair de Lune' – and once a beautiful a cappella rendition of 'Voi Che Sapete' by a boy called Gascoigne.

The second half was all drama, with comedy sketches and short plays and recitations of poetry. Since I'd inherited my father's taste in music, this was when I came into my own. I sometimes played girls. I was The Maiden in *The Tall Tall Castle* – which is described as a Burlesque Mime, whatever that is. Playing The Maiden was the first time I discovered you could get laughs in drag. I also discovered that getting laughs was the greatest joy in all the world and that if I had to play a girl to get the audience to make those wonderful noises, then bring me the wig and the pretty dress and we'll say no more about it. I was also Christopher Columbus and an Airman, neither of which was anything like as funny as The Maiden.

My parents came to these concerts, along with all the other doting mothers and fathers. Francis liked to sit at the front, because of his poor hearing – but since neither half of the evening's entertainment held any interest for him whatsoever, he would fall asleep within the first few minutes and snore quietly for the rest of the show – shaming for my mother, surrounded as she was on all sides by earls and baronets and dukes and princes. As far as my mother was concerned, rubbing shoulders with earls and baronets and dukes and princes was the principal reason why you sent your male offspring to an expensive boarding school in the first place – and why you entered your daughter into the debutante season in the second place, where she could, if she really tried, snag herself a peer of the realm. When my beautiful and clever sister Kerry – having had a most glorious season, ending up as the Debutante Of The Year, no less – when she failed to snap up even a baronet, my mother was mortified. All that money spent on dresses and parties and taxi rides – and all she got for a son-in-law was one Benjamin Spanoghe who, although he'd been captain of boxing at Eton and was as charming as the prince of the same name, didn't have a title at all. It was a great disappointment to my poor mother, who had probably set her heart on Prince Charles, even if he was a bit young for Kerry.

There were two boys at Sunningdale who had very special talents, although mercifully they were never part of the school concerts. Perhaps if they had been, my father might have stayed awake. Charleston would put a drawing pin on the floor and would then kneel on it, embedding the thing into his kneecap. He said it didn't hurt at all. Vokes's trick was to smear the head of his penis with toothpaste. He said it didn't hurt at all. Such devil-may-care attitudes, at such an early age, make me wonder if either of them is still alive.

Chapter 5

At about the same time that I went to Sunningdale, my father decided he could no longer bear living in London. An avid gardener, he wanted to get his hands dirty. He looked around for a suitable place to rent. I don't think there was ever any consideration of buying anything. Rents in 1950 were fairly cheap and we certainly could never have afforded to *buy* Copford Hall, even if it had been for sale, which it wasn't.

Copford Hall was (and still is) in Essex, in the village of Copford, six miles from Colchester. Some sort of residence has been on the site since the tenth century – the seat being held for several hundred years by the bishops of London as their country manor.

The Hall, rebuilt in about 1760 on the bones of an earlier house, has been described as a 'Fine, Listed Georgian Country House, With Extensive Grounds.' My mother said she thought it looked like a lunatic asylum, but my father was determined to have it, and so we took it and lived in it for the next seven years. It proved to be something of a money pit. Francis broke all the rules of the renter, which can be summed up by *Don't Spend Anything On A Place You Don't Own*. My father did the opposite. He resurfaced the driveway, he drained and deepened the two lakes, he spent lavishly on the walled kitchen garden, he refurbished the house from top to bottom, and planted hundreds of exotic and expensive plants in the Extensive Grounds, most of which died off in the bitter Essex winters. He would march some unfortunate, shivering Christmas guest round the garden, pointing out the dead and the dying. 'See that?' he would say, indicating a shrivelled brown twig poking out of the frozen earth. 'Come summer, that's a blaze of colour.'

Every morning, in his business suit and his bowler hat and his umbrella, he would be driven to the station by the Bismuth of the day. A slow commuter train to London, then a taxi to his office on the north side of Waterloo Bridge. Back in the evening on another train, picked up by Bismuth at the station, a late dinner and a lot of whisky and finally, exhausted and fuddled, to bed. Kerry and I hardly saw him at all during the week – he was up before we were and home after we'd been put to bed. The only times he could devote to his beloved gardens were at the weekends, and there were always house guests to be entertained, and lunch parties to be got through, and people to be visited – so, instead of getting his own hands dirty, he employed Mr Norfolk, the gardener, to do it for him. Mr Norfolk sometimes asked his brother Harry to come and help. Harry was the village policeman. He looked like Enid Blyton's PC Plod and was just as jolly.

The parish church was next door to Copford Hall, and the residents of the hall traditionally had their own private side entrance into it, which only they were allowed to use. It was a privilege we didn't abuse; Francis flatly refused to go to church at all. My mother rather liked the traditional Church of

England liturgy so, at Copford, she tried to get Kerry and me to go with her – citing as an attraction the fact that we had our very own entrance into the church and didn't that make us feel special? No, it didn't, not particularly. My sister and I moaned and dragged our feet and so Aileen's Copford church attendances dropped to twice a year, to Christmas and Easter.

The vicar would sometimes come to tea, as vicars are inclined to do. My mother was careful to arrange these visits when Francis wasn't around. The vicar would ask plaintively when we were all going to come to a church service and my mother would promise that we'd be there soon – very soon, when the children (who seemed to the vicar to be in perfect health) had got over their nasty illnesses.

The church itself was a marvel of Norman architecture, one of the finest examples in England – but what intrigued my sister and me was a small glass-fronted frame, about eight inches square, which hung on the outside of the medieval front door. Contained in the frame was a two-inch-square scrap of what looked like dirty leather. This relic was purported to be a fragment of human skin, flayed from the living body of an unfortunate Dane who had been caught raiding in the area. However, local history tells us that,

> Marauding Danes pre-dated the building of the church by 200 years or more. The truth may be that the skin had belonged to a poacher caught harassing the king's deer. The law at the time of Henry I stated that, 'If a man chaseth the deere and mayketh him pannte, if he be free, he shall lose his hand, if bond, his skin.' Forensic examination of the 'parchment' early in the 20th century confirmed that the skin was that of a fair-skinned male.

Marauding Dane or unfortunate poacher, it was no wonder Kerry and I were so taken with the thing.

The best feature of those seven years we spent at Copford – for me those all-important formative years between the ages of seven and fourteen – was the grounds. Twenty-four acres in all, with every sort of landscaping one could imagine: there were extensive lawns where we played croquet in the summer; there were two lakes, both stocked with inedible coarse fish – and, after Francis backed a winner at the races, there was even a small clinker-built wooden dinghy called *Choirboy*, which was the name of the winning horse. *Choirboy* was kept in an eighteenth-century boathouse at the head of the lower lake and I spent many happy hours in it, fishing for roach with a bamboo pole.

There was an orchard, with apple trees producing apples that nobody nowadays has ever heard of – the best being a strange, ugly, rough-skinned ball of deliciousness called a D'Arcy Spice; next to the orchard was a high-walled kitchen garden with greenhouses that grew everything from cucumbers to peaches to grapes; there was a big fruit cage, stocked with every kind of berry – raspberries, blackberries, strawberries, and several sorts of gooseberries. Francis had his own, extra-specially-delicious gooseberry bush from which nobody was allowed to eat except him. It was the closest my father ever got to playing God, I suppose – and with much the same results as God had with Adam and Eve, since Kerry and I ignored the rule and regularly raided his private reserve – 'Jesus Christ, those bloody birds have been stealing from me again – what is the bloody point of having a bloody fruit cage in the first place?'

There was even a small wood, which Francis insisted on calling the 'spinney'. The spinney was home to squirrels – and not the dull grey aggressive species that roamed the rest of the country – these were the real (and increasingly rare) Squirrel Nutkin lookalikes, with fur as red as a fox, with long tufts on their ears and glorious bushy tails. They were so numerous in Essex at that time that the invading grey squirrels had lost the battle and had retreated to areas less well-occupied. The reds were quite tame, too. Kerry once crept up behind one as it chewed at an acorn among the leaf litter. She bent down and scooped it up, holding it in her cupped hands. The squirrel froze – then slowly turned his head over his shoulder to see why on earth he was suddenly three feet off the ground. Kerry and he stared at each other for a moment – she with delight, he with mounting horror – then, with a flick of the tail, he was gone.

Kerry found something else. One day she came across our parents' marriage certificate. She thrust it under my nose. 'Look at the date!' she whispered. Whatever the date was, it was certainly several years after Kerry and I had been born. 'We're *bastards!*' she hissed gleefully.

In summer, when the Essex sun occasionally broke through the Essex cloud cover, my mother would find a secluded spot down by the lake and take all her clothes off and sunbathe. But first she would tell Mr Norfolk. 'I'm going to be down by the lake with no clothes on, Mr Norfolk. Do please stay away, there's a dear.' As far as I know he did. So did Kerry and I. My mother's fondness for taking all her clothes off at the slightest pretext was embarrassing to us children. Aileen was having none of it. 'Oh, don't be so silly. If you see something you haven't seen before, you can throw your hat at it.' She worked hard at getting us to be *au naturel* with her, and sometimes she succeeded. Not with my father of course, whom I never once saw naked – but until some of his modesty rubbed off on me I would sometimes swim bare in the lake, and my sister wore only the bottom half of a bikini long past the time when she should have put on the top half too.

There was a small wooden summer house on one corner of the lawn and this became my shop. I picked daffodils and stuck them in jam pots and sold them to my mother. Nanny was a good customer too; she was prepared to buy back all the stuff I'd stolen from her room. I'd creep in there when she wasn't around, remove a few small trinkets from her shelves and set them up on my shop counter. So fond was Nanny – both of me and her knick-knacks – that she'd visit my store, pick up each of her possessions, examine them closely and critically for their quality, and then solemnly ask how much I wanted for the thing, which was always a penny or two. She would nod judiciously, as if she was in some Arab market and found the prices reasonable – and she would pay up and return to her room and put everything back in its proper place. This terrific marketing wheeze works, I've since discovered, only with somebody who loves you to the point of foolishness.

Having tackled the gardens, the lakes, the orchard and the fruit cage, my father decided that what Copford needed above all else was a pair of swans to glide decoratively round the upper lake and nest under the mulberry tree. Getting a swan to come and live with you proved more complicated than he'd thought. Since all the swans in the UK belong to the monarch, you have to have royal permission to have one on your property. This involves a man armed with some sort of regal authority and a title along the lines of His Majesty's (George VI was still alive and on the throne) Swan Keeper, who comes to your house and inspects your ponds and decides whether or not you might be a suitable swan-owner and not just somebody interested in seeing what they taste like.

A man in a suit and a Knightsbridge accent duly arrived and he wandered around for a bit and then he said yes, we could have a couple of swans, but best to start out with just one, a male. Later, once the bird had become comfortable in his surroundings, then might be the moment to think of a female companion for him. Columbus arrived soon after, in a big wooden crate. He was carted down to the upper lake and set free. He seemed quite happy with his new home and only hissed at us when we got too close.

'Stay away from him,' said my father. 'Bloody dangerous creatures. Chap I knew had his arm broken with one blow of a swan's wing.' This turned out to be a myth, along the lines of Mr Archibald being a cannibal – although it seems to be a myth that is still generally believed by those who don't know much about birds' wings.

Six months later, Filipa arrived. I don't know why Francis wanted to call a pair of swans after the Genoese explorer and his Portuguese wife but that's what he did. Columbus hated Filipa on sight and pecked and bullied and whacked her (ineffectually) with his wings – so His Majesty's Swan Keeper took her away. A month later we tried again, with Filipa the Second. Filipa the Second looked exactly the same as Filipa the First and could well have been the same bird for all we knew. But Columbus decided that she wasn't the same at all and that he liked this one a lot – and we all watched entranced as the pair performed the graceful and lovely courting dance that mute swans do when they decide to mate for life.

What my father hadn't planned on was the volume of excrement two swans can produce, and the arbitrary spots where they choose to produce it. The foulest location was the path that led from the upper lake to the back door. Every morning Columbus and Filipa would hoist themselves out of the water and waddle up the steep incline to the house, dumping as they climbed. They would stand there, hissing disagreeably and rattling their beaks against the windows, and they wouldn't stop until they were fed – mainly dry crusts of bread from a safe distance because you didn't want to get too close to those bone-shattering wings.

There came a day when Columbus felt confined by Copford – or maybe he just needed a break from his wife. He squeezed through a wire fence and managed to get airborne for half a mile before crash-landing in a ploughed field. The family – and Mr Norfolk, who was the only person in England who wasn't afraid of swans' wings – set off in pursuit in the company car of the moment, a funereal black pre-war Rolls-Royce Wraith that my mother called The Hearse.

After a short drive along narrow country lanes, Columbus was spotted sitting forlornly in the middle of a ploughed field. Mr Norfolk marched into the field. He ignored the hissing and the flapping and the stabbing beak and simply scooped up Columbus and tucked him under his arm. His free hand he closed firmly round Columbus's beak, and quite suddenly the enormous bird became meek and passive and subdued – a thoroughly muted mute swan. Without a word Mr Norfolk climbed back into the front passenger seat beside the Bismuth of the day with the swan sitting quietly on his lap. In which stately fashion, Columbus was brought home.

There was a gang of Copford village boys, all around my age, and sometimes they let me play with them. Among six or seven small, pallid Essex faces, there was a single little black one. Nobody commented on it, nobody teased him. He was there, he was part of the scene, he was in the gang. They'd grown up with him. It was *my* presence – the little snob from the Hall – that was sometimes questioned. The black boy was the son of a farm labourer and his wife, both white. During the war, the newly married farm worker was stationed overseas and while he was away his young wife met, and briefly fell in love with, a black American GI, whose regiment was billeted in the Colchester garrisons. She became pregnant by him and in due course had the baby – and the village of Copford held its collective breath for the day when her husband would return.

When he did, his wife tearfully confessed and showed him the newborn. He stared down at the child for a few moments and then he said, 'Well, you 'ave been a naughty girl then, 'aven't you? But 'e's a nice-looking little bugger, isn't 'e? We'll keep 'im, I reckon.'

And they did.

It was an idyllic seven years for all of us except my mother, who preferred Shaftesbury Avenue to East Anglia and could never understand why she'd allowed herself to be buried out in the country, miles from anything that interested her, and with the sort of weather that might just be bearable in Knightsbridge but which was excruciating in Essex. 'It's Arctic and I've no staff,' became her mantra. Arctic it was, at times – but Aileen's definition of 'no staff' was a loose one; at any given moment there was a cook, a butler/chauffeur, a nanny, one and sometimes two gardeners and a couple of friendly girls from the village who would come in and clean twice a week.

For a short while and in a moment of madness, we even employed a Cordon Bleu chef called Raymond Gurton. His food was wonderful and the birthday cakes he made for Kerry and me were architectural masterpieces. When he left us, he went on to become the private chef of Peter Sellers.

It must have come as a relief to my mother when the decision was made to give up Copford and return to London. She'd been left some money by an aunt called Jane Godfrey, who lived in Louisiana and was said to be mad. Great-Aunt Jane left Kerry and me £200 each as well but my mother's legacy was a lot more – enough to buy a house in London, which was something my father could never have afforded since he always spent every penny of his salary, and much more besides, in a determined effort to give his family as nice a possible time while he was alive while ensuring that there wouldn't be a penny in his will for anybody after his death. It was a goal he achieved.

Chapter 6

In 1955, Eton College (founded in 1440 by Henry VI) was still being run pretty much as it had been for the past several hundred years and I hated it from the moment I arrived there at the age of twelve, to when I left it, a little earlier than most, at the age of seventeen.

Many years after my departure, Eton underwent a number of none-too-soon civilising reforms that brought it more in line with the modern world. I believe that nowadays it's a pleasant enough school, but when I was there I loathed it. After the relative comfort and safety of Sunningdale, Eton was a bewildering place.

For a start, it isn't the sort of school that is set tidily inside its own borders. It's within the town of Eton, with twenty-five individual boys' houses – each home to about fifty boys – scattered far and wide, as are the classrooms, the playing fields, the two chapels and the administrative buildings. Immediately, the haphazard arrangement of Eton overwhelmed me. In an instant I went from being a respected senior Sunningdalian prefect, who knew where he was both geographically and in the scheme of things, to a tearfully nervous little new boy who couldn't manage to get to class on time, because (A) he couldn't remember which class he was supposed to be at in the first place, (B) didn't know where the classroom was in the second place and (C) even if he managed eventually to get himself to the right place in the first place, had forgotten to bring the relevant books in the third place.

From the moment you arrived you were treated as if you could do all these things and I couldn't. 'You're so incompetent,' said Francis Cruso, my tutor and housemaster – but of course under Eton's archaic customs, Mr Cruso wasn't 'my tutor' at all, he was *'m'tutor'* – and God help you if you got this sort of nonsense wrong. There were trivial hazards like this round every corner, arcane rules and meaningless regulations enforced, as often as not, by savage eighteen-year-old boys whose authority was not to be questioned and whose only achievements to date had little to do with the development of their minds and everything to do with their prowess on the playing fields.

One of the first trials of a new boy was to learn the names and locations of all twenty-five houses, the names of all their housemasters, the individual house colours (Cruso's was Black and Green quarters, another's might have been Magenta and Brown Stripes) – the names of the captains of the houses, the names of their deputies, the names of the captains of sports – what specific colours went with what specific sporting achievements – the location of every classroom, the location of every sports field, the names and locations of all the school officers, the names and locations of all well-known Eton landmarks – 'Where's the Burning Bush, Ogilvy?' – and all this stuff that you had to learn was being crammed into your head by a child who was only a year older than you were but who still held an authority that was impressive in its powers, because he could complain about your inability to absorb this tedious rubbish to an older adolescent who had the sanctioned power to make your life profoundly unpleasant.

I discovered the horrors of fagging, as did we all. In essence, being a fag meant that, for the first two years of your life at Eton, you were the unpaid servant to an older boy. You tidied his room, put his clothes away, laid out his washing kit and shaving gear, ran his bath, cooked his tea, polished his boots and the brass buttons on his Officer Training Corps uniform, and ran any errand he wanted you to run, no matter how trivial, and no matter that it might be taking you away from doing something important, like your school work. You also had to drop whatever you were doing whenever one of these privileged seniors shouted the traditional boy call – a long-drawn-out wail vaguely sounding like 'Booooyyyyy-uuuupppp!' – which was the signal for all us little fags to run as fast as we could to the source of this noise and line up in front of the noise-maker – and whoever came last had to do whatever this senior time-waster wanted you to do. The often pointless task usually fell, for obvious reasons, to the fattest and slowest of the fags. In my house, in my time there, this was a boy called Lucas. But Lucas wasn't an idiot. He found that, before the pack of faster and skinnier fags could begin to outdistance him, he could use his weight and his strength to hurl out of his way the boy closest to him – and then, using the width of his wide body, he could block any attempt by the boy he'd barged to overtake him. As often as not the barged boy's name was Denny, whose family was in the meat business. Lucas' family was in the business of being immensely rich and owning much of Yorkshire. He was probably the most spoiled person I ever knew. For his fourteenth or fifteenth birthday his father gave him a rare, classic, pre-war racing car, which Lucas used to drive around their vast estate. Lucas once took a bet with the rest of us that he would wear the same shirt, without ever once changing it, for an entire term. He won the bet but smelled appalling.

Lucas got away with this prank because he had his own room – it wouldn't have been tolerated in a dormitory. But then we all had our own rooms. From his first day at Eton to his last, every boy in every house had a room of his own, making the experience similar, in one way at least, to university life. The boy slept in his room, he ate there, he studied there, he played there. He could have his friends to tea. He could decorate the room how he liked within reason – no *Playboy* centrefolds on the wall of course, but Victorian scenes of fox-hunting were encouraged.

Most extraordinary was the inclusion of a fireplace. In every room there was a small but serviceable grate where, in the winter evenings, you were allowed to have a coal fire. No supervision, no thought that it might not be the wisest of ideas to let thirteen-year-old boys have a fire in their rooms – in fact, a scuttle of coal and a bundle of kindling was supplied to each boy, delivered to his room once a week, and what you did with it was your own affair. What I did with mine was I got the fire going and then I burned Nanny's cakes on it. At least once a month, Nanny would lovingly bake me a cake and send it to me. Her cakes were immensely heavy. They must have cost a lot to send. Made to some Estonian recipe unknown outside that country, they contained mountains of sugar, were oddly soggy, and tasted awful. I discovered that I could get quite a good blaze going in the fireplace – better than the feeble flickering I got from my scuttle of cheap coal – if I fed the fire with regular slices of Nanny's inedible Estonian cake. It was the sugar I think, that burned so well. I never told Nanny what I did with her cakes but I told my schoolfellows and within hours of one arriving, my room would full of friends warming themselves at my cake fire.

Corporal punishment, in a variety of forms, was common. Much more common than at Sunningdale, where it was almost unknown. The worst offence could bring the wrath of the headmaster himself down upon you. This rare beating was painful, but the humiliation of the ceremony and its semi-public nature was horrible. The victim was bent over the flogging block, which was a small wooden two-step device, blackened by its own antiquity. Then, under many eyes – some of which must have enjoyed the spectacle for every wrong reason under the sun – the wrongdoer was beaten by the headmaster on his bare buttocks by a collection of brine-soaked birch twigs.

This never happened to me.

My Uncle David visited me at Eton once and, anticipating his reaction, I took a perverse delight in showing him the flogging block. His son was currently being educated at a nice American school and, at the sight of the scarred and splintered object, David went white. 'Dear God,' he said, 'I thought this sort of thing went out before the First World War.'

There was (and still is) an exclusive, self-electing club at Eton called Pop. To get in you had to be very senior and very highly regarded. In my time, Pop was mostly made up of muscle-bound adolescents with hardly a grey cell between them

– sporting achievements then being much more admired than academic ones. There were a few meaningless privileges to being a member. Only members of Pop were entitled to furl their umbrellas, or sit on a particular wall. They could wear grey-checked sponge-bag trousers instead of the regulation black pin-stripes, and they could sport a waistcoat made of any material they liked. I once fagged for a member of Pop who owned thirty-seven fancy waistcoats. One of them was made of real leopard skin. If a member of Pop caught you smoking a cigarette, he could summon you to the Pop library (which, given the average IQ of most of its members, can't have contained many books). There, in front of the entire fellowship, they would force your head out of the window, closing its sash firmly on your neck. Then the senior member would lash at your buttocks until something more interesting came along.

This also never happened to me.

The last and most usual form of corporal punishment was the one administered in-house – administered not, as might be assumed, by the housemaster, but by the captain of the house, an eighteen-year-old boy. He and his fellow prefects, known as the Members of the Library, laid down the law inside the house. They were the judges, the jury and the executioners. Permission had to be granted by the housemaster to cane a boy, but the accused wasn't present at the interview and his point of view was never a factor. All the captain of the house had to do was describe the crime and ask for the right to beat. Perhaps there were times when these permissions were withheld, but I never heard of one.

In my house, the ceremony went something like this: you, the accused, were caught doing something against the house rules by a member of the Library. Your crime was reported to the captain of the house. A discussion would then take place between the members as to whether or not it was an offence that warranted a beating. If the consensus decided that it was, the captain would go off for his short interview with his house-master. Once permission was granted, the junior Library member would be detailed to go and tell you to present your-self outside the Library door at such-and-such a time, which was always several hours in the future, allowing you ample opportunity to contemplate your approaching punishment. Having had plenty of time to get thoroughly frightened, you knocked, fearful and trembling, on the Library door – and you were careful to do it at the exact moment stipulated and not a second before nor a second after.

Delivered from within, in a tone of icy politeness – 'Come in.'

Once inside, you stood while the members, all seventeen- and eighteen-year-old boys with the collective maturity of a warren of bunny rabbits, stared coldly at you as you listened to the captain announcing your crime and punishment. Then you bent over the back of a chair and the captain lifted up the long and protective tails of your coat with the thing he'd been hold-ing in his hands all the way through his harangue – a four-foot cane of thin rattan. The tails of your coat were dropped neatly onto your horizontal back, exposing your pin-striped behind. The cane was raised –

This narrow bamboo stick whistled when it cut through the air, so you knew when to expect the blow, of which there were usually six. They were painful and left red weals. When it was all over, you were expected to thank the captain of the house for making you a better person.

This happened to me twice during my Eton days.

When I myself became a Member of the Library, I was witness to the occasion when my captain, a kind and intelligent fellow called Richard Castle, first beat a boy. I can't remember what the child had done but I do remember sitting in the Library with Richard Castle and the other members, talking among ourselves about the approaching ceremony.

Most of us had suffered beatings during our junior years, so we knew what to expect – but what was utterly *unexpected* was our mutual distaste at what we were about to do. Poor Richard Castle said he actually felt sick at the prospect of hitting a small boy with a stick, and we all said we felt pretty much the same way. I don't know if this reaction made us more mature than those who'd beaten us when we were the young transgressors; perhaps some of them had also felt this unease but had never shown it; others had, undoubtedly, relished the whole thing. But, even feeling the way we did, tradition overruled our sensitivities, and we went ahead with the nasty business. But it must have been a feeble caning, because the victim left the room with a grin of relief – and disbelief – spread across his face. Richard admitted that he'd held back because (since there were no classes offered at Eton in in How To Cane Boys) he had no idea how hard you were supposed to hit them, which was why he'd leaned towards hardly hitting the little boy at all.

If you give seventeen- and eighteen-year-old boys powers like these there are bound to be abuses but on the whole they were rare – and if discovered by the authorities, would be stopped quickly. Of course, in these more enlightened times, it's fair to say that any of these sanctioned treatments of children would now certainly be termed abuse, but it wasn't then because it was part of the same British life that had been going on in the same way for hundreds of years. In 1955, had you been so silly as to call a policeman and complain to him that you'd been assaulted by a teacher or a school prefect or even a parent, he would quite likely have given you a clip round the ear and asked if you thought you were a comedian.

So, while Eton housemasters blithely allowed strapping adolescents to hit small boys ceremonially with rattan canes – because that was then the norm – they were otherwise mostly kindly men who had already spent years as teachers at Eton and who had gained the privilege of running an Eton house by virtue of the virtues they'd displayed during their time there. My own housemaster, Francis Cruso, was typical: a sympathetic, middle-aged bachelor, who loved classical music only a little more than he loved great literature and funny plays. He had a sister called Thallatta or Thallassa (both of which mean 'the sea' in Greek) so it's reasonable to deduce that his parents might have been classicists to saddle their daughter with such a name. Certainly Francis Cruso's education had been a classical one – and, in fact, he had met and had become friendly with another Francis, my father, when they had read Latin and Greek together at Cambridge. He and my father continued to correspond and he did his best with me in a kind and understanding way. So, had Mr Cruso ever been aware of the subtle nastiness I suffered at the hands of one senior boy, he would certainly have put a stop to it. But he wasn't aware because I never told him; you simply didn't do such a thing – and anyway, the nastiness was more relentless than abusive, although to this day I dislike intensely the memory of this senior boy, holding against him the sort of grudge I've never held against the paedo-philiac Mr Spears.

He was the house captain of sport. I was small and light-weight, so I was made the cox of the house rowing eight, of which the captain of sport was also the captain. Being a cox of the house rowing eight should have been a cushy job. All you had to do was sit at the back of the boat, holding a string in each hand; these strings were connected to the boat's rudder. You faced the crew, with the number one oar, called the stroke, right in front of you. You had to learn the orders to start, the orders to stop, the orders to slow down or speed up the rhythm – and you had to learn to steer a fifty-foot-long, two-foot-wide wooden shell that only wants to go in a straight line.

I wasn't good at any of this, but I was the lightest of the new boys, so they made do with me until they could find somebody better. But making do wasn't in the captain's vocabulary, so he decided he would improve me. Or perhaps he just liked hector-ing small boys in their pyjamas. Or maybe he just liked an excuse to look at them. The lumbering thought processes of this lumbering bully remain a mystery.

Once or twice a week during the long summer term the captain of sport would wait until I was ready for bed. He would march into my room, hurl the door shut with a crash and throw all my clothes – which I'd draped on my armchair ready for tomorrow – all over the floor. Then he would sit in the chair and lecture me, and harangue me, and shout at me, and ask me why I was such a dreadful cox and what was it about me that made me so incompetent, and if I didn't improve by tomorrow I would be in serious trouble, and pay attention when I'm talking to you, you useless little twerp – and I was expected to stand there, in my bare feet and my blue flannel winceyettes, and meekly say I'm really terribly sorry over and over again until the awful creature went away. In retrospect what he did was not so frightful; but it was relentless. I started to dread those evenings in my room and, at the same time, I began to build up a burning hatred for this person who could do these humiliating things to me, but who was only five years older than I was. The treatment stopped either when I got too heavy to be the cox, or when the vile fellow left Eton – neither came too soon for me. Many years later, I ran into him at a school reunion dinner. He wore funereal black and his collar was reversed. The house bully had become, to my delight, a vicar.

Added to the list of why I disliked Eton so much must be the Field Game. This sport is played only at Eton. It's an odd amalgamation of soccer and rugby, with all the silliest aspects of both games – and none of the logical ones – incorporated into its complicated rules. Since it's only played at Eton, there can be no inter-school competition. In that respect, it's a little like the World Series of baseball in the USA – a 'world' series played only by Americans inside their own borders; every year, gloriously, the tournament is won by an American team.

I could never see the point of the Field Game and so I never took it seriously. In truth, I've never taken any game involving a ball seriously, because I'm myopic and can't see the ball clearly enough to do anything clever with it. I don't like running, I don't like mud and I don't like being out in the rain without an umbrella, so soccer and rugby and the ridiculous Field Game left me cold. Also wet and irritable.

Even in the summer, at Sunningdale, when cricket came along, I was a burden to my side. I couldn't bat and I threw like a girl. When I fielded the ball and tried to throw it back into play, the stupid thing would only travel a few feet, forcing me to run after it, pick it up and throw it again – and again – and again – until at last I got the ball close enough for somebody on my side to pick it up for me – by which time the two batsmen had scored an enormous number of runs and were ragged with exhaustion.

Many years later my friend the actor Simon Williams was putting together a village green cricket match and asked me to be on his side. I warned him that I would be of no use whatsoever and could, quite possibly, be a hazard instead, but he went ahead and put me in to bat, with himself at the other end. Something extraordinary happened; I hit the ball and we ran. Having reached the other end of the wicket, I became overexcited. I shouted to Simon to run again. He did. Halfway across, the wicketkeeper snatched the fielded ball out of the air and snapped off the bails. I'd run my captain out. Apparently this is the greatest crime you can commit in cricket. That's what Simon has said, quite often, over the years.

Eton allowed me to put my cricketing humiliations behind me. Situated on the banks of the River Thames, Eton is one of only a handful of English public schools that offers, in the summer term, rowing as an alternative to cricket. Rowing doesn't involve a ball, so I elected to become a Wet Bob – the Eton term for an oarsman. (Cricketers were called, logically enough I suppose, Dry Bobs). I wasn't much good at rowing either. Dragging a wooden skiff up the Thames backwards was hard, lonely work; blisters formed on your hands – the cure was to rub purple methylated spirits on them. Apparently this was supposed to toughen your skin. I don't know if it did or not, but it stung and made you smell like a camp stove. When I wasn't hauling my own boat upstream, I was coxing the house eight and putting up with the appalling future vicar. Later, I myself became my house's stroke oar; I was quite good at *acting* the part of a strenuous rower while doing as little as possible, letting the other seven oarsmen do all the work for me. All you have to do to be convincing at this is to grunt, and screw your face up, and hunch your shoulders at the start of each stroke – then you can just lean back and let your oar be pulled through the rushing water by the boat's momentum. It looked good, and I was getting away with doing almost nothing at all. I applied this science of idleness to my academic work too. The over-used phrase 'Could Try Harder' on my school report was always more than deserved.

Eton didn't go in for Drama. Not when I was there. Acting was thought to be an unsuitable activity for boys who were supposed to be training for careers in politics, the military, the church, chartered accountancy and inheriting money. There was no theatre at Eton, only the vast and echoing School Hall, which, while it did boast a raised platform at one end of the floor, was mostly used by visiting lecturers. A school play was permitted, but only once a year; it had to be a classic, prefer-ably by Shakespeare; and, according to rumour, it had to be badly acted, because while bad acting was acceptable in the eyes of God, good acting was profoundly immoral and the Lord didn't like that one little bit. This rumour included the name of the person supposedly responsible for these restrictive rules: Sir Claude Aurelius Elliott, a former headmaster and by this time the Provost of Eton. A keen mountaineer, Elliott was President of the Alpine Club from 1950 to 1952 and, in that capacity, he selected John Hunt to lead the successful 1953 Everest expedition with Edmund Hillary.

Whether or not Sir Claude really felt this way about acting is open to doubt; but *somebody* had put these boundaries in place and, since all I ever wanted to be was an actor, here was another reason why Eton was the wrong school for me. A small outlet for my ambitions was provided by Francis Cruso, who loved the theatre and who occasionally mounted secret, small-scale productions inside the house. I appeared in several of these, still playing girls and still getting my cheap laughs – but when I was about sixteen (and just beginning to resent slightly this insistence by others that I be so often in touch with my feminine side) and Mr Cruso suggested we do *The Importance Of Being Earnest*, with me as Cecily Cardew, I was brave enough to say I was terribly sorry sir, but I didn't want to play girls any more; and, because he was an understanding sort of man, he didn't insist and in fact (without a credible Cecily) quietly cancelled the whole project, which swelled my head and introduced me to the power of the word No.

I did act in two school plays. I was Edgar in *King Lear*, and The Governor Of Tilbury Fort in Richard Brinsley Sheridan's *The Critic*. On the strength of these two performances, I was asked if I'd like to join the Shakespeare Society. This was apparently a signal honour – but it turned out to be an honour only considered signal by the members themselves, since the Shakespeare Society was so select and secretive that nobody else at Eton had ever heard of it. So, boasting to one's friends about the signal honour of being asked to join the Shakespeare Society proved to be almost as unimpressive as claiming to have had the signal honour of going to bed with a Trinidadian girl called Jasmine.

The Shakespeare Society was less about the drama of the plays and more about an academic study of them; but since it did sometimes mount private performances of a few selected Shakespeare scenes, and since the performers were mostly clever scholars without a great deal of acting talent, I was asked to join them because I was considered to be a proper actor, which of course I wasn't, at least not yet. But they said they needed me, so I joined, and I boasted, and I was quite rightly put down by my unimpressed friends, and I performed Trinculo (or perhaps Stephano) from *The Tempest* for our small and select audience, which was composed of senior classics teachers headed by the imposing figure of the headmaster himself, Sir Robert Birley – a man so remote, so distant, that it was unlikely that you, an ordinary schoolboy among 1,400 other ordinary schoolboys would, in the course of your five years at Eton, ever meet the man. And, in fact, although I acted up a storm in front of him and he clapped politely at the end, we were never formally introduced and he never said a word to me.

Birley probably never said a word to Sir Ranulph Twisleton-Wykeham-Fiennes either – something he might later have regretted, since Ranulph (according to the *Guinness Book Of Records*) left Eton to become the 'World's Greatest Living Explorer'. The *Daily Telegraph* included Ranulph in their roster of 'Top 100 Living Geniuses'. The list of his extraordinary accomplishments is very long. He was a member of the SAS until he was thrown out for trying to blow up the film set of *Doctor Doolittle*, which starred Rex Harrison, who – according to reports of his behaviour – probably deserved being blown up. Ranulph was decorated for military bravery by the Sultanate of Oman, where he saw much guerilla action.

When he stopped being a soldier, he became an explorer, visiting the most inhospitable places on the globe, mostly on foot. He lost bits from both his hands from the effects of frostbite, doing some of the surgery himself with an old fretsaw. At the age of fifty-nine, four months after a double heart-bypass operation – and in the course of a single week – he ran in seven marathons on seven separate continents. At the age of sixty-five he climbed Mount Everest. He wrote books about his adventures and more books about the adventures of others.

In case anybody thinks I might have had some small involvement in any of these feats, my acquaintance with Ranulph at Eton was limited to a brief meeting, and later to a session of about twelve minutes, when we did our best not to hit each other.

I was entered, much against my will, in the school boxing tournament – by that same vicar-to-be captain of sport, who now insisted that everybody in Cruso's house under the age of fourteen had to take part. I discovered that, in my first round, I was pitted against a boy called Fiennes. He was in another house, and not in any of my classes, so I didn't know him. It occurred to me that I should sound him out and see if he was as reluctant as I was to get hurt.

Me: I see we're boxing on Saturday.

Fiennes: Yes.

Me: Are you any good?

Fiennes: No.

Me: Why are you doing it then?

Fiennes: Stupid captain of sport.

Me: Same here. And I don't really want to hit you, and I especially don't want to be hit.

Fiennes: Me neither. What do you suggest?

Me: Well, how about putting on a sort of show? So that it looks like we're doing proper boxing but we promise to not actually hit each other at all?

Fiennes: You're on.

So that's what we did. On the appointed day, in front of a crowd keen to watch the early eliminations, Ranulph and I climbed into the ring and flailed away at the air between us for three exhausting rounds. Neither he nor I landed a single punch – but we danced and we weaved and we jabbed and we swung and it must have looked terrific, because at the end the judges declared us to be the most evenly matched pair of boxers they'd ever seen and therefore the fight was a draw – but there can't be a draw, we must have a winner, so both of you will have to get up and fight one more deciding round.

Wearily, we met again in the centre of the ring. Once again we waved our boxing gloves in each other's direction By this time I could hardly lift my arms. Ranulph still could but only just. Two minutes into the three-minute round, he made a dreadful mistake.

Somehow or other one of his wild swings caught me high on my cheek. It didn't hurt but it staggered me a little. I saw Ranulph mouthing 'Sorrysorrysorry' at me, so I knew he hadn't done it on purpose. All the same, I put a little more distance between us, and we went back to the flailing routine – and then the bell rang and Ranulph, on the strength of that one landed blow, was declared the winner, which was a great relief to me because, in his second fight of the tournament, he went up against the school champion in that weight bracket and, in a flurry of blows, none of which he provided, was reduced in the first few moments of the first round to a bruised and bloody mess.

I did master one subject during my school years, although it wasn't on the syllabus. All my friends liked cars, so just to be different I decided to like motorbikes. I subscribed to magazines, I sent off for every catalogue and brochure available, I studied the individual models of now long-defunct companies like Ariel and AJS and Francis Barnett, and I learned to identify a bike just from the sound of its exhaust. Having thoroughly mastered this single subject, I felt that I no longer needed much more education – so, when I reached the age of seventeen, I set about persuading my father that Eton had no more to offer me and that I'd be better off finishing what little was left of my education in London. To my surprise he agreed – probably because the move would save him a lot of money but also, I suspect, because he knew of my growing passion for bikes and partly blamed Eton for my enthusiasm. He said to his old friend, Francis Cruso – 'You've had my son for four and a half years here at Eton and, as far as I can see, the only thing he's managed to acquire from the experience is an encyclopedic knowledge of motorcycles.'

Chapter 7

Having been a lazy and mediocre student in every academic subject, and an unenthusiastic and useless participant in every pointless sport, Eton probably parted from me as happily as I parted from Eton. At seventeen, I came home to London, to my mother's house in West Kensington. All I wanted to do at this point was go to the Royal Academy of Dramatic Art – RADA – and learn to be a film star. But first, according to the agreement I'd made with my father, I had to go to a cramming school to finish my studies.

There were several of these sad little places, many of them around Holland Park. They catered to students who didn't want to do any work, as well as to students who weren't particularly bright. I fitted both categories. The teachers were often rejects from somewhere better and they disliked being there quite as much as the pupils. Playing hooky was easy, so it was hardly surprising that, after six months, I managed to fail two out of my four exams. My father was disgusted, but I was free.

I mooched about during the summer, going to endless films, buying a new motorbike with the two hundred pounds my mad Great-Aunt Jane had left me (for those who are interested in these things, it was a silver blue Triumph Twenty-One 350cc) and finding a girlfriend called Margot. My father liked Margot but his irritation with everything else I was up to swelled until one day he said, 'I will not have you lolling about the place like this. Go and get a job.'

I had no idea how one went about doing such a thing. I imagined somebody who had a job to give away sort of *noticed* you – and having noticed you, decided that you were just the man for the job he had to give away. So, logically, the first thing to do would be to go and hang about somewhere and try to be noticed by somebody – and hope that the somebody who'd noticed you had a job they wouldn't mind handing over. With this vague scenario in mind, I went and hung about – in the manner of a man whose hobby it is to study brick walls – in the alley that leads to the stage door of the Royal Court Theatre in Sloane Square. I studied the brick walls of the alley for several days until at last an exasperated person came out of the stage door and said, 'What do you *want?*'

'A job,' I muttered miserably.

'Why the hell didn't you say so a week ago? Well don't just stand there, come in.'

They let me be a stagehand. I got seven pounds a week. I shifted scenery in a play called *August for the People*, which starred Rex Harrison and Rachel Roberts. I went on the road with the play, travelling to Cambridge in the scenery lorry. We built the set in the Arts Theatre all night and then, a week later, spent another night tearing it down. Then back to London and the Royal Court. I was having a wonderful time. Everybody was very kind to me, particularly when they discovered that I wanted to go to RADA. Actors (not Rex Harrison, who was so astonishingly bad-tempered that I never mustered the courage to tell him I'd been at school with his son) patted me on the head and wished me luck. My fellow stagehands predicted waggishly that when I got to be famous I wouldn't speak to them any more. I promised I would.

When the Harrison play finished, the theatre management suggested I become a student stage manager, to be paid one pound a week, which was a considerable drop in salary from the seven pounds I was getting as a stagehand. But – as they explained to me – the new job was in the nature of an apprenticeship and I was jolly lucky to be offered it because I would be receiving an excellent on-the-spot-training, let alone the honour of working for the great stage director John Dexter – a once-in-a-lifetime experience that was pretty much priceless, so take the job you ungrateful little bugger, or else clear off because we don't need any more stagehands for this production, which is only one set and no scene changes and it's called *The Keep* and are you on board or not?

The Keep was a very Welsh play, full of very Welsh actors like Glyn Owen and Mervyn Johns and Jessie Evans. I had lots to do. An enormous quantity of fake red wine was drunk every night and I had to make it. The bottles had to be washed out thoroughly, then filled with a mixture of water, red food dye (a tasteless substance called cochineal – made, disturbingly, from crushed beetles) and several drops of a dark brown syrup called burnt sugar that you got from the chemist. The brown colouring gave the wine exactly the right tawny look. Then the bottles had to be corked and lead foil wrapped around the top and all placed neatly on the sideboard on the set.

During rehearsals, the director, John Dexter (for whom, I kept being told, it was an honour to be working) asked for a set of ornate castors, which would be put under the four legs of a principal armchair. He didn't want any of those little plastic cup things – the objects had to have some sort of substantial architectural quality to them, or else they'd be rejected. I was sent out to search for the things. In an antique shop I found four splendid heavy glass castors, fluted on the sides and scalloped on the top and substantially architectural in every possible way. Very pleased with myself, I took them back to the theatre and made the dreadful mistake of asking John Dexter if he liked them.

'Very nice. But did I say glass? I did not say glass. I don't want them in glass. Get me four *exactly* like that, but made of wood. Oak.'

Off I went again. I visited antique shops, furniture stores, junkyards and office supply companies. I even found a wood carver, who said he could make them for me but it would take at least six months and the Royal Court would have to take out a mortgage to pay for the things. After several days of wandering fruitlessly round London I returned, depressed and anxious and exhausted, to report my failure to my boss, the stage manager.

'Where the hell have you been?'

I explained about my mission.

'Oh Jesus,' he muttered, pulling me into a dark corner of the stage, where we couldn't be overheard. 'You're a bloody idiot. Just paint the glass ones brown, stick them under the chair legs and don't, for Christ's sake, ask John if he likes them.' I did as I was told and Dexter never mentioned them again. A valuable lesson was learned: don't ask difficult employers for their approval. Just do your job and hope they don't notice.

When I wasn't searching London for things that didn't exist, I was attending rehearsals. Sometimes I was allowed to prompt the actors when they forgot their lines. Having the brain of an eighteen-year-old, with the absorption qualities of Kleenex, the dialogue of the entire play embedded itself in my memory. When it came time for John Dexter to light the play he asked for somebody to stand in for the actors and I was a logical choice.

Dexter and the lighting designer and I were alone in the theatre. I stood on the stage, awaiting instructions. From out of the darkness of the auditorium came the first one.

'Right – could you . . . sorry, what's your name again?'

'Ian, Mr Dexter, sir.'

'Right. Go to where Mervyn comes in at the top of act one.'

Taking my life in my hands, I hurled myself from the top diving board, hoping desperately that the pool had water in it.

'Er . . . I could do the whole play if you like, sir.'

'What?'

'Well, er . . . I know it, you see, sir. So I could do it if you like.'

'You know the whole play?'

'Yes, sir.'

'The whole bloody thing?'

'Yes, sir.'

'And you want to do it all by yourself?

'Yes, sir.'

'Playing all the parts?

'Yes, sir.'

(above left) My mother Aileen, my father Francis, my sister Kerry and I being formal at somebody's wedding. *(Author's Personal Collection)*

(above right) Aunt Betty as Puck in *Fairy Pearls*. *(Author's Personal Collection)*

(left) My grandmother Enid, my mother Aileen and John Mills. *(Author's Personal Collection)*

(above) Post-war parents, Francis and Aileen. *(Author's Personal Collection)*

(below left) My uncle David Ogilvy, in his beloved garden at Château de Touffou. *(Author's Personal Collection)*

(below right) The author – a just-post-war child in St. John's Wood. *(Author's Personal Collection)*

(above) At Sunningdale School – the small, squashed one in the front row. *(Author's Personal Collection)*

(left) A Sunningdale School concert – the author as Airman. *(Author's Personal Collection)*

(above left) My children, Emma and Titus. *(Author's Personal Collection)*

(above right) With John Mills. *(Author's Personal Collection)*

(below) The Queen Mother does her thing – with me, Michael York, Christopher Reeve and a bit of John Mills. *(© Harry Myers/REX/Shutterstock)*

With James Mason in *Stranger in the House*. (© Moviestore/REX/Shutterstock)

The Day the Fish Came Out, with Candice Bergen. (© Moviestore/REX/Shutterstock)

(above) With Boris Karloff in *The Sorcerers*. *(© DDP, Camera Press London)*

(left) The Sorcerers, with Elizabeth Ercy at 90 mph. *(Author's Personal Collection)*

Witchfinder General, with Hilary Dwyer *(© DDP, Camera Press London)*

Waterloo – dancing with Veronica De Laurentiis at the Duchess of Richmond's ball. *(© Arenapal)*

(left) As Edgar Linton in *Wuthering Heights*, with Anna Calder-Marshall. *(© Hulton Archive/Getty Images)*

(below) No Sex Please, We're British – with Beryl Reid, Susan Penhaligon, Ronnie Corbett and Arthur Lowe. *(© Moviestore/REX/Arenapal)*

'This I have to see. Go ahead.'

There was water in the pool. Of course, I could always drown . . .

For the next three hours I galloped about the stage, being Welsh. Occasionally Dexter would stop me while a light was adjusted. Then on again. 'Start with Jessie's speech. The one about the wine glasses. Perhaps a bit less Welsh this time.'

I don't know if Dexter was amused by me but I had a terrific time and the play got lit properly, which was the main thing.

I don't recall much about the run of *The Keep*. It's in the nature of things in the theatre (and indeed much to be desired) for exactly the same events to happen every night, so only occasions of a fairly catastrophic kind stick in the mind. I remember a small catastrophe: one night, when setting the props on stage for the performance, I managed to leave the telephone on the prop table in the wings. In the middle of the play the absent phone rang, as it was supposed to do. The sound came from a hidden speaker inside the sideboard where the telephone, in all its squat, black Bakelite glory, should have been squatting but wasn't. Miss Jessie Evans reached for it. Saw that it wasn't there. Glared into the prompt corner with a look of incandescent hatred. Turned back and looked out over the audience with the air of a woman who was deciding whether or not to be bothered answering the bloody thing at all. The non-existent phone continued to shrill. Miss Evans came to a decision. She took the breath of an actress close to the end of her tether. 'I'll take it in the hall,' she said imperiously and stalked into the wings.

It didn't matter that everybody afterwards said how clever she'd been and how brilliantly she'd managed to ad-lib herself out of a tight spot – Miss Evans was very cross with me. They all were. I was nearly fired, but not quite. It's possible they felt sorry for me – not because my girlfriend Margot had recently dumped me for somebody she liked better than me, but because I'd just failed in my first attempt to get into a drama school and the experience had so disconcerted me, so dumbfounded me, that perhaps they put my carelessness down to that and let me off with a warning.

I had tried out for LAMDA – the London Academy of Music and Dramatic Art – doing their entrance audition as a sort of preparatory try-out audition for the one I really wanted to do for RADA. To my outraged amazement, I failed – which was impossible, surely? I'd been THE ACTOR at Eton. A member of the prestigious Shakespeare Society. My mother had been an actress. My father had been an actor, of a sort. I'd acted in all kinds of things. Nanny had always said I was brilliantly talented. How could I possibly have failed to get into LAMDA – in my uninformed view an altogether inferior place to the school I really wanted to go to? And, if I couldn't get into LAMDA, how on earth could I expect to win over the RADA judges?

Somebody suggested I might find the services of a specialist in audition techniques useful at this point. The name Denys Blakelock came up. I gave Mr Blakelock a call and an appointment was set up.

Denys Blakelock had retired from a distinguished career as an actor because of some sort of health issues, although there was a suggestion that he'd left the profession for religious reasons. Denys was a devout Catholic and it was said that he'd overheard some fatuous priest tell an actress who was dithering with conversion to Rome that the only way to heaven was by abandoning the theatre altogether. I don't believe this was the reason Denys quit acting for he never entirely abandoned the theatre, he simply stopped appearing and started teaching instead, specialising in How To Do Auditions, which was obviously one of my weak spots.

He lived in a dark, cosy flat, filled with his theatrical memorabilia. The first question he asked me was what role had I picked to perform for my failed LAMDA audition?

'Andrew Undershaft, from *Major Barbara*.'

Denys' jaw dropped. Then he laughed. 'My dear boy – we've all heard of miscasting but this is ridiculous. You're a pretty young thing of what – eighteen? With a dear little piping voice, slender as a reed, and as mature as a Pekinese puppy. And you go and choose a character who is half a century older than you, a great bullying bear of a fellow, a billionaire arms dealer and union-busting plutocrat, before whom much of the world trembles in fear. The LAMDA judges are agog, waiting with anticipation for a great, mature, imposing mountain of an applicant to stride confidently onto the stage. And then *you* appear? Well, of course you didn't get in!'

Denys picked my audition speeches himself and he picked right because a few weeks after I'd done my RADA audition, I got a letter telling me I was accepted. It didn't hurt that Denys Blakelock had been one of the judges on the selecting panel either.

Chapter 8

My father had been an actor for a short time. My mother was an actress for a little longer. She was the daughter of a country doctor and, with her younger sister Betty, had been a child performer on the Isle of Wight. There was an article in *The Times* from December 1921 about one of these amateur shows. The conductor in the article, Dr Raymond, was my grandfather George:

> *Children Entertain Convicts. Fairy Play at Parkhurst. An entertainment was given to over six hundred convicts of Parkhurst prison yesterday afternoon. A party of children from Newport, Isle of White, under the conductorship of Dr Raymond, gave a performance of the musical play Fairy Pearls. The prisoners showed their appreciation of the performance by applauding loudly. Aileen and Betty Raymond, the little daughters of the conductor, were especially popular, the former as a Fairy Queen and Betty as Puck. The Fairy Queen's song 'Sunshine and Moonshine' was a special favourite. The thanks of the audience was expressed at the close by one of the convicts.*

I can only imagine what the Parkhurst convicts – who probably didn't have much say in the sort of entertainment they'd prefer – *really* thought of *Fairy Pearls*. Six years later, when she was about seventeen, my mother went to RADA where, in a class of twenty students, there were eighteen girls and two lucky young men. The proportions have since changed.

One of Aileen's first jobs as a professional actress was as a junior member of a touring repertory company, winsomely called The Quaints. In September 1929, The Quaints took an extraordinary number of plays and players on an extended tour of the Middle and Far East. The repertoire included *Hamlet* (in which nineteen-year old Aileen Raymond played either Ophelia or Gertrude, depending on who was available for the performance), *Julius Caesar* (she was Calpurnia in that one), *Young Woodley*, *Funny Face*, *That's a Good Girl* (she was in the ensemble and wrote that she was '. . . the <u>best</u> chorus girl!'), *So This Is Love*, *Mr Cinders* (at one performance she was '. . . quite all right as Phyllis, until "Honeymoon For Far" – she doesn't say what went wrong with the number, but she had gone out before the show with ". . . Mr Knight, in his car and we had a drink or two"). She was in *When Knights were Bold* (she was given the leading role of Rowena on 1 February and opened a week later on 8 February – it was '. . . a <u>topping</u> house – everyone pleased!') Other plays in the repertoire included *The Girl Friend*, *The Man From Toronto*, *A Warm Corner* and *Journey's End*.

I know all this because my mother kept a detailed diary of the tour. The Quaints travelled by ship to India, Pakistan, Singapore, Hong Kong, China, Japan and Burma. Once inside the various countries, there were interminable overnight train journeys to most of the major cities. Many evenings saw the company performing in cabaret at whichever hotel they were staying. My mother had tiffin in the officers' clubs and flirted with the military. A Captain Morgan squired her round Rangoon; she tired of him after several days –'Morgan <u>would</u> make love to me. The beast makes me sick.' She rarely got to bed before three o'clock in the morning.

The company danced to the gramophone in each other's hotel rooms, drank startling amounts of alcohol, had tremendous rows and upsets and woke at noon with appalling hangovers. Several 'heavenly men' bought her presents. In Hong Kong she smoked opium. A member of the company called Chubby declared he was 'violently in love with me!!!!' Several other male members of the company, at one time or another, '. . . tried to be sloppy.' If something was fun, she called it 'topping' or 'ripping'. If it wasn't fun, it was 'rotten'. A poor performance by herself – 'I was rank'. A Japanese man gave her '. . . an exquisitely beautiful liqueur. 'Pousse Café'. Dessertspoonful of each ingredient: (1) French Grenadine. (2) Creme De Mênthe. (3) Cherry Brandy. (4) Cognac. (5) Maraschino. Felt awfully ill.'

She met Noël Coward in Shanghai. Coward was on a Far East tour himself, but he contracted influenza in China and spent his brief convalescence writing *Private Lives*. He was already a major star in England, both as an actor and as a playwright, but he was bored and lonely, and when he heard there was a bunch of English actors passing through, he went and joined them – and one night he even played the role of Stanhope as a sort of guest star in *Journey's End*. He took Aileen to dinner and was '. . . perfectly marvellous. Gave me a lecture.' (She doesn't say about what).

He played Truth or Dare with the company late into the night. When it was my mother's turn to ask Coward a Truth Or

Dare question, she blurted out, 'Which do you prefer sleeping with, Noël – a man or a woman?' The rest of the company were appalled by the impertinence of this very junior cast member and tried to sit on her – but Coward waved them away and said he would answer – probably because he'd got rather a neat reply rehearsed and ready, and wanted to try it out. He said, after a moment of stagy contemplation, 'What a good question, dear. With whom would I rather sleep? Let's see now. Well – for pleasure a man, for comfort a woman.'

The male juvenile lead in The Quaints was a young actor called John Mills. A diary entry early on the tour – 'Johnny plucked my eyebrows. He is a dear boy.' A later entry had her '. . . plucking John's eyebrows, much against his will.' Not surprisingly, with all this plucking going on, John developed an infection in one eye and, in those pre-antibiotic days, my mother spent hours bathing it in warm water. Later, he developed a severe infection in a finger shortly after Aileen had developed a severe infection in her arm, both of which had to be lanced by local doctors. With no penicillin to treat these problems they were potentially limb-and-life-threatening, and John had to spend several days in a Shanghai hospital. A lot of mutual nursing went on. Inevitably, Aileen and John began an affair. 'Exquisite time with John and I am completely drugged with adoration.'

In August 1930 she discovered that she was to be sent home, along with some of the other girls in the company. The tour was winding down and many in the extended casts were no longer needed. John was to stay on for a few more weeks. Their parting was miserable and Aileen cried copious tears.

John wrote in her diary, a secret letter, to be discovered later by her when she was at sea. The language is of the period but the sentiments expressed are obviously deeply felt and, as far as love letters go, it could hardly be surpassed.

I 'spect you're right out in the middle of the sea – do you remember the night in your room when you washed the frock in salt? That's the night I wrote this while you were in the bathroom – I'm sorry if I've spoilt your diary – but I thought this would make you feel I'm with you – as I am always every minute – my love will protect you and keep you safe until I can hold you in my arms again (I am making myself feel terribly miserable writing this – is it a nice surprise?) Darling adorable babe – I love you as I didn't think it possible to love anyone – I adore you, worship you to a state of grovelling! Awful but true – I know the time will fly, 'cause you'll be with me every minute – how I should love to be with you when you find this. I can imagine your eyes – the most wonderful pair that ever happened – glistening and looking dewy – and your soft arms and darling hands – you're wearing my ring, aren't you? And your dearest baby legs and toes, which I want to kiss and hold and never let go. Please take terrific care of your sweet self for me. Darling I must stop now – you've just come out of the bathroom and your (sic) so exquisite. All my love, dearest – and kisses on every bit of your darling body which I adore – John XXXXXXX

Aileen arrived back in England, docking at Tilbury on 29 September 1930, having spent an entire year away from England. John joined her shortly after. They spent a little while living together and then they got married. They stayed married for nine years, some of them unhappily. There were no children and John finally fell in love with a pretty blonde actress called

Mary Hayley Bell. She became the great love of his life. Aileen and John divorced shortly after. He married Mary in 1941 and they lived happily ever after.

With all these actors in my extended family it was inevitable that I would end up as one too. And thirty-one years after my mother had gone there, I started my two-year course at the Royal Academy of Dramatic Art.

I was relatively rich at RADA. I lived at home and the fees were paid by my doubtful father, who also gave me a generous allowance of ten pounds a week. Compared to many of my fellow students, who lived in scruffy bedsitting rooms on tiny grants given to them by their local councils, from which pittance they had to clothe, feed and house themselves, I was Croesus. Compounding my contemporaries' poverty were all the additional expenses that RADA imposed, like books and black tights and strange bone contraptions you put in your mouth as an aid to better speech.

Being slightly rich at RADA could be an embarrassment. We were deep in the era of the kitchen sink period of drama, where everything that was working class had value and where everything that smacked of Rattigan or Coward or Ivor Novello was considered passé at best and, at worst, almost contemptible. My strangulated Etonian vowels were a terrible disadvantage within the walls of RADA. It was hard to be taken seriously when you talked like Prince Charles and had ten pounds a week. I was something of an anachronism – unlike my classmate John Murray. He came from Walsall, had almost no money at all and didn't think much of London.

'Blooody 'orrible place. Well, there's noothing blooody here, is there?' It transpired that all John had seen of London was the walk from his bedsit in Battersea to the local tube station, and then the short walk from Euston Square station to RADA. I suggested he get a motorbike. It turned out he had just enough money for a used BSA. A week later he rode up to RADA on it, hugged me fiercely and said, 'Ehh – blooody Loondon! Ehh – bloody fantastic place!'

John liked to play up his roots. 'You 'aven't blooody lived, mate! You don't know what it's like! Life, mate! *Life!* You've not blooody lived until you've walked down the street with no seat to yer trousis.'

My only riposte to this sort of stuff was to mutter that *he* hadn't bloody lived until he'd had lunch at the Savoy. It was nice of him not to hit me.

Because of my vile background, I was considered – by John Fernald, the principal (and by some other teachers too) – to be something of a dilettante. I tried hard to prove I wasn't. One teacher who seemed to see some sort of potential in me was Jack Lynn.

Jack had been dean of the prestigious Pasadena Playhouse School of Drama in California and had taught Shakespeare to Dustin Hoffman and Gene Hackman and Charles Bronson. Now a leading director at RADA, he'd taught the likes of Ian McShane and Anthony Hopkins and John Hurt. Jack directed me in *The Cherry Orchard*. He had the happy idea of casting everybody against type, so I – the youngest and the freshest-faced in the class – was to play Firs, the ancient and decrepit butler of the estate. Covered in white hair, I hobbled around the stage, bent double and wheezing my few lines straight at the floor. I based my performance on Roy Dotrice's portrayal of Firs in a West End production I'd recently seen, which starred

John Gielgud and Peggy Ashcroft and a very young Judi Dench. Roy Dotrice had also covered himself in white hair, had bent double, and had addressed all his lines to the floor. I copied him exactly. John Fernald, who apparently hadn't sees this prestigious production, said I wasn't too bad and, if I could keep up that sort of standard, he might let me stay the course.

In my second year, Jack Lynn directed a RADA production for the Southwark Shakespeare festival. Our contribution that year was *Measure For Measure*. It starred Gemma Jones, who was already one of the great white hopes of the academy. I played the small part of Barnardine, 'a dissolute prisoner'. Once again Jack covered me in wig and beard and moustache, probably in an attempt to rough me up a little – at least in my outward appearance. He then discovered that a fellow cast member called John Golightly had a strange talent. John had a double-jointed back and could bend himself backwards disconcertingly further than seemed possible. With that in mind, Jack devised a horribly violent scuffle in the jail where John Golightly and I were both prisoners. This entirely superfluous-to-the-plot fight ended with me bending John slowly and sadistically over my knee. With him screaming in agony – and when it looked like his back could take no more stress without breaking – John would suddenly let everything go, flopping into an impossibly tight upside-down U-shape – and at the same moment a stage manager in the wings snapped a piece of wood with a horrible cracking sound. There were screams from the audience and there was a rumour that somebody had even fainted. Jack Lynn was delighted.

It was in this production that *Measure For Measure* gained a new scene. A couple of actors couldn't make their costume changes in time, so Jack Lynn simply wrote a two-minute cod-Shakespeare scene to give them a little breathing space. A critic, writing in one of the better-class London newspapers, commented that it was '. . . so refreshing to see the full folio performed at last.'

Jack was the only person I ever knew who could recite, from start to finish, four or possibly five Shakespeare plays. His knowledge of old films was encyclopedic. He loved rich food and Cuban cigars. He thought Claude Rains was the greatest actor who had ever lived. He didn't care for Laurence Olivier at all. He was a most fond and generous man and he and I became close friends and remained so until the end of his long life. He loved, without reservation, me, both my wives and all my children, and thought of himself as being closely related to us all, a fancy none of us ever felt like denying him.

Unlike Eton, all my classes at RADA were fun – even the dull-sounding ones like Voice (Remedial). In Voice (Remedial) you were taught how to speak standard English. John Murray had to iron out his Walsall accent, Ron Bridges had to correct his cockney, and I had to stop sounding like Princess Margaret. Most of my vowels needed adjustment, except for the way I said 'air'. My 'air' sound was perfection according to Barry, our voice teacher. If anybody wanted to know how to say 'air' Barry would send them round to me, and I would say 'air' at them until they got it right.

I loved the dance and movement classes, and the fencing classes, and the makeup classes, where we learned how to apply Leichner greasepaint to our faces in the time-honoured way. A Juvenile Leading Man of a Healthful Disposition? Simple – a scrub of Number 9 on each cheek and a couple of dabs on the forehead. The same with Number 5. Then rub hard, spreading the thick, greasy mixture all over the face, with care taken to extend it down the neck because we don't want a mask that stops dead at the jawline, now do we? A dot of red in the inner corners of both eyes, to make them sparkle. Heavy black lines on top and bottom eyelid, extending outwards at least half an inch, with a little flash of white painted between them. Outline the mouth in carmine. A straight line of white painted down the bridge of your nose. If wearing a fake beard, be sure to paint a layer of spirit gum first, let dry, then paint a second layer before attempting to stick the thing on. Finish off with a dusting of face powder – the excess can be brushed away using the furry underside of your lucky rabbit's foot.

Of course, no modern actor uses these extremes of stage makeup any more. They aren't necessary, not with the sort of lighting that theatres use nowadays and, in fact, weren't necessary when I was a young actor either. They were simply a hangover from earlier times, when excessive exaggeration of facial features were thought essential to get the point across. In those days, the production photographs of a play were often quite bizarre. The young men and the young girls in the cast all looked like painted harlots and the character actors portraying elderly people seemed to have drawn tramlines all over their faces.

Peter Barkworth and Robin Ray taught technique. How to walk across a stage. How to light a cigarette. How to pour a drink and talk at the same time. Peter Barkworth's speciality was How To Laugh. Laughing was the most useful trick Peter taught, particularly the hysterical sort, when it becomes difficult to speak. 'Before you try to laugh or speak, empty your lungs of all traces of air. Then, *without replacing any of it*, start to laugh and speak.' What comes out is a sort of helpless wheeze, which is exactly the sound we all make when, helpless with laughter, we try to say something. Kevin Spacey is very good at it.

When we weren't in class, we were rehearsing plays, or scenes from plays. I was Orlando in *As You Like It*, Willie Mossop in *Hobson's Choice*, Stuart in *The Dragon's Mouth*. I played two chords on a banjo in an Eleanor Farjeon musical. I was Tarquin the last Etruscan king of Rome in something or other. I got a lot of unwanted laughs in that one, possibly because the RADA wardrobe department dressed me in a very short, frilly tunic in the days when miniskirts were the fashion – what with that and my girlish looks, I probably looked more like a Sloane Ranger called Amanda than a fierce Etruscan king called Tarquin.

Since I was almost entirely without any sort of musical sense whatsoever, it was logical that I should form a RADA rock group called the Wombats. When I say I formed it, I mean I suggested the idea to a couple of friends and they thought the idea wasn't half bad. They changed their minds when they heard me play the drums but by then it was too late – the Wombats was a done deal and RADA students were asking us to play at their parties. I was a terrible drummer – self–taught by a bad teacher – and I could only beat out one particular rhythm, a sort of uncertain swing, heavy on the cymbals, with occasional and daring use of the bass tom tom. We lacked a bass guitarist, so it was up to me to provide the low notes. I loosened the skin on the tom tom until it produced a kind of flabby thump and this was my main contribution to the Wombats – or, as they were once known, Nicky Henson And The *Sensational* Wombats.

Nicky Henson was the son of the great Leslie Henson, a comic actor and music hall artist of genius. Nicky wasn't actually doing the acting course at RADA – at sixteen, he was too young. But, given his theatrical pedigree, John Fernald had agreed to let him come to the academy on the stage managers' course, which lasted a year. If, by the end of that year, Nicky had acquitted himself well enough as a stage manager, he would be allowed onto the acting course, even though he would still have been younger than most students there, some of whom were well into their twenties; David Ryall – easily the best actor in my class and who went on to have a distinguished career mostly at the National Theatre – was close to thirty.

At the end of his successful year of learning how to be a stage manager, Nicky was congratulated by John Fernald and invited to stay on and join the acting course. Nicky declined on the grounds that he didn't really have the time – he was about to start rehearsals of the first West End production of the musical *Camelot*, starring Laurence Harvey. Nicky Henson, at the age of seventeen, was to play the arch villain Mordred. So, metaphorically at least, Nicky Henson told John Fernald that he could take his acting course and stuff it.

In the Wombats Nicky played lead guitar. But so did John Murray, my Walsall friend. There were personality clashes. Nicky Henson did Johnny Cash numbers; John Murray did Frank Ifield songs. A third member of the group was Sean Brosnan, also on the stage managers' course. Sean played rhythm guitar and could adapt to either. I played bad Glenn Miller and couldn't adapt to anything, so everything we played – from country and western through skiffle and all the way to rock – came out sounding like something from a 1940s radio show.

But we were much in demand, mostly at RADA parties; by the time we came on, usually in the early hours of the morning, everybody was drunk and uncritical, so we got away with much. Nicky and John and Sean were excellent musicians but I wasn't, and towards the end of our careers as rockers there were some rumbling noises from the others about getting a proper drummer, or breaking up entirely – or anything, really, to stop having to put up with such a cheesy rhythm section.

Once we played in a real variety show, a single performance at the Winter Gardens theatre in Bournemouth, on Boxing Day. The show was fronted by a popular television comedian of the time, Norman Vaughan, whose catchphrase was either 'swingin!' or 'dodgy!', depending on the context. On the same bill – we were way down at the bottom – was Dusty Springfield and the Springfields. The band music was provided by the Eric Winstone Orchestra (Eric Winstone was one of the very few men who once managed to obtain a court order prohibiting his mother-in-law from ever staying in his house). Also appearing that evening was Roberto Cardinale – 'Italy's Romantic Singer' – (did they only have the one?) – and Nicholas Parsons, who I think must have been the Master of Ceremonies.

Some thought went into our costumes for this show. After all, this was variety and something out of the ordinary would be expected. None of us could afford matching spangly sequinned jackets, so we hunted through our wardrobes for anything we might have in common. We found we all had dark grey suits and white shirts and black ties – except Nicky, who owned the negative – a white suit, a black shirt and a white tie. So, in consideration of the fact that for this one night only we were 'Nicky Henson And The Sensational Wombats', it was agreed (although John Murray was quite unhappy about it) that Nicky should be allowed to stand out in this special way.

Very occasionally we played at debutante dances, at grand houses out in the country. We got these gigs because of my sister Kerry who, two years before, had been picked as Debutante Of The Year by whichever tabloid newspaper happened to be running stories about the Bright Young Things. Because she'd done the season, Kerry knew a lot of upper-crustish sorts of people and it was assumed that I, as her younger brother, would follow her into the season as one of the many young male escorts without whose dubious company most debutantes might have managed to hang onto their virginities for a little while longer. But the season held no interest for me and, rudely, I never replied to the number of gilt-edged invitations to cocktail parties and balls and debutante teas that came through my parents' front door.

However, because Kerry mentioned us occasionally to her aristocratic friends, the Wombats did manage to play at several of these glittering affairs. We would always be the last band of the evening, coming on at well past midnight, when many of the guests were on the point of leaving – so the quality of the music was not so important as, say, a nice steady rhythm for the Bright Young Things to jiggle about to.

Once, after an early-hours gig, we were invited to stay the night at one of these big country houses. When we all met up the next morning, John Murray was quivering with indignation.

'You'll never guess what happened to me last night,' he huffed.

'What, John?'

'I got back to my room and I went in and – you'll never guess – there was a blooody girl in my blooody bed!'

We stared at him, eyes wide. 'A *girl?*'

'In my bloody *bed*. Would you believe it?'

We said we wouldn't.

'And that's not the end of it,' said John, bitterly.

We said we very much hoped it wasn't.

'She was naked an' all!'

'*Naked?*' Our eyes got wider. 'What did you *do?*'

'Well – I wasn't having that, was I? I told her – I told her straight out – "You get out of there!" Blooody disgoosting! Naked girl in my bed! I'm not standing for that! I told her! I said – "Blooody piss off!" She did, I'm glad to say. Blooody naked girl in my bed! Blooody disgoosting!'

We stopped staring at John and stared at each other instead. Either Walsall instilled Christ-like moral sensibilities into its sons or John Murray was barking mad.

Once we were approached by a small, weedy young man who said he thought we had potential and, since he was embarking on a career in music group management and we were a music group of a sort, would we care to take his card and have a think about him managing us for a bit? We thanked him and said we were only doing this as a hobby because what we really wanted to be were actors, so while his interest in us was flattering and much appreciated, thank you but no thank you. Later, we all had cause to remember the name on the card he'd given us.

He was Brian Epstein who, curiously, had dropped out of RADA several years earlier because he said he didn't like being a student – the same Brian Epstein who signed and managed the Beatles' early career, who signed Cilla Black, and Gerry and the Pacemakers, and Billy J. Kramer among others, and who was called 'the fifth Beatle' by the boys themselves – and who died of an accidental overdose of sleeping pills at the age of thirty-two.

Had we signed with Brian Epstein, I wouldn't have lasted long. Pete Best of the Beatles was at least a proper drummer and he was fired in favour of Ringo Starr, who some say wasn't. (John Lennon, it was rumoured, for one. When asked if he thought Ringo Starr was the best drummer in the world, Lennon is supposed to have replied, 'Fuck off – he's not even the best drummer in the Beatles.') Like Pete Best, I would have been ousted in a heartbeat. Nicky and John and Sean might have stayed loyal to me for a couple of days – after all, I was the founder of the Wombats – but the thought of enduring the tedious swing rhythm played by me – on every single number, regardless of tempo or metre, for the rest of their musical careers – would have been quite enough to harden their hearts against me by the time the third day came along.

I had love lives at RADA. They were called Lynne, and Harriet, and Amber. Lynne died tragically young and Harriet went home to Austria. Amber was the best. She was my first proper girlfriend and we were together for at least a year.

When I left RADA I departed with a little more confidence and marginally more talent than when I'd started there two years earlier. I'd also acquired an agent. Aude Powell of Brunskill Management had signed me up soon after my first year. She proved to be the best agent I ever had.

Chapter 9

In England in the 1960s most medium-sized towns and every city boasted a repertory theatre. Every repertory theatre in the land needed a Juvenile Lead. I was, if nothing else, a Juvenile Lead.

Thanks to Aude Powell's powers of persuasion, I started working almost immediately after leaving RADA. I first joined Colchester Repertory Theatre for three plays only – then, with that brief experience under my belt, I was at the Marlowe Theatre at Canterbury for a six-month season, and finally a member of the company at the pretty little Victorian playhouse in Northampton for another six months.

The system was known as fortnightly rep. A new play every two weeks. Rehearse all day from nine in the morning to six at night for the next one, a quick bite to eat in a cheap greasy spoon café and then perform the current production in the evenings. Eight shows a week, with matinees on Wednesdays and Saturdays. Hard work, and wonderful experience for young actors – although older actors would often jeer at us lucky ones and boast about the horrors of the now abandoned weekly rep, with a new play every *seven* days, in which there wasn't even enough time to learn the lines, let alone produce an adequate performance.

Most young actors benefited greatly from the repertory experience, although there were pitfalls. When a play is put on in only ten days, (or, in the case of weekly rep, in five) it's inevitable that shortcuts are adopted, like learning the gist of a speech rather than getting it word for word. Paraphrasing your part in a play is a big sin in the theatre – apart from mangling a playwright's precious words, the improvised cues you might give your fellow actors often tend to be erratic – but in rep, it was almost inevitable and you learned to be quick on your feet. An actor once cut much of his speech to me and ended up with a short improvisation that had little to do with the matter in hand; then he stopped talking and stared at me hopefully. When I didn't respond quickly enough, he said, 'I've finished now. Go on. It's your turn.' Since his made-up-on-the-spot cue rendered my scripted reply pure nonsense, this was hardly helpful.

When there's no time for any sort of profound character development, easy tricks can be substituted. Over time, these tricks can become bad habits. You're playing a Debonair Youth from the British upper classes? Lean one elbow on the inevitable mantlepiece, cross your legs at the ankle and puff on a cigarette. You're an Old Codger this week? Hobble about, bent double, and wheeze at the floor. (I knew this one well). The Funny Neighbour Next Door? Do a funny walk and put on a funny voice and if you're funny enough the audience won't care that you don't appear to know your lines very well. The Police Inspector in a thriller? Write your entire part in your policeman's notebook and refer to it whenever necessary, because you'll never remember it otherwise. The role of the detective – particularly in Agatha Christie plays – is the hardest part to learn; far worse than Iago in *Othello*, say, which is simply very long. But the poor policeman in a Christie thriller is asking the suspects all the questions, many of which are going to be coming out of nowhere, with nothing to do with the previous answer and not much to do with the next one either. Without the links, it's hard to make a chain.

There'd be reviews in the local newspaper. The job of theatre critic was often given to the most junior and least experienced reporter on the paper's staff – probably because most editors of provincial newspapers didn't much care about how good or how bad the local theatre's production of *You Too Can Have A Body* was, so telling the readers all about the show could be done by the least of his employees, and often was. The young fledgling critic who came once a fortnight to the Marlowe Theatre in Canterbury would write mostly glowing reviews of our productions, in which everything was a positive delight, including the welcome she always received from the charming front of house manager, whose name was dutifully listed alongside everybody's else's. But there was one member of the company that this critic actively disliked. Nobody knew why she felt this way about Johnson Bayly, who was a courtly and professional older actor and clearly very good at his job – but she did and, every two weeks, she would inject a sour note into her theatre review, along the lines of, 'Unfortunately, Johnson Bayly gave his usual lacklustre performance.' ('Lacklustre' being the sort of word that, in her mind at least, would probably guarantee her a spot one of these days in the arts pages of *The Sunday Times*). Johnson bore these insults with patient dignity; but one day she went too far.

She wrote that not only did Mr. Bayly deliver his usual lack-lustre performance, but he quite clearly didn't know his lines and on opening night had been forced to take several prompts. This was both untrue and foolish of the reporter to claim, since saying Johnson was a lacklustre actor was a matter of opinion, but claiming he had failed to learn his part was a matter of fact. Johnson was always a stickler for being word perfect and had been word perfect on the night the critic had watched the show.

The entire cast, the director and the stage manager (who never needed to give Johnson any prompts at all) produced affidavits backing him up. Johnson sued the newspaper and won damages, a retraction and a published apology from the reporter who, if not fired, was probably relieved of her job as theatre critic and told to cover the Women's Institute monthly meetings instead. It was a rare instance of an actor suing a critic and winning; usually we just accept the bruises and move on.

Repertory theatre salaries were pitiful. I was paid seven pounds a week at Colchester. This went up to twelve pounds a week at Canterbury and sixteen pounds a week at Northampton. Our rents were usually around three pounds a week – and yet we still managed to clothe and feed ourselves and I was running my first proper car, an old Sunbeam Alpine, which I'd bought from my sister's husband Benjamin Spanoghe.

Benjamin was a recent acquisition of Kerry's. He was glam-orous and charming, an Old Etonian captain of boxing and a wildly successful stockbroker – until it turned out that his wild stockbroking success was based on the idea of not actually investing his clients' money in anything at all but using it instead to buy new cars and take holidays in the Bahamas. When this early Bernie Madoff-style scandal broke, I was interviewed by the fraud squad. They had a suspicion that I had benefited from Benjamin's schemes and, in fact, I had.

My mother had lent me five thousand to buy my first little house in Putney. She didn't know that this money wasn't hers any more, but belonged to some hapless investor who thought Benjamin was putting him onto a good thing. The fraud squad suspected that I might have been in on the scheme from the very beginning but they quickly established that, when it came to money, I was a fool of the first water, so their suspicions of me lifted. Their suspicions of Benjamin didn't and he went to prison. My mother lost much of her money – and yet she continued to keep a soft spot in her heart for her son-in-law. During the trial, she phoned me to tell me that Benjamin had sent her a beautiful bouquet of flowers for one of her opening nights. 'You never do that,' she said. 'Benjamin's so *thoughtful*. You're not.' I said, rather crossly, that I also didn't steal five-figure sums of money from her and that Benjamin's thoughtfulness had cost her upwards of eighty thousand pounds. Kerry agreed with me and sensibly divorced Benjamin and moved on to a better husband altogether called Pierre, who provided her with love, stability and two beautiful children, my nephew Roger and my niece Ariane. But that's where my first proper car came from – my criminal brother-in-law Benjamin Spanoghe.

My father died shortly after I left RADA, while I was a member of the Marlowe Theatre's repertory company. A few days after I'd got the news, I drove the Sunbeam Alpine to London after the evening show and was at my mother's house next morning for the pre-funeral reception, at which every-body told me what a great man Francis had been and how proud I must be of him and how much the world of advertising would miss him – and all the while I was thinking of nothing other than how soon I was going to be able to get away from this wake (and therefore miss my father's funeral altogether) because I had to get back to Canterbury and do a show that night – an attitude that, in retrospect, might seem callous; but, in my defence, there were no understudies in fortnightly rep. If I had failed to appear, there would have been no performance that night, and the audience would have been given their money back. Provincial theatres – even then – teetered on a seesaw of insolvency and already their ends were in sight. So muttering my thanks and appreciation for all the sympathies and condolences and good wishes I was receiving, I ducked out of my father's funeral, got into the Sunbeam and raced back to Canterbury in time for the evening performance. My mother understood my decision; she was an actors too and The Show Must Go On.

During the year and a bit I spent in repertory, I played every-thing from a polar explorer to an impotent husband, a fake vicar to a genie of the lamp, a vicious killer to a hapless victim. I was briefly – until the producers realised that mothers and sons don't mix very well in the theatre, particularly when asked to play certain roles – both my own mother's nephew and then, creepily, her lover. My mother came out of retirement at about this time. Aileen, now a widow and with encouragement from Kerry and me, went back to the professional stage. We worked together twice – in *Pride and Prejudice* (I was D'arcy, she was Lady Catherine de Bourgh) – and in *The Browning Version*, when she played the sexually predatory Millie Crocker-Harris to my young schoolteacher, Frank Hunter.

Frank Hunter spends much of the play trying to rebuff Millie's loving advances. With Aileen lunging erotically in my direction, her lips puckered for a decidedly unmaternal kiss, the rebuffing part wasn't difficult. The producers, mistaking my particular discomfort at working with my mother during *The Browning Version* for a general discomfort at working with my mother at all, suggested that since I obviously hadn't enjoyed the experience very much, they would in future hire somebody else to play the female character roles. My mother and I never worked together again, but she had a long and satisfying career appearing in reps throughout the country.

Having left the profession for many years, and having not bothered to do much studying of the changes effected on acting styles over the years by people like Paul Schofield and Marlon Brando, Aileen continued to use the techniques taught to her at RADA in 1928. Clear articulation, graceful movements, head up, eyes sparkling, teeth ditto. A 180-degree stage turn was performed by walking like a runway model and then, at the appointed spot, pivoting neatly on the balls of the feet, both of which must be planted firmly on the ground. Actors who put their hands in their pockets were anathema. When speaking, face front, with occasional small head turns to establish the person you're addressing. Never, on any account, slouch, even if you're playing one. These dated acting techniques appealed to the majority of repertory audiences, most of whom were of Aileen's generation; they remembered the old acting styles fondly and recognised immediately the theatrical effects my mother was going for. She was a favourite for many years at repertory theatres up and down the country – until Basingstoke in 1979, where unfortunately for her it all ended while appearing in *The Curse of the Werewolf.* She fell off the mountain she was climbing and broke her hip. There was no front curtain at Basingstoke, so she lay on the stage in full view of everybody in the auditorium, smiling bravely through the pain, while the audience stayed in their seats and watched, with morbid fascination, the drama of her being loaded onto a stretcher and carted off by a pair of embarrassed paramedics – a drama that obviously proved to be at least as entertaining as *The Curse Of The Werewolf* because, when the management offered the audience free drinks in the bar while poor Miss Raymond was being tended to, not a single spectator left their seat. After that, Aileen didn't feel like acting any more, so she didn't, retiring happily to her small flat off the Fulham Road.

If audience attendance at the rep theatre started to decline, there was an easy solution: put on an Agatha Christie thriller. Provincial audiences loved Agatha Christie plays. I was in two: *Spider's Web* – and, startlingly now, *Ten Little Niggers,* which was renamed – when the 'N' word became anathema – *Ten Little Indians.* When even that title was considered too racist to be tolerated, the play ended its days as *And Then There Were None.* The plot of this uncertainly titled play concerns the deaths – one by one under mysterious circumstances – of a number of puzzled guests on a private island. I was the first to die – from poison. I discovered a useful trick about dying from poison in an Agatha Christie play. If you're going to do a lot of spectacular gurgling, and staggering, and throat-clutching, and rolling-of-eyes during your last moments of life – (and really, what is the point of being poisoned on stage if you can't put all that in?) – then make sure you're near the back of the sofa (there's always a sofa in an Agatha Christie play). Then, when the poison eventually overcomes you – (and I say *eventually* because dying of poison can and usually does involve terrific opportunities for lengthy histrionics, which can last as long as the director and your fellow actors will stand it) – when finally you allow yourself to be overcome, it is imperative to fall *behind* the sofa, out of sight of the audience. If you die in front of the sofa, you have to lie there in full view, keeping absolutely still and hardly breathing, and it can get very uncomfortable. If I have any advice for a young actor who is scheduled to die in an Agatha Christie play, it's locate your sofa and put a good book on the floor behind it so that you have something to read while you're dead.

In *Spider's Web* I was the murderer, so the whereabouts of the sofa didn't matter. What did matter was the mistake I made when somebody accidentally upset a tray of sandwiches and a bridge table of playing cards all over the floor – seconds before the inspector comes on to question us all in a scene where everything should appear to be quite normal. A floor scattered with cards and sandwiches was not normal, so we had to do something about it fast. I left the cards to somebody else and concentrated on the sandwiches. The mistake I made was to pick up as many as I could and then, inexplicably, stuff them into my mouth. I suppose in my panic it seemed to be the logical place to put them, although with a perfectly good tray staring me in the face, I have to wonder how good I was back then at making instant decisions. One of my fellow actors, realising I would be useless for some time to come, hissed at me, 'Go and stop whoever is going to be at the door at any moment from coming in!'

I went to the door to tell the inspector we weren't quite ready for him yet, but with my cheeks bulging with bread and butter, I couldn't tell him anything. So I shook my head and waved my arms and the actor whispered, 'What?' 'What?' '*What?*' at me until everything was put back in order. A useful lesson – the mouth is not the proper place in which to store props.

Another lesson was given to me by Nigel Hawthorne.

Long before Nigel Hawthorne became famous (and knighted) he was, like the rest of us, just another struggling actor. He joined the company for a couple of shows at the Marlowe Theatre in Canterbury and he and I played the older and younger brothers in Neil Simon's *Come Blow Your Horn*. After the first week – and with only a week to go before we moved on to the next play – I got bored and decided to see if I could make Nigel laugh. There was a moment in the play when he asked me where I'd been, and my line was, 'I went downstairs for a sandwich.' On this particular night, I thought I'd insert a little extra something.

Nigel: Where have you been?

Me: I went downstairs . . . for a *peanut butter* sandwich.

(There was a nasty pause, while Nigel gazed at me dispassionately – and without a flicker of the hoped-for smile. Then –)

Nigel: For a *what?*

(This wasn't Nigel's next line. I felt a twinge of panic. Had I bitten off more than I could chew?)

Me: Um – a peanut butter sandwich?

Nigel: (*Slowly, and with horrible emphasis on each word*) A. Peanut. Butter. Sandwich. Really? So, this peanut butter – was it smooth or crunchy?

(Oh God. I'd made a terrible mistake)

Me: Er . . . smooth.

Nigel: Smooth, huh? Funny, when you were a kid you always used to like it crunchy. So when did you change?

Me: Um . . . Oh, a while back.

Nigel: Yeah? A while back, huh?

Me: Yup. Look, do you think we could move on—

Nigel: No. Does Mom know?

Me: What?

Nigel: Never mind, I'll tell her. She won't like it. So – this sandwich – where did you get it? This oh-so-smooth-peanut-butter sandwich – where did you get it, huh?

(OK, please stop Nigel, I swear I'll never do this again)

Me: Um – at Jack's place.

Nigel: Jack's place? *Jack's place?* Don't lie to me, kid – Jack's place has been closed for over a year . . .

I don't remember any more of this agonising cross-talk act we were doing, so perhaps it was about now Nigel decided to let this poor, inexperienced sap of an actor off the hook. I've been grateful to him ever since – not for being let off the hook, although when he did it was a relief – but for the lesson he taught me. It was a lesson I needed to learn – don't ever try to mess with your fellow actors on stage, the chances are they're better at messing with you.

We all rented rooms in theatrical landladies' houses. Theatrical landladies of that period were a breed apart. They liked to talk incessantly, usually about the actors who had stayed with them last season and who were much more famous than you were. Arms folded across ample chests, they'd buttonhole you in the hallway and tell you what was wrong with your performance and how much that lovely Sir Laurence Gilligood had enjoyed their Yorkshire pudding when he'd stayed with them in 1953.

The Northampton landladies told tall tales of Errol Flynn, who had started his career at the same little Victorian theatre where I was currently performing. The stories were told with roguish relish, most of them concerning the number of children Flynn had supposedly sired during his brief stay in Northampton – none of whom any of us company members ever met and who were, I suspect, mostly figments of the imaginations of lubricious landladies.

Politics rarely came up – although I once heard the famous Manchester landlady Alma McKay exclaim, with much shaking of her permed curls, 'Ooh, that Ian Smith and his Rhody-see-yah. You want to give him a good smacking, don't you?'

A popular landlady story (the story was popular – I don't think the landlady was) concerned a young actor newly arrived at his digs. His landlady showed him to his room and, while unpacking his few belongings, the actor felt a sudden and urgent need for a bowel movement. The bathroom on his floor was occupied. He remembered seeing, on his way in, a small lavatory on the ground floor, close to the front door. He hurried down there and locked himself in. A minute or two later there was a knock at the door.

Landlady: Who's that in there?

Actor: It's Mr Wooffall.

Landlady: What are you doing in there, Mr Wooffall?

Actor: Oh, well – look, I'm sorry, but the bathroom on my floor was occupied you see—

Landlady: Never mind all that, Mr Wooffall. What are you *doing* in there? This toilet is *special*.

Actor: Special?

Landlady: Yes. Well. It's not for *solids*, you see.

Another landlady hurled open an upstairs window and shrieked down to her departing actor/tenant, who was now on the other side of a busy main road – 'Och, Mr Standing, dear – when you use your chamber pot in the middle of the night, would you kindly not replace it beneath the bed? The steam rises and rusts the springs.'

To avoid conversations like this I tried not to stay with theatrical landladies at all. In Northampton, I shared a flat with another actor called Alec Lightfoot. The flat was over a local hair salon and on Saturday mornings giggly sixteen-year-old trainee hairdressers would give Alec and me free trims.

Working in repertory was a happy experience and an educational one too, but we all looked forward to the time when we could move on to more lucrative and less provincial employment. Like a job on television – or the ultimate dream, a part in a film. When that happened – rather sooner than I expected it – and I found myself making a film in Rome, and playing the juvenile lead in it too, I found to my disappointment that I was to be paid only a little more than I got for a month's work at Northampton rep; but at least you couldn't say it was provincial.

Chapter 10

My agent Aude Powell called.

Did I know somebody called Mike Reeves?

I did know Michael Reeves but I hadn't heard from him for a long time.

We'd first met when we were both fifteen years old. Michael was at Radley School, I was at Eton, but a mutual friend suggested we meet. 'Mike wants to be a film director and you want to be an actor,' said Paul Vestey, 'so why don't you get together?' With Paul's help, we did. Mike and I got on wonderfully well, discovering many mutual likes and dislikes and spending hours discussing films, a subject he knew far more about than I did. We quickly became the best of friends. He was tall and thin, with a strong narrow jaw and dark hair that flopped into his eyes. He most closely resembled the French actor, Gérard Philipe, who died young at the height of his fame of liver cancer at the age of thirty-seven.

When the next school holidays came around, I went to stay with Michael and his widowed mother Elizabeth Reeves at their house in Suffolk, and we made our first movie, a twenty-minute thriller called *Carrion*. Mike shot it all on a little 8mm camera, in black and white. It was about a wheelchair-bound girl, alone and vulnerable in her snowbound house. (The snowbound bit was added after Suffolk serendipitously received a heavy snowfall on the first day of shooting). Mrs Reeves' tea trolley served as a mobile camera platform. I played a deranged murderer, recently escaped from the local lunatic asylum. After struggling through the snow for a bit, I come across the isolated house and, being a cold and wet deranged murderer, I of course assault the lonely girl – but her boyfriend, who looks like Gérard Philipe, returns unexpectedly and interrupts me right in the middle of my attempted rape and there's a terrific fight that rages all over the lonely girl's house and ends only when Gérard Philipe smashes a bottle over my head and gouges out one of my eyes, a wound from which I swiftly die. The blood was chocolate sauce.

Mike invited me down to Suffolk during the next school holiday, with the idea of reshooting the movie – only, this time, using semi-professional equipment and calling it something different. I'd had such a good time making the 8mm version of *Carrion* that I assumed making the 16mm version of *Intrusion* would be double the fun. But I came down with a bad dose of influenza the day before we were to start shooting, and had to be put to bed and fed chicken noodle soup by Mrs Reeves, which meant I couldn't play the maniac this time. Instead, when I recovered a week later, I played the very small part of the Spanish butler – a part that had to be specially written for me because, in *Carrion*, there hadn't been a butler at all – but, to give me something to do in *Intrusion*, the poor wheelchair-bound heroine was now not quite so poor any more and could afford a teenage servant in a white jacket with just the one line, which was, 'Will there be anything else, Miss?'

Having (temporarily at least) exhausted the possibilities of girls in wheelchairs and homicidal lunatics and the effects of broken glass on human flesh, Mike and I parted on the friendliest of terms – he promising to put me in a real movie one day, and me promising to be in it.

We lost touch over the next few years, while we both did some growing up. I went to RADA, got jobs in provincial theatres and played small parts in a few television productions. Several things happened to Mike, the most significant being when he inherited a lot of money and went to America. He made his way to Hollywood, found out where his hero – the then-B-movie director Don Siegel – lived and knocked on his door. When Siegel opened it, Mike said, 'Hello. My name is Mike Reeves and I've come all the way from England to see you and I think you're the greatest film director in the world.'

This hyperbolic compliment, addressed to an American B-movie director by Gérard Philipe's double in the tones of a well-brought-up English public schoolboy, must have charmed Siegel enough to invite the kid into his home and let him live in the pool house for a few days. At the time, Siegel was conducting tests on an Elvis Presley vehicle called *Fun in Acapulco* and told Mike he could be the audition dialogue coach. Michael jumped at the opportunity. He spent several days as 'Don Siegel's Dialogue Coach'. All the job entailed was to help the auditioning actors remember their lines in their screen tests, so it was hardly a position of importance. All the same, Mike relished the experience and remained forever loyal to his teenage assessment of Don Siegel's talent as a film maker.

After his success with Don Siegel, Mike came back to England and looked around for some other influential movie person to hang with. The Reeves family had a connection with the film producer Irving Allen and Mike managed to wangle his way onto the set of *The Long Ships*, a Viking saga starring Richard Widmark. When that film finished, Irving Allen used Mike again, on *Genghis Khan* with Omar Sharif. Mike worked in a number of minor positions on these films, mostly as a runner or very junior assistant director. He met Paul Maslansky during the shoots – an American production manager operating out of Rome – who offered him a number of similar jobs on a low-budget horror film he was producing in Italy, called *Castle of the Living Dead*. This movie is now known primarily for being the film debut of a very young Donald Sutherland. It was produced and directed by Warren Kiefer. Sutherland called his son Kiefer in honour of the man who gave him his first movie role – or roles plural, since Sutherland played at least three of the parts, including a Macbethian witch. Mike was mainly involved with shooting some of the second unit sequences. His footage impressed Paul Maslansky enough to give him his own shot at film-making – if Mike could come up with most of the money. Mike could and did.

So, when Aude Powell called me and asked if I knew a Michael Reeves and if so did I want to play the leading role in his film – (title yet to be determined and the salary is lousy – but you will be in Rome, Ian, and that'll be nice, won't it?) – I said yes.

The She Beast – or *La Sorella Di Satana* – or *Vardella* – or *Il Lago Di Satana* – or *Revenge Of The Blood Beast* – or whatever title it's known by – is a dreadful little film. We shot it a few miles outside Rome, in twenty-one days, for a budget of fifteen thousand pounds. It might have cost more – but at that time the Italian licence to shoot a documentary was considerably less than the one they issued for making a feature film, so we pretended to be making an archeological movie called '*RUINI ETRUSCI*'– at least that was the title chalked on our clapperboard.

I was paid a very small salary and a very small amount of daily living expenses. Neither was enough for a proper hotel, so I stayed in a cheap and depressing *pensione* at the top of the Spanish Steps. I had to pay extra to have a bath. Mike and his girlfriend Annabelle were genuinely too busy to spend much time with me after work was done for the day, so I spent lonely evening hours wandering around Rome and trying to find somewhere cheap to eat. I lived on spaghetti and oranges, which led me to the conclusion that cheap Italian food was just as awful as cheap food anywhere – except France, where you could eat well on pennies. Nobody has ever agreed with me about this – but then nobody who has disagreed with me about this has ever wandered around Rome as hungry and as poor as me.

The plot of *Revenge of the Blood Beast* involved the reawakening of a vicious four-hundred-year-old witch called Vardella who goes on a vengeful rampage, killing the descendants of those who murdered her. Vardella was played by a man – a middle-aged black American dancer and actor called Jay 'Flash' Riley. As Vardella, Flash wore a ragged old dress, a straggly wig and a knobbly latex rubber mask of tremendous hideousness. His hobby was to go off in this costume during the lunch hour and hide in the bushes by the side of the main highway to

Rome. When he heard a car approach, he would jump out and try to hitch a ride. The longer the black skid marks the cars made as they swerved violently to avoid the ghastly apparition hopping dementedly about in the middle of the road, the better Flash liked it.

The star of the film was Barbara Steele. Barbara was the undisputed queen of the schlock horror films that were being churned out by the hundreds every year during the Italian 1960s. *Revenge of the Blood Beast* occupied her for all of a couple of days and she moved on almost immediately to another, probably similar, film – so it's not surprising that Barbara claims to have no memory whatsoever of being in Michael Reeves' first movie, of playing my loving wife, of rolling around half naked with me in our bed scene – of any of it, in fact.

The budget was so tiny, and the schedule so short, that much of the film had to be adapted on the spot to whatever inconveniences fate chose to throw at us. Each day we shot what we planned to shoot – and if it was an exterior scene and it happened to be raining that day, the scene would quickly become an interior scene, shot anywhere that was available. We were nothing if not adaptable. An old Roman siege catapult, left over from some biblical epic, became our witch's ducking stool. Once we were in some sort of barn, with rusty farm equipment lying everywhere. The scene involved Vardella attacking a Transylvanian peasant with a sickle, cutting him to ribbons. Mike stood behind the camera hurling blood everywhere. (When there was blood to be hurled, Michael didn't trust anybody else to do it. In fact, hurling blood was probably a significant reason why Mike wanted to be a film director in the first place).

So, after being thoroughly slashed and doused with gore, the Transylvanian peasant dutifully fell dead and Vardella cast her bloody sickle aside and rushed out screaming her customary witchy gibberish. We were about to move on to the next set-up when Mike saw an old hammer lying on the floor. He placed the hammer just so, set up the camera pointing down at it – and then, our single camera rolling, Mike himself took the bloody sickle and threw it down – where it landed in exactly the proper spot across the hammer, forming a perfect emblem of the Communist party – and in one take only because we didn't have time for two. There are serious students of the films of Michael Reeves who study this lousy little movie just to relive the hammer-and-sickle moment.

Our producer Paul Maslansky, and another expatriate American called Amos Powell, played two comic Transylvanian policemen. Paul was an excellent producer, and Amos a good writer, but they were lousy actors and not in the least bit funny, so the decision – halfway through filming and by somebody other than Michael Reeves – to introduce slapstick comedy into the movie would have been fine had there been any competent funny men on the set, which there weren't.

But who was I to judge? I was just as bad as Paul and Amos. Even after two years of vocal training at RADA my voice was high and reedy and childish and with an accent originating from somewhere behind Harrods. When it came to looking tough and dangerous, I looked about as hard as custard. Everything I did was entirely predictable and therefore was entirely uninteresting – but luckily Mike didn't know very much about acting, other than when it struck him as being particularly atrocious – and I wasn't quite that – so my performance seemed to satisfy him at least enough to promise to use me again. I was game too, which might have added to his appreciation of me. If Mike asked me to jump into a lake of sulphurous water, I did. If he asked me to lie on the centre line of the main road while a truck drove straight for me, I said sure. Ride a horse? Of course. A motorbike? Naturally. Without a helmet, at 90mph along the M1? Why not? Have flammable black sump oil poured all over me? Lead me to it. Nude scene? Well, up to a point. I had inherited my father's modesty and refused to expose anything below the waist. I always played my love scenes in bed wearing a pair of grey flannel trousers – because I knew Mike was quite capable of reaching out in the middle of the scene and whipping the sheets off me and my lover, but he wouldn't bother if all the camera would catch was a pair of grey flannels.

Mike's professional relationships with actors on his film set was always a slightly aloof one. He was in awe of actors and their processes of producing a performance, and preferred to leave them alone to get on with their jobs, without much more input from him than an occasional tentative request that, on the next take, might they perhaps do it a bit faster? This neglect of his casts sometimes worked and sometimes didn't, but since it was something that his idol Don Siegel practised – (Siegel famously said that he knew nothing about what actors did and got his wonderful performances simply by casting his films correctly in the first place) – then Mike felt justified in doing the same. Some actors thought he didn't like them; in fact, Mike loved actors and enjoyed their company – but he was nervous about delving deeply into what they did and how they did it.

This sensitivity about the actor's craft made Mike resistant about going to watch them in the theatre, because awful things could happen in live performances, like the set falling over, or the performers forgetting their lines, and Mike couldn't bear to be a witness to the poor actors' resulting distress. He said that, when forced to go to the theatre, he would spend the entire two hours of the average stage play waiting in trepidation for something to go wrong – something that could never happen in film, which was why Mike felt completely secure in a cinema – so much so that he was capable of seeing four or five films in one day without the slightest discomfort. Except ones with scenes in which the individual features of an actor's face became completely obscured, by mud or slime or blood, or anything that rendered the face no longer recognisable as a face. For some reason images like these disturbed Mike terribly and he was unable to watch them. He never saw, for instance, the war film *Ice Cold In Alex,* starring John Mills and Sylvia Sims and Anthony Quayle, because Quayle at one point sinks into the mud of the Quattara Depression and, when pulled out by brave John Mills, his face is nothing but a dribbling mass of mud. Not only would Mike not watch such a scene, he wouldn't even enter a cinema where a film with such a scene was playing. It was an odd, and unexplained, phobia.

By the time we finished *Revenge of the Blood Beast* – of which we were all inordinately proud, if only for the accomplishment of having made a real film – Mike and Annabelle and I were once again firm friends. He'd bought a small house in Yeoman's Row, a cul de sac off the Brompton Road in London, and he and Annabelle opened their front door to any friends who happened to be passing and wanted a free drink. We played

Monopoly endlessly, under Mike's house rules, which meant
that any time anybody approached one of his properties, the
game would stop while Mike sold all his hotels on the opposite
side of the board and moved them over to the sites his oppon-
ents were nearing. This could take a long time, calculating the
differences in the hotel costs and the resulting rents we were all
about to incur, but it did guarantee that Mike would usually
win the game outright. Since we Monopoly losers were drinking his alcohol and eating his food, it seemed a small price to
pay. Once he brought home the strategic board game
Diplomacy, but by then we had had enough of his cardboard
deviousness. A resourceful somebody threw away the rule book
when Mike wasn't looking (and before he'd had a chance to
learn how the game was played and certainly well before he
could work out how to adapt the rules to his benefit) and that
– to everybody's relief – was the end of Diplomacy.

Mike had a 16mm film projector and he would rent movies
and show them in his living room. Most of the films were Don
Siegel's B movies. His favourite – and the film he considered
the best ever made, by anybody, from anywhere and at any
time – was Siegel's *The Killers*. The film starred Lee Marvin,
Angie Dickinson, John Cassavetes and the oddly named Clu
Gulager. It was a B thriller and featured, as the main villain,
Ronald Reagan. *The Killers* was Reagan's last movie before retiring from acting and becoming a politician. Mike ran *The Killers*
at least three times a year, which, in the age before DVDs and
streaming films and Netflix and all the rest of the current aids
to watching whatever movie strikes one's fancy, was a fairly
complex thing to do. You had to be friendly with a movie rental
company; they had to have in their libraries the film you wanted

to see; you had to have enough money to rent a 16mm version of it and it wasn't cheap; you had to lug home the big tin cans that held the multiple reels; you had to have a film projector and know how to lace it up; and you had to put up with the groans from your audience when it was time to change the reels. All of Mike's freeloading friends, myself included, saw *The Killers* many times over. We also saw *Invasion of the Bodysnatchers* and *Baby Face Nelson* and *Riot in Cell Block Eleven* – all low-budget B movies made by Don Siegel before he hit it big with *Madigan* and *Coogan's Bluff* and *Dirty Harry*.

Mike soon set about getting his next project underway, which turned out to be another low-budget affair called *The Sorcerers*. Mike had met a young American producer called Patrick Curtis in Rome. Curtis was married to the statuesque Raquel Welch at the time and they were a glamorous and helpful couple to know. Patrick liked the *Sorcerers* project and started shopping it around. He ended up with Tony Tenser's Tigon Productions, a tiny D-list film company operating out of even tinier offices in Wardour Street. Being in the business of making extremely low-budget horror films, Tony Tenser had heard about Mike Reeves and *Revenge Of The Blood Beast*, so he was at least aware of this new young film director.

The Sorcerers was exactly the kind of project he wanted at the time and he agreed to be a partner in the venture with Patrick and Raquel, with Mike Reeves to direct. For some reason Tony chose not to watch *Revenge of the Blood Beast;* he said he 'didn't need to see it.' This must have come as a relief to Mike and it certainly did to me but, having got away with our primary producer choosing to live in ignorance of the mess we'd made of our first movie, we were determined to make as little mess as possible of our second one and, on the whole, and with a budget of only about thirty-five thousand pounds, we succeeded.

The Sorcerers starred Boris Karloff and Catherine Lacey and me. Boris and Catherine played an elderly impoverished couple, reduced to putting advertisements in tobacconists' windows advertising Karloff's talents as a hypnotist. But they have a secret – a Heath Robinson machine that enhances the hypnotist's skills to the point where they can control their subject from afar just by *thinking* at him, which allows Boris and Catherine to *think* me (the hero) into doing all sorts of exciting things, all of which they experience themselves, albeit at second hand.

So, under their baneful influence, the hero steals a fur coat, and rides a motorbike, and beats up his best friend, and swims in the Dolphin Square swimming pool with a beautiful French girl and, because this was a Mike Reeves film, eventually starts murdering people – but never (for reasons that wouldn't be valid today but were valid in the 1960s) gets to indulge in any sexual activity while under their influence, which one might have imagined would have been the first thing that wicked old Catherine Lacey would have thought of. In the initial script Boris was just as wicked as Catherine Lacey but he asked for changes to redeem his character – an interesting demand from a man who had played villains for most of his life, but who now late in life obviously wanted to leave behind a kindlier image of himself.

Boris was delightful and charming and funny and cooperative and I am proud of having worked with him. He was one of very few actors who couldn't pronounce his esses and still managed to have a career. Sean Connery is another – his esses come out as a slushy 'sh' sound – but Boris actually *lisped*. He was old and unwell at the time and therefore uninsurable, which meant some producers were reluctant to take on this once great star. Boris solved this by always asking for a sum that anybody could afford. He earned eleven thousand pounds a film, regardless of the budget of the movie or the size of the part – eleven thousand for one line or the lead, it didn't matter.

This fee reduced our budget to twenty-four thousand pounds, so once again we found ourselves making do, and improvising, and cutting corners, and not bothering with silly things like stuntmen. This was the film in which Mike had me riding along the M1 motorway, without a helmet but with a pretty French girl on the pillion, at 90mph on a Norton Commando motorcycle. The pretty French girl was called Elizabeth Ercy and she was terrified. Mike himself was lying in the relative safety of the open boot of a Jaguar, the Arriflex camera cradled in his arms as he shot backwards down the motorway. 'Come closer!' he kept shouting, and I would try to oblige, all the while ignoring the French-accented shrieks from close behind me.

This was also the film in which Mike asked me to sit in the back of a police car during a chase scene, because he was missing an actor that day who should have been in the police car – so would I mind being a shadowy figure in the back seat? Mike was once again tucked into the boot of the car in front – (in fact the car I was supposed to be driving during this chase scene) – and was filming the pursuing police racing along narrow London side streets. At one point the driver of the police car – with me inside it – quite accidentally lost control and we spun 360 degrees down the centre of the street, remarkably missing the cars parked on either side. Mike was delighted with the shot and it's in the finished film. The fact that I'm in the pursuing, spinning police car, and not in the car I was supposed to be driving, is one of those useless little snippets of information that real film buffs like to know.

The Sorcerers was one of Susan George's first films. She doesn't include it in her résumé. She was very young. She bounced into the audition that Mike and I were holding and won us over immediately. She was on set for perhaps two hours until I killed her with a pair of scissors. Mike hurled a lot of blood over her and then she went home. In her mind the experience was probably (and understandably) not worth mentioning.

In the film Boris goes searching for a likely candidate on whom to try out his Heath Robinson machine, and he comes across me – a moody young antiques dealer – eating a hamburger in a Wimpy Bar. It was a night shoot and Boris and I had been there for hours while they lit the scene. Knowing how cost-conscious we were being, I had eaten something before coming to the set, but it turned out that Boris hadn't and he was getting hungry – but drawing the line at Wimpy burgers. Nobody had been anywhere near us to see if we needed anything. Outraged on his behalf, I started to make a small fuss. Boris stopped me. 'Don't bother that young director, he'th got quite enough on hith plate. *I* haven't, but there you are.'

Boris's concern for his young director wasn't matched by Mike's concern for Boris. With Mike, the film was everything so, while he loved him dearly, he had Boris fall over onto a hard floor, he had him struggle with Catherine Lacey in a geriatric fight scene, he had him sit for hours on bare boards with a thick layer of black, burn-to-a-crisp makeup all over his face and hands – and Boris never once complained. Early in the shooting, the sound man went to Mike and said, 'Every time Mr Karloff moves, I'm picking up a squeaking sound.' Mike apologetically broached the subject with his star. Boris shook with laughter. He rolled up one trouser leg, revealing a metal brace, articulated at ankle and knee. It was a support for a badly arthritic leg. 'Bring me thome bithycle oil!' he said, and applied it himself to the squeaking hinge – an oddly Frankensteinian moment.

I asked him if he'd ever felt typecast as an actor. 'Don't believe there ith thuch a thing as typecathting. You naturally play the parts that thuit you. Lucky to be working at all. Betht day of my life wath when they catht me to be Frankensthtein's month-ter. Before that, they didn't know what to do with me. After it, they did.'

He and I waited endlessly behind a scenery flat for a cue to enter, which took a long time coming. 'By the time thith cue arriveth, I shall probably be dead,' muttered Boris gloomily. 'Then they'll be thorry.'

Fourth billed in *The Sorcerers* – after Boris Karloff, after the almost entirely unknown Elizabeth Ercy, and after me – was Victor Henry, who played my friend Alan. Victor and I had been RADA contemporaries. He was everything I was not. He was a northern lad, solidly working class, with a head of bright ginger hair and a prodigious and exciting talent. Why he bothered with our little film is a mystery; he was much in demand on television, in films and in the theatre and was regarded by everybody in the profession as one of the most interesting up-and-comers of his generation.

At RADA he'd been a wild man, raucous at student parties and unpredictable in class. I was in a play with him; he would stand in the wings when I was on stage, stripped naked, madly waggling his dick in my direction. He was funny and imaginative and brave and we were all in awe of him.

If Victor's talent was prodigious, so was his capacity for beer. There was a dialogue scene in *The Sorcerers* between Victor and me, at night, outside a pub. It was a cold evening, close to freezing, so Mike suggested we keep warm inside the pub while he and the crew set up the shot outside. This was a mistake. I drank half a pint of bitter and then stopped. Victor drank several pints of the strongest brew available. We chatted away and he seemed quite unaffected by all the alcohol he'd absorbed – until it was time to shoot the scene and we had to step out from the warm embrace of the pub and into the freezing London air. The cold hit Victor like a sledgehammer. Almost immediately he became very drunk. He swayed slowly from side to side. His eyes became glassy and unfocussed. His tongue stopped working and his hands, looking for somewhere warm to bury themselves, fumbled in vain for his pockets. We filmed the scene but Victor was obviously paralytic. Mike was torn between finding the situation funny – and knowing that the footage was unusable and would have to be reshot.

Next day, Victor and his agent were invited to come to a screening of the previous day's rushes – a Godfather-ish sort of invitation, which left Victor and his agent in no doubt as to whether or not they should attend. I sat with Mike behind the two of them in the darkened screening room, watching the train wreck unfold before us. The hardest part for Mike and me was to remain stern and unforgiving and silent – because what was happening up on the screen was not only appalling but also darkly comic. Victor's attempts to not appear drunk were funny enough, but the movements of his hands – out of shot and persistently failing to find his pockets all the way through the scene – made it look as if he was surreptitiously masturbating. Mike stuffed a handkerchief in his mouth.

At one point during this retributive screening Victor simply slumped in his chair and buried his face in his hands. The agent never moved a muscle. When the lights came up, Mike and I pulled ourselves together. Mike took out the handkerchief and we straightened our faces and tried to look grim. Victor and his agent turned to face us. Victor was almost in tears and abject in his apologies. The agent was more practical; he and Mr Henry would pay in full to reshoot the scene. Mike accepted the apology and the offer and no more was said on the subject.

Some years later, I don't know when, tragedy – in the shape of a bus or a lorry or a car – hit Victor Henry as he was standing sober and sensible on a London pavement. He remained in a hospital bed until he died without ever regaining consciousness at the age of forty-two. A remarkable talent and a dear man, his unfulfilled life ironically snuffed out by a drunk driver.

But *The Sorcerers* was a happy shoot. I had done a lot of work between *Revenge Of The Blood Beast* and *The Sorcerers* – more television, more theatre, more film parts – and was a slightly better actor for the experiences. Mike had a bigger budget and a better script – and a real star in Boris Karloff. We were on familiar ground and everybody knew just a little bit more about the business of making films.

Mike was in charge of the car chases – in *Revenge Of The Blood Beast* these had been handled by an incompetent second unit with a misplaced sense of humour, which resulted in some ridiculous sequences involving speeded up vehicles, an unexplained stranger on a little motor scooter, and a silly musical soundtrack accompanied by silly whizzbang sound effects.

The car chases in *The Sorcerers* were serious events and, given our restricted budget, effective too. We even had a glamorous movie star producer, in the pneumatic shape of Raquel Welch, who sometimes helped out in the wardrobe department. But it was still a make-do affair and many of the scenes in the film were snatched when nobody was looking. Permissions from the authorities – to speed along motorways without helmets, or to zoom dangerously around London side streets in old Jaguars, to swim at night in Dolphin Square's locked and private swimming pool, or to strap our cameraman to the top of a car with washing line and hope he wouldn't slide off on the corners – these permissions were never given because they were never asked for. We simply stole our shots and moved on before anybody noticed us – until, that is, we blew up the big old Jaguar (with me supposedly inside it) on a sunken building site somewhere in Notting Hill.

Mike slyly told the special effects man to fill the petrol tank to the brim, on the basis that if ten gallons would make a big explosion, seventeen gallons would make a bigger one, seventeen gallons being all that the Jaguar's fuel tank could carry without spilling some. The resulting fireball blew out windows all around the building site and a woman two streets away complained that her cooker had jumped a foot away away from the wall. The special effects man and his crew wisely and hurriedly packed up their gear and ran away, but foolishly a lot of us stayed on to admire the blaze. Several police units and three fire engines arrived and the inferno was extinguished – but not before one particular young fireman singled me out and, pointing furiously at a tiny blister on the corner of his mouth, screamed, 'It's people like you who cause things like this!' Names were taken. We felt like naughty schoolchildren.

In the moments before the upside-down car explodes, a bloody hand is seen scrabbling weakly through the smashed front window. The hand was Mike's. Since this was a scene involving no actors, neither I nor the makeup department had been called that day. I was there because I wanted to see a car being blown up but I drew the line at crawling about inside an upside-down Jaguar with seventeen gallons of petrol packed into its petrol tank – which is why it's Mike Reeves' hand you see impersonating mine. Without a makeup team on set, there was no blood available and Mike couldn't have a death scene with no blood, so he made do with red house paint. It is quite obviously red paint, which somewhat spoils the scrabbling hand effect – but you forget all about the red paint a moment later when the Jaguar blows up in an enormous fireball, breaking windows and sending cookers jumping away from walls.

The Sorcerers was considered good enough to get a West End release, opening in London in June 1967. Boris was delighted. He hadn't seen a film of his play in a major London cinema in many years. He was even happier a year later when the film was selected as the British entry for the international festival of science-fiction in Trieste, where it picked up the first prize in the shape of the 'Golden Asteroid' – which turned out to be a big, rectangular lump of glass with a hole in the middle. It was almost too heavy to lift. Tony Tenser flew me (possibly because

I was the strongest surviving member of the cast) to Italy to pick it up. There were other awards too – Catherine Lacey, who had hated both the film and her role in it, won a Silver Asteroid, and a specially created award went to Boris. *The Sorcerers* also won the Grand Prix at the San Sebastian science-fiction film festival and was sold to Allied Artists for release in the USA.

Such was the success of this little film that Tony Tenser immediately started to hunt around for something else for Mike to direct. He came up with *Witchfinder General*.

Witchfinder General has been a cult film for over forty-five years. It's been discussed endlessly, written about voluminously, and nominated by several people who know about these things as one of the greatest films ever made. It has also been vilified in the press, most notably by the playwright Alan Bennett, who described it at the time as being '. . . the most persistently sadistic and morally rotten film I have seen. It was a degrading experience, by which I mean it made me feel dirty.'

It was the violence he was objecting to. In 1968, movie violence was nowhere near the pitch that is seen today and the brutality pictured in *Witchfinder General* appears mild by contemporary standards. But in 1968 it was considered by some to be a dangerous and immoral film and questions were asked about it in the Houses of Parliament. All this controversy did wonders for its success at the box office and helped to propel it to the cult status it still enjoys today.

Tony Tenser bought the film rights to the book of the same name by Ronald Bassett. It was an effective, pot-boiled and fictitious history of the real Matthew Hopkins, the self-righteous and self-appointed witchfinder general, who travelled around East Anglia between 1645 and 1647 with his assistant

John Stearne, discovering suspected witches and executing them in a variety of interesting ways. It is believed that, in those two years, Hopkins and Stearne were responsible for the deaths of over three hundred women. Tony Tenser saw the potential in the story for a lot of blood hurling, which made it a perfect fit for Mike Reeves.

Mike agreed. He and his old friend and writing partner Tom Baker (not the *Doctor Who* actor – this Tom Baker was a quiet and self-effacing man, which can hardly be said for the *Doctor Who* Tom Baker) put together a script, pencilling me in as the hero, which was flattering for me and comforting for Mike. By now he felt safe with me and would probably have used me in these kinds of roles forever, or at least until one of us had got too heartily sick of the other to continue.

Once I was on board, Mike and I had discussions as to who should be the leading lady. I pushed for my old girlfriend Nicola Pagett and we set up a meeting with her, but there must have been something in the air at this meeting that smelled a little noxious in Nicola's nostrils. Perhaps she took us for a pair of amateurs, or maybe we mentioned the nude love scene too often, or possibly it seemed unprofessional to be holding the casting meeting in my flat – whatever it was, Nicola decided to treat the whole thing with an air of mild disdain and, after she left us, Mike said he didn't think she wanted to do it, and if she didn't want to do it then he didn't want her to do it either, and we'd better look elsewhere. With no help from me, he found a newcomer, Hilary Dwyer, who not only played the part to perfection, but who looked far more like a country parson's niece than Nicola Pagett's dark exoticism ever could.

Tony Tenser started to hunt around for a financial partner to carry half the load. He found it in AIP – American International Pictures, the Californian film company responsible for a slew of stylish horror films, most of them with titles from Edgar Allen Poe stories and most of them starring Vincent Price.

AIP promised half the budget on one condition: Vincent Price was to play the witchfinder. But Mike Reeves and Tom Baker had somebody else in mind. They envisaged the character as a small, flea-bitten man, an unattractive, diminutive clerk with ideas above his station, resentful of the laughter his unprepossessing appearance engendered and vicious in his revenge on those who would dare to snigger. They wrote a scene where Hopkins is helped onto his horse and, before the animal takes a step, Hopkins falls off the other side. They wrote a weakling, a sickly little man, with bad breath and staring pale blue eyes; a creature who hated the hand the world had dealt him and was prepared to deal with the world accordingly. A cold, quiet, calculating monster, whose power lay not in his physical presence but in the dark recesses of a warped and vicious mind. In Mike and Tom's eyes, there was only one actor who could embody all these ideas and that was Donald Pleasance.

What they got was Vincent Price.

Vincent Price – he of the imposing stature and the long handsome face, with its long, aristocratic nose leading to the pencil moustache that hovered above a pair of lips designed expressly for the sardonic quip. Vincent Price – famous for his nasal vowels and his queenly consonants. Vincent Price – known mostly by contemporary audiences for his roguish, eye-rolling, over-the-top performances in the Edgar Allen Poe films he made with Roger Corman, with titles like *The Pit and the Pendulum, House of Usher* and *The Masque of the Red Death.*

Vincent was under contract to AIP, with one more film to make for them. AIP's executives, Sam Arkoff and Jim Nicholson, decided that the *Witchfinder General* subject could be shoe-horned into a vaguely Edgar Allen Poe-ish sort of concept – and sold as such in the USA under the nonsensical title *The Conqueror Worm*, a phrase Arkoff and Nicholson picked at random out of a Poe poem. This was pretty much the extent of their influence over the film, although Mike did get occasional messages from across the Atlantic asking for more blood, more naked people and, if possible, more blood *on* more naked people. Mike ignored these messages.

I met Vincent while I was trying out my film horse for the first time. The horse they gave me was called Captain and he was huge and excitable and – once into his favourite gait, which was a full-out gallop – almost unstoppable. I was also trying out my crimson Roundhead uniform, with its pair of fetching, thigh-high black boots, its steel lobster-tail helmet that had a tendency to fall over your eyes whenever you or your horse made any sudden movements, and its enormous rowel spurs that jangled Western-like whenever I got off Captain and walked.

Captain and I were cantering along a gravel lane. In the ditch bordering the lane was what looked, at first glance, to be a pile of old black rags in a top hat but which turned out to be Vincent Price in his witchfinder uniform, having a rest by the side of the road. As Captain and I rode nobly by, I heard a famous voice. 'Oh my Ga-a-a-ad, would you fucking *look* at her. She's so *pretty* and she rides that fucking horse so *well*. I *hate* her.'

Vincent didn't hate me. He didn't have time to hate me. We have very few scenes in the film together because our story lines run parallel and separate through most of the movie and we only meet briefly at the beginning and end of the picture. I also didn't give him any particular reason to hate me, apart from in the final scene, when I hit him several times with an axe made out of hard rubber – but as Vincent was fairly drunk at the time, he probably didn't feel much pain from the blows.

For Vincent, it was not a happy shoot. There were several reasons: somebody tactlessly let slip that Mike had wanted Donald Pleasance for the role; Vincent missed the comforts of studio filming in Hollywood and found working in draughty old aircraft hangars in the wilds of Norfolk unpleasant; he had to do a lot of riding and he didn't like horses; and worst of all, he didn't get on with Mike. The feeling was mutual and there was friction from the start. The upstart pipsqueak of a young director either ignored Vincent, or told him not to do things – things that Vincent had been doing successfully for many years and which, as far as Vincent was concerned, had contributed to his enormous popularity with his fans. But Mike was determined. If he couldn't have the actor he wanted, then at least he would do his damnedest to get something good from the actor he didn't want – and for the first time he actually tried to direct his star's performance. But it was all in the negative. 'Don't waggle your head so much, Vincent.' 'Could you not flap your hands like that?' 'A bit less of the eye-rolling, Vincent.' At one point, Vincent – exasperated to breaking point by this director who seemed stubbornly unable to understand just how fabulous Vincent Price was – reared up to his full height of six foot four inches and said, 'Young man, I've made ninety-three films in Hollywood. How many have you made?'

'Two good ones,' said Mike tersely.

In the evenings, at the Angel hotel in Bury St Edmunds and away from Mike and the horse and the draughty aircraft hangars, Vincent was able to relax and have fun. He would sit in the bar, poised and elegant and witty, his wrists jangling with turquoise and silver bracelets, telling stories of Hollywood. Once, Nicky Henson – my old RADA and rock group friend, whom Mike had cast as the Hero's Best Friend – appeared beside him sporting several bits of modest jewellery of his own. 'Don't push it, Alice,' drawled Vincent and went upstairs to put on more turquoise.

Since I only interacted with Vincent in a brief scene at the beginning of the film and a couple of scenes at the end, I saw little of the conflict between him and Mike and, for most of the time, enjoyed myself. I charged about the Norfolk countryside on my enormous horse being impossibly heroic. I had a naked-apart-from-my-trousers bed scene with Hilary Dwyer. I spent cheerful hours with Nicky, who decided, without any prompting from me or Mike, that the Hero's Best Friend was to be a comedy turn. The first scene Nicky shot was a single line addressed to me. He leaned nonchalantly into the doorway and said, in a growly cockney, 'Well – I'll see you in the tavern with the others, then.' For some reason Mike thought Nicky's delivery of the line so staggeringly funny that he lay helpless on the floor for several minutes, clutching his ribs and wiping away the tears that streamed from his eyes, while Nicky plaintively said, 'What? What? *What?*' in the background.

We burned witches, and drowned witches, and strung witches up in trees. We dropped live rats on Rupert Davies, who, in a long and distinguished career, had probably never sunk so low. Our producer Philip Waddilove was press-ganged into playing a Cromwellian officer. The Battle of Naseby was fought off screen because we didn't have a budget for a battle, but we did import – for one day only – the impressive Patrick Wymark to play Oliver Cromwell. We also imported Wilfred Bramble of *Steptoe and Son* fame to play a horse dealer, a tiny scene that Wilfred managed to turn into a tour de force of leering campiness. The film's music composer, Paul Ferris, was roped in to play a bereaved husband. Jack Lynn, my beloved old RADA teacher, was an innkeeper. I broke a toe during a fight scene and spent the rest of the film trying to disguise a limp. The insurance company paid out ten thousand pounds for my injury. Mike said, 'Thanks very much. Now I can shoot three scenes which Tony-bloody-Tenser has arbitrarily cut from the script because he says we can't afford them. Now we can. Could you see your way to breaking something else?'

One of the last sequences we filmed was in Orford Castle, a well-preserved twelfth-century keep near Ipswich in Suffolk. We had the castle for a limited time, one night only, from six o'clock until midnight, and Mike had set an almost impossible task for himself, involving at least thirty-five shots, with complex lighting, in many different parts of the ancient building. This was the night Vincent decided to turn up drunk. He was truculent and inclined to be uncooperative – on the very night when Mike needed everybody to pull together. Everybody except Vincent did pull together. We fumbled our way through the multiple set-ups, doing the best we could do under the circumstances and, by the time the scene in which I attack the witchfinder with an axe came round it was nearing our filming deadline and Mike was blazing with fury.

'I want you to hit the bastard,' he hissed in my ear. 'I want you to hit him really hard.'

'I'm not going to do that, Mike,' I said. 'I'll try to make it look real but I'm not going to hurt him.'

'It's just a rubber axe. It won't hurt him. Anyway, the bastard's drunk. He won't feel a thing.'

The rubber axe wasn't sharp, but it was as hard as wood and weighed as much.

'No, Mike. Not going to do it.'

'You bloody will.'

Mike and I hissed our arguments at each other in a corner of the dungeon, and Philip Waddilove, our producer, managed to hear just enough of them to get an idea of what Mike was after. He hurriedly gathered a lot of foam rubber padding and stuffed it under Vincent's costume. When Mike called 'Action!' – in a tone of unmistakably savage glee – I went after Vincent with my rubber axe just a little harder than I would have normally, and probably bruised his ribs a bit – and all of it was quite pointless, because most of the blows ended up on the cutting room floor, victims of the censor's disapproval.

When *Witchfinder General* was released in the U.K, the British Board Of Film Censors was headed by John Trevelyan, who was described as having '. . . a face like a 1933 walnut case radio set – comfortable, reliable, emitting the Home Service sounds of English common sense and autumnal bronchitis'. Opinions on Trevelyan's tenure of the post of censor differ markedly. Roy Ward Baker – a film director I worked with several times and admired unreservedly – said of him, 'Trevelyan had that schoolmasterly habit of pigeon-holing people. If you were in the box marked 'art cinema' you could tackle anything, however controversial: sex, violence, politics, religion – anything. If you were in 'commercial cinema' you faced obstruction and nit-picking all the way. He chose these categories and allocated everyone according to his estimation of them. He was a sinister mean hypocrite, treating his favorites with nauseating unctuousness'.

Mike Reeves, on the other hand, liked and respected him – possibly because John Trevelyan seemed to have put Mike at least partially into his Art Film category, or maybe because they just happened to be distant cousins – or perhaps it was a combination of the two. There were still clashes between them about what should go and what should stay and Mike fought hard against every proposed cut in the film, while Trevelyan bent over backwards to let him keep as much as possible. But in the long run the BBFC had its way and much of the excessive violence was removed – but still leaving more than enough to outrage Alan Bennett. When Mike saw the final version of his film, with all the offending sections gone, he found himself pleasantly surprised. The overall effect of the cuts hadn't really harmed his movie at all and he even admitted – admittedly reluctantly – that leaving more to the imagination and less to the eyes and ears was perhaps no bad thing when it came to manipulating audiences' emotions.

When AIP's Sam Arkoff and Jim Nicholson screened the finished film in California, it was reported that one of them turned to another and said, 'Jesus Christ, we got a fucking *art* movie on our hands!' And when Vincent saw it, he was moved to sit down and write a letter to Mike, both of appreciation and of remorse, in which he pretty much admitted that Mike had been right all along, and he had been wrong all along, and that the performance that the young genius had wrested from him was one of which he was genuinely proud. Mike wrote back. 'I told you so.'

Revenge of the Blood Beast, *The Sorcerers* and *Witchfinder General* were all made between 1965 and 1968. The budgets for all three films added together amounted to less than two hundred thousand pounds. Of the three, *Witchfinder* is easily the most accomplished film – with *Blood Beast* being almost unwatchable, and *The Sorcerers* somewhere in between. *Witchfinder General* has, deservedly, stayed prominent in the minds of all serious movie buffs – helped in no small part by the efforts of producer Philip Waddilove, who over the years has fought not only for its promotion, but also to preserve its original integrity in every possible way.

After *Witchfinder General*, Mike seemed to lose his way. Annabelle had moved on, her own career offering her opportunities she didn't want to resist. Her departure had nothing to do with Mike's subsequent problems. He was always prone to mood swings but now he sometimes plunged into a black depression, drank heavily and swallowed lots of sleeping pills. He worked in a desultory fashion on a number of projects but they came to nothing. He became reclusive. His friends saw less of him. I went on to other projects in film and television and theatre – some of them abroad – and didn't notice this decline as much as some others who stayed closer to Mike. So it was a devastating shock to hear that my closest friend had died, of an accidental overdose of barbiturates, on 11 February, 1969. He was just twenty-five. I was numb with grief – not only at the loss of my close friend, but at the waste of a life that held such promise.

There's not a lot to be said for dying young, other than the obvious and cynical observation that it's one way of becoming legendary, particularly if the deceased was working, with moderate success, in the arts when he died. Had Michael Reeves survived his accident, I don't think he would have achieved the status he now enjoys in death. But I do believe he would have gone on to make bigger and better films, that he would have enjoyed a long and prosperous career – and that he would have ended his life a famous and respected and prolific film director. I also like to think I would have been in some of his movies, and that we would have remained close friends until the end.

One person who was present throughout almost all of my short but rich association with Mike Reeves was Diane Hart. Through me she was part of the group that met regularly in Mike and Annabelle's Knightsbridge house and she was the resourceful somebody who had the foresight to throw away the Diplomacy rules before Mike could get his hands on them. She had enormous affection for Mike – we all did – but Diane understood him better than most. Both of them suffered from periods of depression and self-doubt – Mike rather more than Diane, but the shared experience certainly gave each a sympathy for the other – and, towards the end of his life, it was Diane who cared for – and about – Mike more than any of the rest of us put together.

I met Diane Hart on the way to Rome. Whether it was waiting in line at Heathrow Airport, or on the plane flying to Italy, or at Leonardo Da Vinci-Fiumina airport when we got there, I can't remember. All I can recall was seeing a beautiful but nervous girl, about my own age, sitting alone and studying, with ferocious concentration, a film script.

Diane Hart and I were flying to Rome for the same reason. So was a young actress called Natasha Pyne and a young actor from the National Youth Theatre called Michael York. Four of us, all unknown, on a plane to Rome, to test for roles in a star-making movie.

Franco Zeffirelli was set to direct a film version of *The Taming of the Shrew*, produced by Dino de Laurentiis and starring Richard Burton and Elizabeth Taylor. Zeffirelli needed a youthful couple for the younger Shakespearean lovers, Lucentio and Bianca, and he'd held auditions in London, whittling the likely men down to Michael York and me, and the likely women down to Natasha Pyne and a lovely girl he'd seen modelling clothes in a fashion magazine. The lovely girl's face was, in Zeffirelli's eyes, perfect for the role of Bianca, and on the strength of her face alone, he was bringing her to Rome to test her for the part. It was no wonder that Diane was nervous. She wasn't an actress, she'd never done any acting, and she didn't particularly want to attempt it now. I thought she was adorable.

The film tests were something of a media circus. With Burton and Taylor already on board, the search for two young unknowns was designed to whip up even more interest in the project, and all four of us young hopefuls came under the scrutiny of the Italian press. Diane became even more nervous than before. I was nervous too, but for a different reason. The moment I'd set eyes on Michael York, I suspected I wasn't going to be Lucentio. I knew I was nice-looking, and so was Michael – but Michael's face was *interesting*. He had an interesting broken nose and interesting blond hair and interesting high cheekbones and I knew immediately that if I was Zeffirelli I'd pick interesting Michael York over not-quite-as-interesting Ian Ogilvy in a heartbeat.

Michael was paired with Natasha Pyne for his audition. I was partnered with Diane. Diane sometimes wryly blamed herself for my failure to land the part of Lucentio, but her performance in the audition (which was fine, by the way) had nothing to do with it. It was Michael York's nose that settled my fate – that and Alberto de Rossi, the patriarch of the Italian makeup department.

Michael and Natasha were to test first, so they were the first in the makeup chairs. Alberto was entranced by Michael's face. Every time Franco Zeffirelli walked past the open door, Alberto would grab him and drag him to Michael's side and, gesticulating wildly at the interesting nose and the interesting cheekbones and the interesting hair, he would hiss, 'Che viso *straordinario! Formidabile! Meraviglioso!*' Sitting in the makeup room and waiting for my turn, I couldn't help but overhear Alberto's hoarse endorsements, and I couldn't help but notice that Zeffirelli seemed to agree with them. And when Alberto put a short golden beard on Michael's chin, each small clump of hair glued on by hand and then curled into perfection with a pair of miniature curling tongs, which transformed Michael into a young Greek god who had once come in second in a boxing match, I resigned myself to rejection.

The Greek god climbed out of the chair and I climbed in. Alberto De Rossi looked at me dispassionately, sighed heavily, dabbed a bit of colour on my face, spread spirit gum under my mouth and shoved a hank of black hair onto my chin. I looked in the mirror and saw, staring gloomily back at me, an Amish farmer with low self-esteem. Alberto studied at me again, this time with disgust. He shook his head. Then he ripped the hair off my chin and wiped away the spirit gum. 'Ees good like that,' he muttered. 'No beard for you.'

I remember little about the actual film test, other than a sense of gloom that hung over me like a small black cloud. The gloom was offset somewhat by the beautiful girl I was acting with and the prospect that, if she found me only a tenth as attractive as I was finding her, she might agree to see a bit more of me back in England, when all this silly Shakespeare nonsense was done with.

When it was time for us four hopefuls to go home – by which time the four hopefuls had decreased to two hopefuls – Michael York said he might stay on in Rome for a few day – 'to see some friends'. It was the first we'd heard of any friends of Michael living in Rome. That was when I knew for sure I wouldn't be playing Lucentio in Zeffirelli's *Taming of the Shrew*.

Diane had never held out any hope of landing Bianca and the prospect of going home on the first available plane and forgetting all about the horrible experience was appealing to her. We comforted each other all the way back to England and, soon afterwards, she moved into my flat on the King's Road, bringing her three-year-old daughter Emma with her. Emma quickly became *my* daughter too. In due course I proposed to Diane and was accepted, and in due course we were married, in secret, at the Wandsworth town hall registry office. Afterwards we went home and telephoned all our friends and relations and told them the news – and that evening we had a party to celebrate. My mother came and was displeased – not at Diane, but at the thorough *commonness* of the site we'd picked for our wedding and the fact that, common or not, she hadn't been invited.

For a long time – through the end of the 1960s and on into most of the 1970s, Diane and I were happy. We went everywhere together and rarely spent a day apart. If possible (and most of the time it was possible) she came with me when I went on location. She was there when we made *The Sorcerers*. She came to Greece with me for the dreadful *The Day the Fish Came Out*. She was a regular on the set of *Witchfinder General*. She came to Russia with both our children to be with me while I filmed the epic *Waterloo*. She held everything together while I made the *Return of the Saint* television series, and even appeared briefly (and I think reluctantly) in an Italian episode, playing a lost but lovely tourist.

We moved from the King's Road flat – the rent was £10 a week – to a little house my mother helped me to buy (it cost ten thousand pounds) in Putney. There, in 1969, Diane produced my son Titus, whose middle name is Michael, in memory of my friend who had just died. Later we moved from Putney to a modern house on Kingston Hill, then to an Edwardian house in Raynes Park. Finally, in about 1980, we went to live in the country, in a wooden house near Guildford, with nine acres and a small lake. And that's where our marriage fell apart.

An unsettling restlessness sometimes comes over men in early middle age. It came over me – this male pattern boredom – and I started to wonder whether this was all there was to Life, or if there was Something Else. And if there was Something Else, perhaps I should start looking for it before it was too late. It's an ugly and selfish state of mind that causes some men to leave their wives and strike out in search of some sort of adventure – an adventure that might allow them to think for a while that they're younger and more vibrant and more interesting than they really are. Some men regret this decision, others don't. I'm one of those who had few regrets – other than a crushing sense of guilt for having behaved so badly to a woman who most certainly didn't deserve any of it.

I looked for an exit. I found it in an affair with Maria Aitken, while on tour with her in Birmingham. Diane voiced her suspicions and I couldn't deny them. The break-up was agonising for us both, but much worse for Diane; I was ripping her rug of stability out from under her, removing in a few days everything that she'd built up and lived for over the past twelve years. I also had the fun and excitement of an affair to keep my mind off things – and the prospect of freedom from a marriage that now bored me.

Chapter 11

When you ask an actor which of the four media he prefers to work in – theatre, film, television or radio – he might (if he was me) tell you that he likes film for the financial rewards, television for the regular, bread-and-butter aspect of the work, radio because you don't have to learn the lines or struggle into uncomfortable costumes, and theatre because that's where the material is nearly always better than that written for the other three media. He might (if he was me) also mention that in the theatre, the actor is king.

Theatre is at the root of what we do. It's where we rule. Where we are not interfered with. Where nobody comes between you and your audience. Television and film and radio have legions of technicians who stand between the actor and the observer, and performances in those three media are canned and pasteurised and improved upon and – by the time the observer gets to observe – are already old. But the theatre is immediate and fresh and belongs to the actors – and the playwrights and the directors of course – but during the actual act of performing the play in front of a paying audience, it belongs only to the actors.

Through most of the 1960s, after my stints at the three

repertory theatre companies, I was fully occupied doing film and television work and it wasn't until the early 1970s that I won my first part in a West End play. This was *The Waltz of the Toreadors*, a period comedy by the French playwright Jean Anouilh. The producers – one of whom was my old drama teacher Jack Lynn, who had moved up in the world – had assembled a pair of stellar leads. Trevor Howard to play the old General St Pé and Coral Browne to play his hypochondriac wife. I was to be his secretary, Gaston.

Trevor hadn't been on stage for many years, being busy making films and earning vast sums of money. He had a reputation for being a tremendous drinker – it was said of him that no film director in his right mind would bother shooting scenes that involved Trevor any time after lunch. Coral Browne was a formidable actress with a reputation for searing wit and a libido to match. Shortly after I worked with her she embarked on a two-year, torrid affair with Christopher Cazenove, who was thirty years her junior. Christopher had been a contemporary of mine at Eton but, unlike most Etonians, he had beautiful manners. When I asked him how on earth the affair had started, he said, 'Well, she suggested it and it seemed so churlish to refuse.' Many years later, when she was quite old, Coral Browne married Vincent Price. She called him Vinnie and he called her Madame and, by all reports, they were very happy with each other.

We opened *The Waltz of the Toreadors* at the beautiful Theatre Royal Haymarket in 1974 and all went well for several weeks. The reviews were mostly favourable. The audiences were large and respectful. Trevor remembered his lines and Coral didn't try to seduce anybody. Then one night the management came round to our dressing rooms while we were getting ready for that evening's performance. 'We think Trevor's been drinking. He's got these Schweppes ginger ale bottles in his coat pockets and we've checked and they're full of neat whisky. Well, actually, right now they're half full. Well, actually some of them are empty. Also, he's having difficulty putting on his shoes. He's trying to stuff his left foot into his right shoe and vice versa. There might be a problem.'

That evening, for the first time since opening night, the entire cast was clustered in the wings to watch the opening of the play. Moments before the curtain rose, Trevor sat quiet and alone behind his desk on the darkened stage, looking fine in his general's uniform. He seemed composed and steady. Then, on cue, the curtain went up and the lights flooded the stage. Trevor frowned and leaned forward and stared out at the audience.

'FUCK OFF!' he roared.

Several members of the audience guessed correctly that, even in the freest of translations from its original French, this was probably not the opening line of Jean Anouilh's *The Waltz of the Toreadors,* and those who were sufficiently offended took Trevor's instruction to heart and fucked off. We heard the banging of many seats as the affronted ones hurried from the auditorium. Satisfied at having winnowed away all the people he wouldn't care to have watching him act, Trevor settled down to do the play – but only in the vaguest way and almost entirely in his own words – or mine, come to that. As his secretary, nearly all my scenes were with him – just the two of us on stage, with the General having the lion's share of the lines. But not on this night. This night I said most of Trevor's lines for him. It was lucky that I'd spent time with him helping him learn his part, because I knew it better than Trevor did, so the moment Trevor looked blank when it was his turn to speak – which was often – I would jump in and say his entire speech for him, transposing the subject and object pronouns as I went through it, and changing tenses – from past and present to *subjunctive* past and present and then back again – according to what would make sense if I was telling the story on his behalf, which of course I was. At the end of a speech – and as often as not – Trevor would blink owlishly up at me and say, loudly enough for the audience to hear, 'That was *bloody* good. Do that one again.' And I would jump to his next speech and say, 'Ah, yes indeed, General – what you mean to say is . . .' and off we'd go again.

Zena Walker, playing the General's mistress, sobbed quietly in the wings. 'I won't go on with that man,' she moaned. When her cues came, a stage manager gave her a push, propelling her into her scenes whether she wanted to go on or not.

One particular speech was a favourite of Trevor's. It was General St Pé's reference to the story of the brave Spartan youth and the purloined fox. In the play, the speech goes:

You have been bred on the classics, you say? I do not therefore have to teach you the fable of that Spartan youth who, having stolen a fox and hidden it beneath his tunic, preferred to have his stomach gnawed away sooner than confess his theft.

On this night, during this *Titanic* of a performance, Trevor decided that this was one speech he would do with no help from me.

Ian Ogilvy

'Shut up. My turn. So, there was this kid, see? An' - an' - an' - he'd got this fox, see? An' - an' - an' - he stuck it under his jumper, right? An' - an' - an' - the fox went, "*Wurrer wurrer wurrer – wurrer wurrer wurrer.*" He was worryin' him, see? Ha ha. Well, I'd be fuckin' worried, wouldn't you? Havin' a fox doin' that, right?'

I was used to this by now. Besides, it was strangely fascinating, which was why I encouraged him by saying, 'Doing what, sir?'

'Doin' what? Doin' *what?* I'll tell you what. Bitin' him, he was. All over his tumtum. An' - an' - an' - then - you'll never guess – he *ate* him. Ate him right up. An' - an' - an' - the chap never said a dickie bird. 'Cause he was a fuckin' *Spartan.* They don't talk much apparently. Truth.'

The only scenes Trevor played properly were his moments at the bedside of his invalid wife. Trevor was frightened of Coral Browne and behaved himself during their one scene. But once it was over, he came galloping back to mischief. By the time the final curtain fell I was drenched in sweat. There might have been a couple of dozen audience members left open-mouthed in the auditorium. Most had walked out at the interval. Many demanded their money back. Coincidentally, that night Diane had come to see the play again and she stayed until the end. As she said afterwards, it was one of the most extraordinary evenings she'd ever spent, anywhere – and, if she had paid for her ticket (which she hadn't) she would never have asked for her money back.

The next day Trevor came into the theatre beaming with general joie de vivre. 'Went quite well last night, didn't it?' he said, entirely without irony.

I did a season at the Chichester Festival Theatre, playing John Worthing in *The Importance of Being Earnest* and Dick Dudgeon in *The Devil's Disciple*. Hayley Mills played opposite me in *The Importance of Being Earnest*. We didn't discuss my mother's marriage to her father at all, but when John came down to Sussex to see his daughter perform, he spotted Diane in the bar before the show. Had she seen it already? Diane said she had. 'How is Hayley?' Diane said, truthfully, that she was lovely. John looked both pleased and relieved; Hayley Mills was known almost entirely by her superlative film work and was – before her Chichester appearance – something of an unknown theatrical quantity.

John Mills had stayed friendly towards my mother, but was always careful not to hurt the feelings of his adored wife, so for many years what little communication passed between him and Aileen was brief. But on the rare occasions when I would run into John – usually at some professional event – he would always ask, 'How's Mum?'

Mum was fine and was returning to her old life as a professional actress. Sometimes she would appear at the Richmond Theatre in Surrey. John and Mary Mills lived on Richmond Hill. One day my mother got up the courage and sent them an invitation to her first night. To her astonishment, both John and Mary turned up. To her further astonishment, they all got on very well, with Mary showing Aileen nothing but friendliness. After that, communications became a little easier, although still rare.

Much later, when Mary developed Alzheimer's disease – and when she no longer was aware of anything very much – John took to visiting Aileen in the old ladies' rest home where she lived for the last twelve years of her life. I think, with his wife away in her own shrinking world, John was lonely. When my mother died, John sometimes took my Aunt Betty out on an occasional date. Betty had always liked John but, in old age, she found him irritating. Whether it was her old age or John's old age that irritated her, or a combination of the two, the effect was the same. They stopped seeing each other after a few dinners and that was that.

Later, there was another play for me at the Theatre Royal Haymarket – this time it was *The Millionairess,* by Bernard Shaw. A bad film had been made of it, starring Peter Sellers and Sophia Loren, and it was time for a London audience to see the real thing again. Our version starred Penelope Keith, and my old friend and attitude-adjuster, Nigel Hawthorne.

Penelope was one of the funniest women on British television and had become a star by playing Margo, in the situation comedy *The Good Life*. Margo was an imperious blinkered snob, an appalling creature whose sole redeeming feature was that she was funny – a part Penelope played to perfection. Nigel was, by this time, a highly respected stage actor and serious about his craft. The problem between them lay in Penelope's interpretation of the role of the millionairess, Epifania. She played her if not exactly like Margo then with Margo-ish overtones. Nigel thought that Epifania couldn't possibly be played that way, that it made no sense and was a cheapening distortion of Shaw's original intent. Penny said that she would play Epifania the way she wanted to play it and that was that. At one point – and point-lessly – they appealed to me. What did I think? I thought that we all had to work together over the next few weeks and that to side with either one against the other would cause lasting frictions that would make the run of *The Millionairess* a misery for every-body. So I said lamely that I thought there were points to be considered on both sides and then slunk away.

Privately and silently I thought that Penny should play Epifania the way her countless fans would want her to play it – and, after all, the Theatre Royal was going to be filled primar-ily with the fans of Penelope Keith. At the same time, Nigel's point that Epifania and Margo were not interchangeable char-acters was undeniable. For the rest of the short run Penelope played the theatrical Epifania the way she wanted to play her and Nigel seethed quietly in the background.

At the end of the 1970s I played the iconic character Simon Templar, in a revived television series of *The Saint*, taking over the role from Roger Moore who had vacated it a good ten years before. After the series ran – and for most of the 1980s – I was unwelcome in UK television and films. Not rejected by the fans, but by the producers, who thought that I was so identified with the character of Simon Templar that nobody would believe it if I played anything else. The result of this exclusion was that I spent most of the 1980s on stage in London, where I was welcome, up to a point. It was one of the best things that could have happened to me because it was in the West End that I began to learn what acting was all about.

It was disgracefully late to discover what a run-of-the-mill actor I really was. I'd come into the profession in 1963 and had produced a number of perfectly adequate and perfectly unmemorable performances in films and television produc-tions and theatrical plays for the past eighteen years. The realisation of just how inadequate I was hit me when I went to the Liverpool Playhouse to play in *The Devil's Disciple* – in the same role I played later at Chichester where, in the light of what my wife said to me in Liverpool, I hope I was a lot better. Diane came up to Liverpool to see me at the Playhouse. After the show, she was quieter than usual.

'Well, come on,' I said. 'What did you think?'

Diane squirmed uncomfortably. 'I thought you were good.'

'Good? Is that it?' Actors are insecure, and need a lot of praise just to get up in the morning.

'Well – isn't Dick Dudgeon a star part?'

I said Dick Dudgeon was one of those Shavian roles that could absolutely be described as a whopping great star part.

'Then why,' said Diane, 'why did I feel you were just another member of the company?'

'What?'

'Well, you were very good of course. I just didn't think you stood out enough.'

Diane was right. I didn't stand out at all. This was something of a wake-up call to me and I began to think about what I'd been doing – or rather *not* doing – for the past few years. It still took another half decade before I fully realised what I should have been doing from the first day I became a professional actor. I'd been getting away with a lot, simply because I looked nice. I wasn't a horribly bad actor – I'd been improving steadily over the years, with much room for it too – but being merely a *good* actor is not quite enough in our profession. There are thousands of good actors out there, and more joining the ranks every day. So many people can act; so many can act well. To rise above the rest, to be *great* in fact, you have to deliver something extra. Laurence Olivier said that if you give an audience what they expect, they'll despise you; but give them the unexpected and they'll love you forever. Since Liverpool, I've spent the rest of my career trying, with varying results, to be a little bit more unexpected. It's just a pity I didn't think of starting sooner.

I remember Liverpool for something else. I was asked by a policeman if I'd murdered an old man.

I was back on motorcycles when I worked in Liverpool and my transport there was a 350cc, two stroke Yamaha. After the show one night, I rode my bike back to my digs in Huskisson Street. The house was a tall, once-elegant building, filled with actors – and mercifully, no landlady. The rent was five pounds a week, which was all I could afford on the salary the Playhouse was giving me. As I neared the house, I saw what looked like a shifting bundle of clothes at the foot of the steps that led up to the front door – and, as I pulled to a stop, a figure detached itself from the bundle, zipped through the beam of my headlight and raced away down the street. I got off the bike. The bundle of clothes stood up. An old man, tall, well over six foot, in a long black overcoat, wheezing and clutching at his side.

'Bugger mugged me,' he said.

'Are you all right?' I said.

'Bugger punched me.'

'You'd better come inside. There's a phone.'

The pay telephone was up on the first floor landing. The old man and I climbed the flight of stairs. He was bent double, breathing heavily, his hand still clamped to his side. I asked him about the attack. 'He was a half-caste,' said the old man. I dialled 999 and when somebody answered, I handed him the telephone. He took it. He had just enough time to say, 'Hello? Right, yes. Look, I've been mugged—' Then he stopped. The receiver dropped out of his hand. He stood up ramrod straight, like a soldier coming to attention. Then his eyes rolled back in his head and he keeled slowly backwards, his body rigid as a falling tree. The crash when he hit the bare floorboards shook the house. The telephone receiver was swinging dramatically at the end of its cable and I could hear the dispatcher calling out, 'Hello? Hello? Hello?'

I grabbed the receiver. 'He's just collapsed! He's been mugged! Huskisson Street! Quick!'

The old man looked awful. His false teeth were halfway out of his mouth and he was making an unpleasant gurgling sound deep in his throat. While we were waiting for the help to arrive, I thought the least I could do was to try to make him comfortable, so I went to my room and got a pillow off my bed and put it under his head. Gingerly, between finger and thumb, I removed his dentures and put them on the floor next to him.

Several actors, roused by the crash, came out of their rooms and clustered round. I explained what had happened. One of them went off to make the old man a cup of tea, because – as he explained – when the poor chap woke up, a cup of tea was going to be just what he'd need.

Soon two ambulance men arrived, which was a relief because up until then I had seemed, reluctantly, to be in charge of the situation and, with their arrival, I could pass the responsibility on to them. They had uniforms and I didn't, which made all the difference.

One of the ambulance men peered closely at the old man. 'Well, he's dead, isn't he?'

'No, he's not,' I said. 'He's been making this funny noise—'

'Yes, well. That's called the death rattle, sir. No, he's definitely dead.'

I didn't argue. They had uniforms.

Minutes later the house was filled with policemen. I had to explain about the mugging and the pillow and the false teeth, and how I really hadn't seen anything in the darkness of Huskisson Street, other than a human shape, which had flashed through my single headlight. A plain clothes detective bundled me into a car, squeezing me between two burly cops in the back seat, and we started to drive at high speed through the dark back streets of Liverpool, looking for a man of mixed race whose face I'd not seen and who was only thought to be of mixed race because the old man had told me so. Every time we passed a dark pedestrian, one of the policemen would ask, 'Is it that one?' And I would say, 'Sorry, I don't know.' As a witness I was turning out to be next to useless.

Around one o'clock in the morning, they took me to the police station to make my statement. A friendly detective took it all down. At one point he looked at me with that steady, level-eyed, expressionless sort of gaze I imagine they get taught in police school, and said, 'I've got to ask you this, Mr Ogilvy. You didn't do it, did you?'

I said no, I had *not* done it, and the detective said he didn't think I had for a moment, it was just routine, and he hoped I hadn't minded being asked. I said I was delighted. For the rest of my life, I could dine out on the story of how I was once accused of murder.

'Didn't actually *accuse* you, sir.'

'But I was a suspect?'

'Oh, yes. Technically you still are. I'm afraid I have to ask you not to leave Liverpool without notifying us.'

We discussed what had killed the old man. The detective thought it was most likely a heart attack. 'Not that easy to get a murder conviction – not with a heart attack,' he said glumly.

I was driven home. The house was still full of policemen and sombrely excited actors. The old man still lay where he fell but now he was wrapped up in layers of thick polythene sheeting. The ambulance men were waiting to cart him off to the mortuary. But first, I had to identify the body.

'I'm sorry,' I said. 'Identify him? Why? He hasn't gone anywhere has he?'

'Just a formality, sir. If you wouldn't mind?'

The polythene wrapping had been done efficiently and it took a fumblingly awkward couple of minutes to unveil the old man's face. The staccato, machine-gun sound you sometimes hear when Sellotape is ripped off plastic sheeting has always reminded me of those moments. When finally revealed the old man looked disconcertingly different. He could have been somebody else entirely. The ruddy face was now the colour of candles, the plump cheeks were now hollow caves, and his chin seemed to have receded so far into his neck as not to be a chin at all.

I said that if I was going to be entirely honest – (and the policeman with the most gold braid on his hat said that under these circumstances that was the best thing to be) – then I wasn't sure it was the same man at all, and the policeman with the most gold braid explained that a corpse always looked a bit different after a while, mainly because of gravity, which had the effect of pulling the blood and skin and the muscles towards the centre of the earth, which causes a general alteration in the physical aspect and . . . yes, well, not to worry, sir, it's definitely the same chap and, once again, just a formality, and we can wrap him up again now, gents – quick as you like, because we all want to go to bed, don't we?

They'd brought a tin coffin, painted the colour of dried blood. The old man was too tall for it. They put him in it anyway. The last I saw of him were his knees. They had folded them double in order to fit him into the casket. His bent knees lent the dead old man a slightly casual, even jaunty air as he was carried in his tin coffin down the long flight of stairs.

Next morning – after an unaccountably peaceful night's sleep with my head resting on the same pillow as the one I'd put under a corpse's head – I was walking down Huskisson Street when I saw the detective (whose technical suspect I was) walking up the street towards me.

'Just coming to see you, sir. Thought you ought to know something. In case you felt at all bad about making an old man about to have a heart attack climb all the way up a long flight of stairs – it turns out it wasn't a heart attack at all. We got him to the mortuary and got him undressed and when we were down to his vest we noticed there was a couple of spots of blood. Nothing much, just a couple of spots. Got the vest off him – found he'd been stabbed three times – and twice straight through the heart, with a very fine, stiletto-type blade. So, there was nothing you could have done for him, sir. He was a walking dead man, you see.'

The walking dead man's name was Mr Jones. I went to the inquest. I gave my evidence and was thanked by the judge and dismissed. On my way out I was approached by a tearful middle-aged woman. She was Mr Jones' daughter, profuse in her gratitude. I said I'd done nothing and that I was sorry for her loss. She said she was just grateful that somebody had been there and had taken care of him at the end. I didn't argue with her version of events. Maybe she'd heard about the pillow.

I don't think they ever caught the mugger. A curious coda to this story is that, looked at in one way, Mr Jones' attacker did him a favour. At the inquest it was revealed that the old man had an incurable cancer, one of the nastier kinds that causes a painful and lingering death. But neither Mr Jones nor his family knew he was ill. So, instead of months of agony and fear and hospital beds, of operations and chemotherapy and radiation, all Mr Jones suffered were three sharp blows to his chest, done with such speed and efficiency that the old man never even knew that a knife had been involved; he thought he'd merely been punched.

Perhaps we should all be so lucky.

I did no theatre work for a while, not because I was traumatised by the Liverpool affair but because I was busy with the television show which gave me, for a while, a famous face. Then, when that show ended unexpectedly at the dawn of the 1980s – and I found myself suddenly avoided by British television producers – I took the offers that the West End theatre managers were extending and was grateful to be offered them.

A new Simon Gray play was running at the Vaudeville Theatre in the Strand. It was called *Stage Struck* and it starred Alan Bates. I was asked to take over the leading role when Alan's contract was up. I went to see the play. It wasn't one of Simon Gray's best, being a thriller along the lines of *Sleuth* or *Deathtrap* – a genre into which Simon had more or less (and temporarily) drifted, if only to see if he had sufficient theatrical éclat to put together a drama like that. He could. *Stage Struck* isn't great but has several fine *coups de théâtre*, with moments that make an audience gasp with shock. It's a lot of fun to play and to watch, and I thought I could be good in it. I had two weeks to rehearse.

After the first week I was feeling confident. Simon Gray came in to see a rough run-through. Afterwards, obviously perturbed, he took me to one side.

'Sorry – but what are you *doing*, Ian?'

'Doing? Well – er – I'm doing what Alan did. Well, I'm *trying* to do what Alan did. Obviously not very successfully yet—'

'But I don't want you to do what Alan did. I want you to do what *you* do. I *hated* what Alan did.'

Alan Bates and Simon Gray went together like Simon Gray and Harold Pinter went together. Harold Pinter directed nine of Simon's plays (in one of which, *The Common Pursuit*, they thoughtfully cast me) and Alan Bates starred in most of them – so for Simon to say he hated what Alan had done with his thriller was surprising.

'Look, don't get me wrong, I love Alan, he's a great actor and an old mate. But I didn't write this for him. I don't know who I did write it for, but I didn't write it for Alan. I made a stupid mistake; I sent it to him. All I wanted was his approval, but the bugger took it as an offer and here we are. But please don't think I want you to do it like Alan, because that's the last thing I want.'

The trouble was, I liked what Alan had done with it. It was hard not to – Bates was always an actor to admire. So I did what Alan did but in my own way and Simon seemed satisfied. It was a flamboyant role and, with my name in neon lights up on the Vaudeville theatre Marquee, for the first time in my life I tried to be brave. I stuck my neck out. I took chances – and for the first time in my professional life, I felt I might have achieved something just a little out of the humdrum.

I even got my name in the papers – not because of the excellence of my take-over (critics rarely re-review a play just because its cast changes) but because of what I persuaded Simon Gray to take out of the script. There were several '*fuck*'s and a couple of '*fuckings*' scattered through my part. I went to Simon and said, 'The people who come to see Alan Bates in a Simon Gray thriller are different from the people who come to see *me* in a Simon Gray thriller. Many of the people who will be coming especially to see me will be fans of my family-oriented television show, and will be uncomfortable with the obscenities. If they bring their children, which is a possibility, they'll be appalled. Any chance we might take those words out out?' I spoke with little hope of persuading him and, in fact, expected a curt refusal – which of course I would have accepted – but, to my surprise, Simon agreed immediately.

'Actually, to be honest, I never liked them myself,' he said. 'They're gratuitous. I don't know what I was thinking. Get rid of them.' The story filtered to the press. The reaction was predictable. I got letters vilifying me for being a prude and for arbitrarily altering a great playwright's intent; others praised me to the skies for my one-man campaign to clean up the filth currently passing for British entertainment. I bleated to anybody who would listen that neither was true, but it was no use; for a short time, until everybody forgot about it, I was a reactionary philistine for the Left, and a cultural hero for the Right.

Maria Aitken and I appeared for one night only, at the May Fair Theatre, in a charity presentation of a new work by

Sheridan Morley, called *Noël & Gertie*. It was an affectionate tribute to the theatrical partnership of Noël Coward and Gertrude Lawrence, and was made up of sketches and songs in which they'd both performed, and letters they'd written to each other. Edward Fox was booked to do it, but he stepped aside at the last moment and I stepped in. It was the nicest thing Edward Fox ever did for me. It was the *only* thing Edward Fox ever did for me – apart from giving me, many years later, an oblique sort of compliment; I'd had some small success writing novels, for adults and children, and he heard about it. 'Good lord,' he's reported to have said. '*Books?* Well done him. I have a hard time writing a bloody letter.'

The one performance of *Noël & Gertie* was a success – so much so that, after the show, a short, slim and deeply tanned older man sought Maria and me out among the post-performance crowd. 'Fabulous, the pair of you. You should do *Design for Living*. In fact, I'm going to reserve it for you.'

Graham Payne could do that. He'd been Noël Coward's lover and life partner throughout most of the second half of Coward's existence and was in control of the Coward estate – which was why, soon afterwards, I found myself rehearsing *Design for Living* with Maria Aitken, Gary Bond and Roland Curram.

Design for Living is a curious play. By some estimates it's the best of Noël Coward's works, in others it's a piece that is more rewarding to perform than to watch. Either way, we were given a glittering production by our producer Duncan Weldon, who spent lavishly on sets and costumes, even using, to dress Maria, the talents of the great Japanese designer Yuki, who made her look so stylishly glamorous as to take away the breath of many of the London critics and cause them to write so ecstatically about the bewitching and brilliant Maria Aitken that there wasn't much room left in their columns to say nice things about the bewitching and brilliant Gary Bond, Ian Ogilvy and Roland Curram.

We opened in Birmingham, which was where Maria and I, violently attracted to one another all the way through rehearsals, finally fell on each other one night and then went on falling on each other for all the nights to come – and even continued to fall on one another in the breaks between the shows on matinee days. The affair broke up the marriage that I wanted broken up, and then petered out amicably during our respectably long run at the Globe Theatre on Shaftesbury Avenue. Maria and I have stayed friends ever since.

At one performance, while Gary Bond and I were playing the scene in which Leo and Otto make fun of Gilda's American dinner guests, I made the mistake of thinking ahead. It's something all actors do at one time or another and the effect can be disastrous, particularly in a long run of a play. We'd been doing *Design for Living* for several months, with eight shows a week and, with that many performances under your belt, there are times when an actor wonders if the line he's about to say surely wasn't said by him only a moment ago? It's the close familiarity with every word and the sheer number of times that you've said them that can cause, paradoxically, a momentary loss of memory. This lapse happened to me during the teasing scene. It was coming up, I knew – that line about the volcano in South America – and, try as I might, the name of the volcano wouldn't come to me. Bizarrely, I knew what the name *sounded* like – it sounded like Chappaquiddick – but I couldn't say, 'Have you ever been to Chappaquiddick?' – because that place was notorious for being the spot where the Democratic Senator from Massachusetts had behaved with such dishonour, and the audience – and the cast – might think that if I said, 'Have you ever been to Chappaquiddick?' that I was going for a cheap laugh. Gary Bond was an inveterate giggler and this could reduce him to helplessness. Or he might do something else – I remembered my experience when I tried to be clever with Nigel Hawthorne. And finally, there was the geographical aspect to consider: Chappaquiddick is an island near Cape Cod; it's not a South American volcano.

All this was going through my head with the line only half a page away – and still the name wouldn't come. The situation was getting desperate. I was sitting next to Gary on a cream sofa, the two of us impeccable in white tie and tails. I leaned close to Gary and muttered in his ear, 'What's the name of the volcano?'

Gary looked at me as if he thought I'd gone mad. '*What?*' he hissed.

'What's the name of the volcano?' I hissed back.

'How the fuck should I know?' he whispered furiously – and this after hearing the actual name of the volcano from my mouth eight times a week for the past six months, which had led me to believe, not unreasonably, that Gary might just have the lost word available for me. But no – all I got was, 'How the fuck should I know?' Then – after a moment's pause, during which it occurred to Gary that he *ought* to know it, having heard it so often, and the fact that he didn't might be cause for shame, he decided to go on the attack rather than admit his failings. He hissed, accusingly, 'It's *your* bloody volcano.'

All this angry whispering was not entirely out of character for Leo and Otto, and so far I thought we'd got away with it.

But still the only place name I could think of was Chappaquidick, and that was no use. There was only one thing I could do. 'Excuse me a moment,' I said to the company and strolled casually off the set and into the prompt corner.

The prompt corner is called that because if an actor is unlucky enough to forget a line, it's from this corner that he can reasonably expect to be prompted. When I went into the darkness of the prompt corner, I saw an assistant stage manager – (whose only job is to come to the aid of an actor who has forgotten the name of his volcano) – sitting on her stool and staring vacantly into space.

'What's the name of the volcano?' I whispered.

'What?'

'The. Name. Of. The. Volcano.' Even with heavy emphasis, I still managed to whisper.

'*I* don't know,' she said, a little affronted, as if I'd asked her the way to the nearest strip club.

I stopped whispering. 'It's on the fucking *page* – it's right there in *front* of you . . .'

I shouldn't have been so intense. The ASM looked like she might cry. Quickly, I scanned the script. There it was. The word I'd said almost two hundred times so far that year. Many more times than that, if you count all the rehearsals. Casually I strolled back on stage, trying to look as if I was deep in thought. Then I turned to the dinner party guest. 'Have you ever been to Chuquicammatta?'

After that, I had the name of the volcano written on my shirt cuff in indelible marker ink.

In spite of mistakes like that, I think I must have been improving as an actor. The critic Ned Chaillet wrote in *The*

Times – 'The surprisingly fine partnership of Gary Bond and Ian Ogilvy . . .' – a backhanded compliment if ever there was one, but one which I treasured because, in Ned Chaillet's eyes at least, I'd obviously surprised him by being better than he expected. Gary, on the other hand, was a little peeved. He thought, justifiably, that he'd always been terrific.

Ray Cooney's enormously successful farce *Run For Your Wife* was still early in its long run – and still at the vast Shaftesbury Theatre – when I took over the part of Stanley-the-idiotic-neighbour from the comedian Eric Sykes. James Bolam – a superbly funny actor with the face of a lugubrious haddock – took over the part of John Smith, the hapless and bigamous taxi driver, from Terry Scott. Eric Sykes and Terry Scott were not the original players; they were the leading men of the second cast, and James Bolam and I were the two leads in the third.

During the immensely long run of *Run For Your Wife*, Ray Cooney replaced his two leading men every three months. This was a popular move with the two leading men, because three months is the perfect length of time to spend in the West End, doing the same thing every night. You don't get too bored, the end is in sight, the pay is good, and with *Run For Your Wife* you were guaranteed full houses every night. Of course, the rest of the regular cast probably didn't enjoy these changeovers so much. It must have been a wearying business, adjusting to each new replacement pair, if only because of the radically different playing styles between people like Eric Sykes and people like me.

When I was offered the three month job, I went to see the show. Sykes and Scott were about as funny as two men could be, with Sykes regularly stopping the show to explain matters that the audience might have missed – like why he was standing *here* when he should really have been over *there*, and *would* be over there except for the fact that he was holding the telephone receiver and, unfortunately, Mr Scott was standing on the phone cable and he, Mr Sykes, couldn't go anywhere until Mr Scott took his considerable weight *off* the cable, thus releasing the receiver and allowing Mr Sykes to go where the director had asked him to go –

It was one of the funniest evenings I've ever spent in the theatre and at the end of it I was weak with laughter. When I told Ray Cooney how much I'd enjoyed Sykes and Scott he made a non-committal noise and shrugged and said, 'Yes, very funny of course, but they do add about twenty minutes to the running time of the show and that's never a good thing with farce. Frankly, I prefer to have actors and not comedians doing my plays. Comedians are inclined to turn them into variety shows. Actors let the play come through and, as it's *my* play that's coming through, I like that.'

Ray taught me two fine bits of comedy business. The first involves a glass of whisky and a nudged elbow. It is possible, when theatrically startled, to jerk the hand holding the whisky glass upwards in a single, short, sharp and precise movement, so that the liquid shoots out of the glass and up into the air and *remains in one piece* – or rather in a single large wobbling globule – which, if you do it right, you can then catch (with it still in one piece) back into the glass again.

The other bit of comedy business was one of Ray's favourites and is entirely unconnected with reality. 'Ian, you know when you go to the door and open it and say your last line and exit? Well, just before you exit, could you do this?'

This was a bit of bizarre and meaningless physical business, nothing to do with furthering the plot, but designed to get a laugh merely on the strength that it looks funny. It's easy to do: right hand to the bottom of your imaginary zippered flies; left hand behind your back, at the bottom of an even more imaginary zipper that supposedly runs up the crack of your backside; in one neat movement, pull up both imaginary zippers – while, at the same moment, dropping halfway down to a squat with your knees to the ten o'clock and two o'clock positions; then, when the two zippers are at their respective apogees, return them smartly to their original nether starting points – while at the same moment straightening your knees to regain your full height. The whole thing lasting not more than two seconds. Preferably one and a half.

I did as I was asked, every night for a few weeks, and got the laugh Ray wanted me to get. Then one evening James Bolam put his mournful face round my dressing room door. 'You know that bit of business you do?' he said. 'You know, that fucking bobbing zipping thing?'

I said I did know it and what about it?

'Would you mind not doing it any more?'

'No, I don't mind. But why not?'

'Because I fucking *hate* it,' said James, with what I thought was more venom than the business deserved.

For the sake of good relations I stopped doing the bobbing zipping thing, because accommodating your fellow actors is a friendly and sensible thing to do – as long as the accommodation doesn't deprive you of something that might be relevant to the plot or to your character. I once asked an actor to not do something on stage and, considerately, he didn't.

At Chichester, during rehearsals for *The Devil's Disciple*, that excellent actor Graham Seed (best known perhaps for playing Nigel Pargetter for many years on the long-running radio series *The Archers*) was cast as my younger brother. I was standing heroically on the dining table, heroically doing one of the hero's big heroic speeches. In a moment of exuberance, Graham suggested to Peter Dews the director that might he – Graham – perhaps run on during my speech and, in a moment of inspired comedy, comedically grab a biscuit from the plate between my feet and then run off with it – a bit of business that might, Graham thought, get quite a nice laugh? When I – through gritted teeth – suggested he not do that because (A) I was in the middle of a big heroic speech and didn't need any funny upstaging distractions thank-you-very-much Graham and (B) if he did insist on running on and comedically grabbing a biscuit from between my feet right in the middle of my big speech, he should bear in mind that, since I was standing on a table, I was in a convenient position to kick his teeth in, which, come to think of it, might actually get a bigger laugh than the biscuit business. Graham recognised the weight of my argument and sensibly dropped the idea immediately.

Run For Your Wife was one of the most joyous experiences of my professional life and I learned how to do English farce. The play is about as theatrically lowbrow as you can get. But occasionally it achieved something that higher-brow drama can't: a handful of audience members would always be waiting at the stage door after the show. Several times I heard, 'We've never been to the theatre before – always thought it a bit stuffy, you know? But our friend – he's a taxi driver, you know – he told us to come. And if this is what the theatre is really like, we'll go again!' Lots of taxi drivers recommended the play to their friends because it was about one of their fraternity, but a mere recommendation isn't enough. The play itself was what generated that sort of enthusiasm from first time theatre goers and for that alone *Run For Your Wife* deserves its place in the list of all time great comedies.

A play that's on this list already is Ben Travers' classic farce *Rookery Nook*. I went back to that great barn the Shaftesbury Theatre to play one of the two male leads; the other lead was Tom Courtenay. Tom and I had made a film together in the 1960s called *The Day the Fish Came Out* – a film so bad that nobody nowadays has ever heard of it – so, while not the closest of friends, we did at least know of one another. I also knew the wonderfully funny Lionel Jeffries, with whom I'd recently made a comedy television series called *Tom, Dick and Harriet*. The fine character actress Peggy Mount was in the cast too, and the splendid Nichola McAuliffe, who could play imperious, bullying wives better than anybody alive. Derek Smith played her hapless hen-pecked husband with such quivering, pop-eyed timidity that he pretty much stole the show.

Peggy Mount knitted me a blue sleeveless pullover in her spare time but she must have dropped a few stitches in the making, because the thing unravelled into a pile of wool within a few days. In *his* spare time, Lionel asked if he could polish a pair of my shoes. It was something he'd learned to do in the army and it had become a hobby. Some men like to play golf; some men like to listen to music; Lionel liked polishing shoes. 'It's all in the spit, you see, Ian.' When I got them back, they were so embarrassingly shiny I didn't want to wear them.

Princess Alexandra was the sister of my old Sunningdale contemporary, Prince Michael of Kent, and was one of the most popular members of the royal family. She was married to Sir Angus Ogilvy, younger brother of the Ogilvy clan chieftain. She came to see *Rookery Nook* and afterwards the cast did the traditional line-up to meet her. When she got to me the princess said that her children were big fans and, having the same last name as I did, were keen to know if they were related to me? I said they were. When princesses ask if you're family, you say yes.

Forty-three years after my mother toured the Far East with The Quaints company, I followed with the Derek Nimmo touring company, visiting several of the places she'd seen back in 1929. It was an eight-week tour all over the Middle and Far East, taking Neil Simon's comedy *Barefoot in the Park* to Dubai, Abu Dhabi, Bahrain, Oman, Singapore, Kuala Lumpur and Hong Kong.

Derek Nimmo was one of England's finest comedy actors. I once saw him in the popular old farce *See How They Run*, playing a bishop. At one point in the play he sat down on a sofa, plonking his ample bottom on top of a World War II gas mask – the kind that sports a corrugated rubber hose sticking out from the nosepiece. Derek arranged it that, once he'd sat down, only the gas mask's hose was visible to the audience. He also made sure that the hose dangled over the edge of the sofa and appeared to originate in the neighbourhood of his crotch. Derek's elderly bishop suddenly notices the hose – registers shock and horror at what he takes to be an accidental but nevertheless thoroughly indecent exposure of his private parts – and then spends the next few minutes surreptitiously trying to stuff the whole thing back into his trousers. You had to be there, of course but, for me, it was the funniest and wickedest bit of stage business I'd ever seen.

When he wasn't starring on television, or appearing in London in some great comedy or other and making me laugh until tears streamed down my cheeks, Derek ran theatrical tours to unlikely places. These tours made him a lot of money, but I think the primary reason he had started them up was because he himself was an inveterate, passionate world traveller and couldn't understand why so many of his colleagues in the acting fraternity weren't. The tours were designed to put this right. The pay wasn't much but, as Derek explained, you weren't doing it for the money, you were doing it because you shouldn't spend the rest of your life regretting all the extraordinary places in the world that you'd never seen, not when he was prepared to send you to lots of them, and once there put you up in the best hotels, and give you just enough money so you could buy a handmade suit in Hong Kong – and in return all you had to do was put on a play in the ballrooms of the best hotels, doing eight dinner shows a week to a bunch of boozy expatriate British and American and German and Scandinavian engineers and, in the process, make Derek a small fortune.

Friends like Simon Williams and his wife Lucy Fleming had done Nimmo tours, so I knew what to expect – so, when Derek put the idea to me and then flattered me further into the scheme by asking me to pick the play, I said 'Yes' immediately. I chose *Barefoot in the Park* because I'd always liked it. The part of the newlywed husband Paul was undemanding and I thought the play was stuffed with good one-liners that would go down well with our audiences. What I hadn't taken into consideration was the average summer time temperatures of all of the places we were to visit, which often hovered around 100°F – and the setting of *Barefoot in the Park*, which is New York during a particularly bitter winter. At one point snow is supposed to flutter down through a broken skylight. This meant wearing a lot of warm winter coats and boots and gloves and woolly scarves, and a lot of foot-stamping, and hands-rubbing, and general purpose cold weather acting. The ballrooms of the hotels where we performed the play were air-conditioned, but inevitably they were much warmer – and much more humid – than any theatre I'd ever appeared in before. On stage, sweat would be pouring down our faces even as we characters complained about how cold it was and why weren't the radiators working? The audience thought this was funnier than most of Neil Simon's one-liners.

There were other small hazards to playing in the ballrooms of large hotels, to dinner guests who often had drunk more than they should. The leading lady was the pretty and well-endowed Susan Denaker. Her first appearance in the play was sometimes met with raucous shouts of 'Get 'em off, girlie!'

The snow, by the way – and the best kind if you want the fluttering effect – was made from the corners cut from Rizla cigarette papers. I don't know if these tiny triangular scraps of paper are still available from Rizla but they were in the early 1980s, and Colin, our stage manager, carried a big polythene bag of them all the way through the Middle and Far East. Occasionally he had a hard time explaining our 'snow' – what it was and why we needed it – to suspicious customs officers.

Colin was a kind, sweet small man who said sweet, kind, small things like, 'Give me a cup of tea and my pipe and I'm a happy man.' He was, at the time of the tour, a bit down on his luck, although in the past he had been, apparently, a quite successful psychic who told people's fortunes and predicted the future. 'But surely,' said Derek Nimmo, 'if you could predict the future you wouldn't be down on your luck now, Colin?' Colin said it didn't work like that but Derek remained unconvinced.

The tour would have been more fun if Tony Jay hadn't been in the company. Tony was a good actor but he should never have joined the cast in the first place because it turned out that among the many things in Life that Tony Jay hated, the absolute worst were sun, sea, sand, foreigners, foreign food and flying. The only place and people other than England and the English of which he approved was South Africa and the South Africans (the white ones) – and this at the time when South Africa, with its appalling record of social injustices, was one of the most anathematised countries in the world and one scrupulously avoided by Equity members at the specific request of our union.

Tony's distaste for all things not Anglo-Saxon or Dutch-Boer was exacerbated by fear. He was frightened everywhere we went, because everywhere we went had foreigners wandering about the place – but in the Middle Eastern countries his fear was palpable. He thought he looked Jewish – which led him to the unshakeable belief that if he were ever to put his head outside the hotel doors, he was sure to be attacked by a horde of enraged Arabs and quite probably killed. We pointed out to him that if he looked at all ethnically Semitic – and he didn't, not particularly – that it couldn't matter in the least because everybody else out there, being of similar ethnicity, was going to look just as Semitic as he did and therefore wouldn't give him more than a passing glance – but Tony wouldn't buy any of this. He resolutely stayed inside the hotel and hardly ever went anywhere. Even safe inside, there were problems; the food was one. In South Africa the food was excellent and why couldn't he get that sort of thing in Abu Dhabi? Once in Hong Kong he was persuaded to come out to dinner with us. Cruelly, halfway through the meal, I told him we were eating dog. It took me twenty minutes to reassure him out of his gag reflex.

Derek Nimmo was with us at the start of the tour in the United Arab Emirates, to show us the ropes, as it were. On our day off, he organised a coach trip for us, to take the company from Dubai and across the desert to a white sand beach on the Gulf of Oman. Halfway there we stopped at a remote village, dominated by an ancient Bedouin fort. Tony Jay stayed in the bus, wrapped in his own paranoia, but the rest of us – Guy Siner, Susan Denaker and Joyce Grant among others – were herded like sheep by Nimmo, who was determined we should admire the old fort as much as he did. We tramped over the stony ground and into the primitive little mud-walled hamlet. A stream ran through the place and the villagers had built a large, square concrete trough into which the stream was diverted. This was the communal bath of the village and was full of half-naked men sitting in the flowing water. We walked slowly past the tub, our eyes respectfully averted. There was a sudden excited shout – and an excited pointed finger – and a lot of excited turning of heads – and all excited eyes directed at me.

'Saint! Saint! *Saint!*' yelled the man who'd spotted me, and the rest of the bathers took up the chant and there was much smiling and nodding and salaaming and waving, and then Derek hustled us away to look at the Bedouin fort – but for months after he would tell the story of how, in the middle of the desert, on a patch of sand somewhere between the United Arab Emirates and the Gulf of Oman, in a tiny village made of mud with not a television aerial in sight, a half-naked Arab man sitting in a communal bath had turned out to be a fan of Ian Ogilvy's.

There were other plays for me during my personal TV and film famine of the 1980s. When I came back from the Far East, Maria Aitken was waiting for me with a wonderful role in a revival of Giles Cooper's strange black comedy, *Happy Family*, which she was to direct and produce, with Stephanie Beacham, James Laurenson and Angela Thorne. Maria did both superbly, particularly with me – so much so that Jack Tinker, who had just been voted Critic Of The Year, wrote, 'If Ian Ogilvy has ever given a better stage performance then I am the poorer for having missed it.' Since I felt I was slowly improving with each performance I was glad Jack Tinker must not have noticed any of the ones I'd done before.

One night, during the run of *Happy Family*, I stopped the play. It happened right at the start, when Stephanie answers the door to her brother, played by me. This time, Stephanie yanked open the upstage door and made a lot of faces at me in the open doorway, and did a bit of head-jerking and eye-rolling, which I took to mean that something odd was happening in the auditorium. It was only when I stepped into the light that I became aware of it – what seemed to be a furious row between two women in the stalls. I decided not to say my opening line and wait for a moment until the disturbance died down. It didn't. If anything, it got more furious. There was only one thing to do; I stepped forward and said, 'Ladies and gentleman – sorry about this but I think we'll start the play again when whatever is causing this ruckus is sorted out.' The audience gave me a big round of applause and the stage manager lowered the curtain and ushers took charge of the row, which turned out to be between a German lady and an English lady, the English one objecting to the German one sitting on her fur coat and the German one oddly refusing to move off it, causing the English one to become distraught because the fur was extremely precious and quite new and who won the fucking war anyway?

It was a short run but a happy one and Maria, having cut her directing teeth with this play, went on to direct many more – and most successfully too.

She didn't direct *The Common Pursuit*, a new play by Simon Gray about university undergraduates founding a literary magazine. It was to be given a pre-West End production at the Lyric, Hammersmith. I was offered the part of Martin, the non-intellectual member of the group who provides the funding for the venture. I read the script, thought it wonderful, accepted immediately – and a few days later got a telephone call.

'Hello – is this, um, Ian Ogilvy?'

'Yes. Who's this?'

'Um – this is Harold.'

'Harold Who?'

'Um – Harold Pinter.'

I kicked myself for not recognising those dark brown, slightly self-deprecating tones. Before I could apologise, they went on:

'I'm directing Simon's play. Just wanted to say how delighted we all are that you – um – are going to do it.'

'Well, I'm even more delighted, Mr Pinter.'

'Harold, please. Well, that makes all of us delighted then. Jolly good. See you at rehearsals.'

At first, rehearsals were a hushed affair. Simon Gray sat at the back of the rehearsal room, nursing glasses of red wine and watching for signs that his play was being tampered with. Harold, dressed always in black, was darkly serious up front. A lot of the communication between playwright and director, and director and cast, was conducted in whispers. My friend Simon Williams was playing Peter. After a couple of weeks he could stand it no longer.

'I'm sorry, but it's like working in Chartres cathedral. It's all so reverential. We have to have some jokes.'

Simon Gray said, huffily, that he thought there were quite a lot of quite good jokes in his play and he was in fact quite proud of several of them.

'No, I meant the rehearsal atmosphere. It's all a bit earnest.'

Harold apologised. 'Sorry. I've – um – I've just given up smoking and it's making me tense. Feel free to have all the jokes you want.'

The atmosphere relaxed a little, allowing Simon at a later rehearsal to muse to Harold – 'I wonder, Harold, if I sort of moved over here, if that might take the curse off this line?'

From the rear of the rehearsal room, from an affronted Simon to a Simon with his foot in his mouth – 'And what curse would that be, may I ask?'

Clive Francis, Nina Thomas, Robert East and Nicholas Le Prevost made up the rest of the cast. All were wonderful in their roles and the reviews of the play mostly reflected this; sour notes were reserved for the play itself. Several reviewers referred to one of Simon Gray's best jokes (and one of his bravest, considering at whom it was aimed). It was a line about a media personality leaving his television programme to become theatre critic on *The Sunday Times* where '. . . they seem to be impressed by his lack of qualifications.' With lines like that, we were lucky not to be lynched – and, perhaps partly because of lines like that, it wasn't surprising that the play failed to transfer to the West End and finished its run at the Lyric, Hammersmith.

A dinner was arranged, at a restaurant in Kensington, partly to celebrate the run of *The Common Pursuit* and partly to allow us all to get together for one last time to commiserate with each other that it wasn't going to run any longer. The evening started out fine. We all of us – cast, crew, writer and director, together with one or two wives and husbands and other loved ones who were along for the free food – sat round a big circular table in the restaurant's private dining room. The advantage of a round table is, in the words of Simon Gray (who wrote in his published diary about this peculiar evening) that, 'No quarrel need be confined to an area at the top, or the bottom, or the middle, as in a long table. By simply swivelling your head in the course of delivering a sentence you can see at a glance the face of everyone you're insulting with it almost simultaneously. In short, you can get from tranquillity to complete uproar with a single ill-judged remark.' I was the one who provided the ill-judged remark.

I was telling Simon Gray's wife Beryl about something that had happened at my son Titus's boarding school. On the day of a visit by the widow of the late Airey Neave – (Airey Neave was a war hero and politician who had been assassinated by an IRA bomb in 1979) – a few staggeringly tactless and cruel boys had thought it a tremendous prank to construct a fake bomb and plant it somewhere where it was sure to be found by the security people who always precede these visits. Sure enough it was discovered. Diana Neave's motorcade was turned back and the guilty boys confessed and were instantly expelled. I happened to say to Beryl – in a sort of jokey hyperbole – that, had Titus been one of the perpetrators, I would have 'broken both his legs and smashed his teeth in.'

Simon Gray was sitting on the other side of his wife and overheard my plan to maim my son. He though it excessive, and said so, quite crossly. He also suggested that perhaps the school might have taken some of the responsibility on themselves and kept the boys on, rather than brushing the problem under the carpet by expelling them. Nick Le Prevost – whose jacket lapel always wore out before the rest of his coat because of all the badges espousing left-wing causes he had pinned to it – chipped in with an interesting concept, which involved the idea that there were good bombs and bad bombs, and good bombs were the ones that were used against people with whom you disagreed – who, in Nick's view at that time, seemed to be most of the British establishment.

This inflammatory tangent took Simon Gray a third of the way towards apoplexy and quite soon everybody was joining in with their respective opinions on the matter, and things around the table were getting heated – except in the neighbourhood of Harold Pinter and his wife Lady Antonia Fraser, where things were very (and very unnaturally) quiet indeed. This was the proverbial calm before the storm, because quite suddenly the profoundly liberal Harold Pinter metamorphosed into an enraged retired colonel from Tunbridge Wells, bellowing that everything his old friend Simon Gray was saying was arrant and dangerous rubbish, that Ian was quite right to think of breaking bones, that he'd never heard such a collection of ridiculous ideas in his life – and Simon took up the challenge and started to bellow back – and then Harold picked up a heavy glass ashtray with the vague idea of hurling it at Simon's head and Simon, not to be outdone when it came to offensive weapons, started hefting a diminutive butter knife in his right hand. Beryl Gray was weeping into her napkin and muttering, 'Shutupshutupshutupshutup,' – but nobody except me heard her and I'd long since shut up anyway, due to the shame I was experiencing for causing all this in the first place. Lady Antonia Fraser, in an appropriately ladylike attempt to lighten the situation, proposed that we should all play a game. 'How about In The Manner of the Word – and do let's start with 'Aggressively', shall we?'

Waiters scurried in and out, looking increasingly worried with each visit. Occasionally somebody would try to reassure them by calling out that this was merely a little something to do with the common pursuit, which explained nothing and probably served only to make them more anxious than ever. Eventually the passions cooled and a strained silence hung over us all.

Harold got up and made a short, embarrassed speech thanking us all for our hard work, and then Simon Gray did the same only in slightly different words and with a slightly redder face, and then the party ended and we all went home.

The next day I called Harold and apologised. He was kind and exonerated me from blame; he said we were all tired and tense and things had got out of hand and I wasn't to spend another moment thinking about it. Then I telephoned Simon Gray and apologised and got pretty much the same reassurances from him – that we were all disappointed after our valiant efforts, that I wasn't to concern myself, and that he and Harold were of course the best of friends. But I discovered that it was still several days before they broke their dignified silences and resumed their old affections – and I suspect the ashtray and the butter knife were never entirely forgotten.

Harold and Simon shared a passion for cricket. Harold also wrote poetry. One of his shorter (and cricket-related) pieces went something like this:

> *I saw Len Hutton in his prime.*
> *Another time, Another time.*

Harold sent the poem to Simon for his appraisal. Several weeks went by with no word from his old friend. At last Harold could bear it no longer. He telephoned Simon –

'Hello. It's Harold.'

'Hello, Harold.'

'Um. I sent you a poem. Was wondering what you thought of it.'

'Yes. So sorry I haven't got back to you – only, the thing is – I haven't finished reading it yet.'

The disappointment of *The Common Pursuit*'s failure to get a West End run was offset for me by a fine production of *Three Sisters*, directed by Elijah Moshinsky, which started at the Greenwich Theatre and then transferred to the Albery in Saint

Martin's Lane. I played Vershinin, opposite the Masha of the exciting Joanne Whalley at Greenwich and then, in the West End, opposite the Masha of the equally exciting Francesca Annis.

In Greenwich, Joanne Whalley electrified the critics by creating a wonderful moment for herself and playing it to perfection. During the emotional parting from Vershinin, when he tries to push her away from him, Joanne made the rejection look violent by falling – and then somehow sliding – halfway across the stage. When Francesca took over, she decided to create her own moment of supreme drama – but not by any falling and sliding business; that belonged to another actress. Instead, she would scream – a dreadful, primal shriek that went on and on and was as theatrically effective in its way as Joanne's slide had been. What Francesca didn't know was the fun the rest of the cast, lurking close to the Tannoy speaker in the Green Room, had with her scream. The moment I left the stage I would run to the Green Room to hear the latest reason for Francesca's distress.

'Francesca Annis has just discovered that she hasn't got top billing.'

'Francesca Annis fails spectacularly during her audition for the role of Tosca.'

'Francesca Annis finds out that she's being paid ten quid a week less than anybody else.'

In fact she was being paid rather more, I later discovered. I didn't mind. Like so many of Francesca Annis's leading men, I was besotted with her.

Sir Anthony Quayle – the same Anthony Quayle whom Mike Reeves never saw in the film *Ice Cold In Alex* because of

the mud from the Quattara Depression that caked his face –
sent me a letter.

> *Dot and I came to see your Three Sisters at the Saturday matinee*
> *and were bowled over. And it was a joy to see your Vershinin. If*
> *I may say so, I think you are just getting better and better as an*
> *actor and I do urge you to do more and more of that kind of*
> *work.*
>
> *That's a silly thing to say, I know, for we all do what has to be*
> *done, or what offers and so on. But you know what I mean.*

I did indeed. I was also pathetically grateful that any improve-
ment I might be making in my acting had been noticed by
somebody as distinguished as Anthony Quayle – distinguished
not only because of his body of work as an actor, but also for
his eight years of directing plays at the Shakespeare Memorial
Theatre, where he was primarily responsible for laying the
foundations of the Royal Shakespeare Company.

I knew Quayle only slightly and the acquaintance was
through my daughter Emma. She had become a stage manager
and was so good at her job that Quayle – after working with
her once – insisted that she go on working for him forever after.
At the time, Diane and I were still together and living in the
country, in the wooden house in Pirbright. Emma used to
come home at weekends. One Friday she rang us. Could she
bring a couple of friends for Sunday lunch? Diane and I said of
course she could. We didn't bother asking the names of the
friends, assuming them to be some junior colleagues of hers on
the stage management staff. She turned up with Sir Anthony
and Lady Quayle.

After lunch, Anthony grabbed the sledgehammer I'd been using to break up some concrete slabs I wanted to be rid of and he laid into them lustily for half an hour until Lady Quayle – who was the equally distinguished actress Dorothy Hyson – told him to stop because he was getting his clothes all dirty.

Emma once asked me what I did about my props in a play. Did I go to the prop table in the wings and pick them up for myself, or did a stage manager hand them to me just before I go on stage? I said I picked them up for myself and why did she want to know?

'I always hand the props to the actors,' said Emma.

'Why?'

'Because if I don't they'll pick up the wrong ones,' she said. 'Or not pick up anything at all.'

'Really? Why do you think that?'

'Because actors are so *stupid!*' she hissed through gritted teeth. Obviously she'd had some bad experiences, although not with Anthony Quayle – and with that level of contempt for the abilities of actors to think for themselves, it was probably for the best that soon after she left the theatre and became a chef in her own restaurant in Marbella. Her partner at the time was Carol Mailer and their restaurant was called Ogilvy & Mailer.

When my uncle David Ogilvy heard about this, he was slightly displeased. 'I don't think they should have done that,' he muttered. I said I thought he should take it as a huge compliment, which of course it was – and, since he'd established that I was the head of the family and *I* approved of it, perhaps *he* ought not to disapprove so much. Amused, he dropped his objection immediately.

In 1934 the Reverend Walter Reynolds wrote a play called *Young England*. It wasn't his first; in the years leading up to the death of Queen Victoria in 1901, he'd written a dozen melodramas with titles like *A Woman's Truth*, *A Mother's Sin*, *Church and Stage* and *The Shamrock and the Rose*. He'd also produced a number of travelogues – *Recollections of Japan*, *Snapshots of Africa*, and the archly entitled *Lillel Ole Noo York*. He'd been an actor, appearing with Sir Henry Irving in 1904 and then touring the provinces with the great man. Later he became a justice of the peace and represented Hampstead on the London County Council for nearly a quarter of a century.

The Reverend Walter was a Victorian gentleman of sound moral principles and, with those moral principles in mind – together with an admiration for the way things were done in the nineteenth century – he sat down at the advanced age of eighty-three to write a play that would exemplify all those fine Victorian qualities that were so conspicuously lacking, in Walter Reynolds' eyes at least, from the contemporary theatrical scene. Once *Young England* was finished, he set about getting it produced. Quite how he managed that is a bit of a mystery, but he did manage it and it was mounted at the Victoria Palace Theatre in 1934. Later, it went on tour round the provinces, then returned to the Holborn Empire theatre for a further run. It's one of the worst plays ever written and, unintentionally, one of the funniest.

Young England deals with drunkenness, drug addiction, decadence, gambling and fraud in big business. Here to solve all these social evils are the Boy Scouts and the Girl Guides of Young England, led by the hero of the play, the incorruptible scoutmaster Hope Ravenscroft. The two Jabez Hawks – *père et fils*, a couple of the vilest villains ever seen on any stage – are the wicked evildoers.

The writing was innocent and intensely melodramatic, and audiences in 1934 found the play so riotously funny that it became a cult. People would return to see it again and again. Noël Coward brought parties of friends. Quite soon, the audience knew the play better than the actors; it became a fad to shout out upcoming lines at the poor performers before they had a chance to say them for themselves. Unable to beat them, the actors joined in the joke; they would let the audience yell out their lines and then repeat them themselves – but with subtle differences designed to make the audience laugh at their cleverness. It was difficult, at times, to know who was behaving the worst, the actors or the audience.

Apart from the ludicrousness of its sentiments, the cast of *Young England* numbered about forty-five, making it doubly impossible to mount these days – impossible that was, unless your name was Ned Sherrin and you had a lot of friends.

Ned Sherrin was a writer, a producer, a director, a critic, and a radio and television personality. When he wasn't being famous and highly paid, he sometimes gave his valuable time to putting on, for one night only, a charity evening of some special performance, where major stars appeared in both large and small roles, where the tickets were expensive, and where a lot of money was raised for various good causes. It was Ned who had put Maria Aitken and Edward Fox (and then, when Edward was no longer available, me) together for *Noël and Gertie*, and it was Ned who persuaded me to appear for one night only in a lavish production of the pantomime *Cinderella*. I played Dandini opposite Joanna Lumley's Prince Charming. Peter

O'Toole had one line as The Herald. Somebody had to ask him, 'Does the Prince approach?' The Herald's line was, 'He does, My Lord.' Peter O'Toole grinned evilly and said, 'Fucked if I know.'

Each scene in *Cinderella* had been written by a different comedy writer, with contributions from John Cleese, Barry Cryer, Michael Palin, Michael Frayne and several others. Naturally the show was gloriously filthy and also wildly under-rehearsed – precisely the aspects that made shows like this such fun for both audience and casts; and these were those sorts of evenings that Ned Sherrin put on when called to do so.

But *Young England* was something special. This was a real play with a vast cast and the actors who would be asked to contribute their time and talents for nothing would be facing several weeks of unpaid rehearsal time. Naturally, when asked to play the villainous Jabez Hawk junior, I said, 'Yes'. Patrick Ryecart (that rare creature, a good actor *and* a natural blond) played the impossibly heroic Hope Ravenscroft. The rest of the cast positively glittered and included Anthony Hopkins, Alan Bates, Millicent Martin, Bonnie Langford, John Hurt, Gwen Watford, Fenella Fielding, Lindsay Anderson, Geraldine James, Alec McCowen, Christopher Cazenove, Frank Finlay, Felicity Kendall, Maria Aitken, Victor Spinetti, James Bolam, Eileen Atkins, Jean Marsh, Nigel Hawthorne, Tim Curry, Daniel Day-Lewis, Rupert Everett, Tom Hulce, Elaine Paige, Roger Rees, Prunella Scales, Omar Sharif, Esther Rantzen, Ronnie Barker, Jane Asher, Simon Callow, Lionel Blair – and many other luminaries who turned up on the day and were incorporated into the show in various walk-on parts.

Gaye Brown played my mother. Perhaps because she had

other things to do, she missed some rehearsals and on the night of the performance was rocky on her lines. It didn't matter; audiences for these events were prepared for mishaps and even looked forward to them – so when Gaye dried on a line and looked hopefully at me to help her out and I said, 'It's no good looking at me like that, Mother – it's your turn not mine,' the audience was delighted. I was as delighted as the audience because they entered into the spirit of the evening from the moment the curtain rose; they cheered Patrick Ryecart whenever he struck a heroic pose, and they booed and hissed me whenever I slunk villainously from the wings, and I hissed back and shook my fist at them and everybody had a wonderful evening – which was the main reason I always said, 'Yes' to these events; not so much from charitable inclinations, but rather more for the selfish reason that I knew I would see many old friends, and meet some new ones, and probably have more fun than I deserved.

I went to America in 1989, to try out a new career in Hollywood and become a film and television star. I became neither. I did a lot of television work and appeared in several films, but nobody was sufficiently excited about my being there to make any great difference to my career so far; so between those paying gigs I went on working (often for no pay at all) in the American live theatre in Los Angeles. I played Garry Essendine in Coward's *Present Laughter* and the show was a small hit; Gene Kelly and Martin Landau came to see it. I did *Sleuth* at the Pasadena Playhouse and very few people came to see that. I was in the original American production of Oliver Cotton's *Wet Weather Cover*. I played Henry Higgins in three separate productions of *My Fair Lady* – the only musical I could ever do because the role was written for Rex Harrison, who could sing only a little better than me, which meant he could hardly sing at all. I was in *Love! Valour! Compassion!* by Terence McNally, playing the double roles of the English twins John and James – probably the two best theatre parts I ever had.

Love! Valour! Compassion! is about a group of gay friends who meet regularly at the upstate New York house of one of their number, and there was a lot of male nudity in it. I was the only member of the cast allowed to keep his clothes on. It was disconcerting to be standing in the wings with the rest of the cast waiting to make a collective entrance, surrounded by naked men, several of whom – in attempts to look bigger than they were when in their un-aroused state – would be busily playing with themselves. Self-fluffing, as it were. Occasionally I had to have words. 'Oh, do put that thing away, Randy.'

Three times I returned to the UK to fulfil theatre jobs, once to play *Sleuth* again for a short run in Shaftesbury Avenue and twice to take a couple of plays on tours of the provinces. But a problem was developing. Ever since the first production of *My Fair Lady* – at the enormous American Musical Theater of San José, in Northern California – I had been suffering from a strange and gradually worsening form of stage fright.

Two hours before the first night of *My Fair Lady* I began to feel deathly ill – so ill I could hardly stand up. The symptoms were flu-like, and so debilitating that I was convinced that I wouldn't be able to walk on stage without falling over. But there were two thousand people out there waiting to see the show; somehow I pulled myself together, and tottered on and got through it, gradually feeling better and better as the show progressed. But ever after, whenever I appeared in the theatre, these sick feelings would sweep over me, and each first night was worse than the last; the subsequent nights of the run were not quite so painful, but they were still unpleasant. It all came to a head during the second of the English tours.

The play was *Dangerous Obsession*, by N.J. Crisp. It's a good, taut thriller, with only three roles. I played the lead, the man with the dangerous obsession, and it was my character who had the most lines and who drove the play forward. Having accepted the role, and having looked forward to the job, I found to my distress that within a day of starting rehearsals I hated the play and my part, and now the feeling of sickness was with me permanently. I couldn't sleep, so I started taking the sleep aid Ambien every night. But it was ridiculous to be in such a state. Nothing was wrong. I'd learned most of the play before we'd started to work on it, so remembering the lines wasn't a problem. I understood the character and had made a perfectly intelligent choice as to how to play him. My fellow actors – Lisa Goddard and Martyn Stanbridge – were friendly and fine. The dates we were to play were first rate. The director was sympathetic and helpful. So there were no particular problems associated with *Dangerous Obsession*, apart from the state of my mind, which, unknown to me, was fraying at the edges.

Three weeks later we opened in Aberdeen, but only just. I felt so ill I spent every day in bed, only getting up to drag myself to the theatre. I knew that this sickness was psychological, and that there was nothing physically wrong with me, but knowing this didn't help. It was still a struggle to get myself on stage, and another struggle, once I was on, to stop myself from keeling over in a dead faint.

I tried to hide this from the rest of the cast and crew but they must have sensed something was wrong because later they told me that, during the eight-week tour (or seven, as it it turned out for me) I became progressively odder and odder – manic one minute, depressed the next and, during the day, a virtual hermit locked inside my hotel room.

It was in Brighton that my mind (like Peggy Mount's blue pullover) finally unravelled. It was the penultimate week of the tour. We were playing at the lovely old Theatre Royal, a familiar stage I'd worked on several times during other touring productions. After Brighton, there was only one more week to go, at the pretty little Richmond Theatre, where most of my friends would be coming to see me. Something to look forward to. The end of the road and a lot of familiar smiling faces telling me how good I was.

It was a Thursday night. That evening, sitting in my dressing room ready to go on stage, I felt no better and no worse than on any other evening of the tour. But then I began to wonder – what was my first line in the play? I couldn't think of it. This is not uncommon among actors – a momentary lapse of memory – but what was rare was the fact that, try as I might, it still wouldn't come to me. I began to feel the first flutterings of a panic attack. I didn't have a copy of the play in my dressing room so I went to the prompt corner and opened the stage manager's copy and looked at the first page of *Dangerous Obsession* – and found myself staring at a play I'd never read before. I recognised none of the lines. The stage directions made no sense. I couldn't even find my character's name.

That's when the shaking started.

All careers have their own particular nightmares. Each person has their own variation of their profession's frightening dream – perhaps a surgeon faced with an emergency case can't find the right scalpel, maybe a journalist with a deadline can't get his computer to work – and actors are no different. I've asked friends and colleagues what their nightmares consist of and, while they differ in the details, they're similar in the terrors they invoke; my actor's nightmare is usually in the form of finding myself in a strange theatre, with a strange cast, about to play the leading role in a play with five minutes to go before curtain up – but for some reason I've never spent a moment rehearsing the play and have never even read the script. In the five minutes left before my first entrance, I roam the theatre desperately searching for a copy of the play, if only to get an idea of the plot – but nobody has one. There isn't even a copy in the prompt corner – the one place where there's *always* a copy. The minutes tick by and I become more and more frantic. Then, with only seconds to go before I have to march on stage and perform this unknown role in this unknown play, I'm rescued; the dream-state terror reaches such a pitch that it wakes me up.

But this horribly *real* moment in the prompt corner of Brighton's Theatre Royal was my actor's nightmare made manifest and I wasn't waking up. I was confused and very frightened because something was obviously wrong with my brain. But then I decided to ignore whatever it was and let my internal computer take over . . . if I just relaxed and didn't think about it, everything would be fine . . . good old Doctor Theatre would come through for me and whatever problem I'd just come up against in the dark corner would go away all by itself . . .

Shaking all over, I got myself ready in the wings. When the curtain went up, revealing Liza Goddard alone on the stage, I knew what I had to do – it was what I had done for the past fifty-three uneventful performances. All I had to do was do it again. I walked slowly along the back of the set, past the floor-to-ceiling windows and thus in view of the audience, crunching my way over the gravel laid on the wooden floorboards of the stage. I went to the front door and, as usual, rang the doorbell. As usual, Liza opened the door and looked at me in the way one does when surprised by an unexpected caller. It was time for my first line.

Which wasn't there.

Doctor Theatre, on this occasion, turned out to be a quack. I gaped pathetically at Lisa, opening and closing my mouth like a goldfish. She tried to help me out, doing something similar to what I'd done so many years before with a drunk Trevor Howard. Still I said nothing – but now I was starting to cry. Liza tried another prompt, but it was no use, I was crumbling in front of her eyes. I shook my head in a mute attempt to say I was sorry. Then I stumbled away, out of sight of the audience, sat down in the wings and started to sob in earnest. People clustered round. The curtain was lowered. An announcement was made about a sudden illness. Liza suggested I breathe into a paper bag. Martyn Stanbridge rubbed my shoulders. Somebody went to make a cup of tea. I would have preferred a brandy.

I was helped to my dressing room, still weeping – which is something I never do because my generation was brought up to believe that big boys don't cry. At Sunningdale school, my father's old Cambridge friend Philip Squarey would reward a boy who didn't cry when hurt on the rugby field with a paper star. Crying was for sissies. Today, when I see a grown man like a famous soccer player or a chancellor of the exchequer sobbing in front of the television cameras I find myself despising him. I am lachrymose intolerant. So the shame I felt at this uncontrolled weeping I was doing was intense.

The shame was made worse when the paramedics arrived in my dressing room to have a look at me. Obviously summoned by the company manager – the thought of his kindness set off another attack of wails – the paramedics were a young man and a young woman, looking efficient in their ambulance uniforms. They patted me on the shoulder and said everything was going to be all right and, when I lifted my crumpled, tear-stained face to thank them for their kindness, the young man said, 'Oh blimey, it's the Saint!'

This brought on a renewed burst of tears, this time of humiliation. On a list of the people who should never cry, the Saint would surely be in the top ten? There was more shoulder patting, together with soothing reassurances that they'd both seen this sort of thing before and that I wasn't to be embarrassed, it happens to all sorts of people – 'But not to me!' I hiccuped. 'Never to m-m-me!'

The kind company manager found a kind Brighton doctor who was prepared to see me and the kind young paramedics put me in their ambulance and took me to him. By the time we arrived at his consulting rooms I was feeling a little better, because on this particular night the one thing I'd been dreading doing, I didn't have to do. I didn't have to do *Dangerous Obsession*. Somebody else – my unfortunate understudy – was at this very moment doing the play for me. The relief was enormous. It was as though a skilled surgeon had removed, painlessly, a ten-pound weight that had, for the last seven weeks, been lodged in my head. He'd also taken away another heavy lump of something or other that had been sitting in my chest cavity.

Everybody in Brighton that night seemed impossibly young. The doctor was a mere child, but a wise one all the same. After questioning me closely about what had been going on in my recent life, he said, 'Well, it's nothing terribly serious. You've been under a lot of strain and you've had a small nervous breakdown.'

I said was he sure it was a small one? Because it felt like quite a big one, actually.

'No, no. A bad one and you'd be baying at the moon. But you might like to give the stage-acting a bit of a rest for a while.'

'A rest? For how long?'

'Until you feel like doing it again. You'll know when. Or maybe you won't.'

'Won't what?'

'Maybe you'll never feel like you want to go back. And that's all right too.'

Oddly, it was the young doctor's *permission* that clinched it for me. Not *having* to go back. That was exactly how I felt – and how I've continued to feel ever since. I found I wasn't alone. Many actors have suffered this sort of debilitating stage fright – which is the worst kind, because it often comes over you relatively late in your career, by which time you should have developed into a mature and confident actor and not a quivering, anguished wreck. I'm comforted by the knowledge that the great Ian Holm went through a similar experience. He described it during an interview for Masterpiece Theatre Online:

Something just snapped. Once the concentration goes, the brain literally closes down. It's like a series of doors slamming shut in a jail. Actors dry up all the time. Well, I wasn't just drying; I was stopping.

Ian Holm eventually returned to the theatre and, when he did, he said he couldn't think what all the fuss had been about. I like to hope that one day – before I get so old that I can't remember my own name, let alone speeches in a play – I'll think the same way.

Chapter 12

There's no point denying it; I've made a lot of rotten films and very few even passable ones. But even the bad ones had interesting people working on them.

Expectations were low for my first film, *Revenge of the Blood Beast*. They dropped a lot lower for my second. The director was Michael Cacoyannis, who the year before had enjoyed a huge success with his film *Zorba the Greek*. On the strength of this, he was given a lot of money by excited investors to make them another hit.

Cacoyannis came up with a monumental flop called *The Day the Fish Came Out* – a futuristic story set in what he assumed would be the giddy, gaudy 1990s, about a lost container of nuclear materials jettisoned over a Greek holiday island by a pair of incompetent bomber pilots, played by Tom Courtenay and Colin Blakely, who spend most of the film half naked and hiding in bushes. A military team headed by Sam Wanamaker and me are detailed to dress up as tourists and conduct undercover searches for the missing materials. An American archeologist (nineteen-year-old Candice Bergen) arrives to look for statues. She takes a fancy to me and we nearly have sex but not quite. A goatherd finds the missing container and chops it open with an axe and then, disappointed that it doesn't contain anything he can sell, dumps the whole thing into the ocean. All the fish – and presumably everybody else on the island – die. Hence the title.

Michael Cacoyannis not only wrote and directed the film, he also designed all the costumes – the ones he supposed (in 1966) that we'd all be wearing in 1996. He couldn't have been more mistaken. The women's clothes – what there was of them – looked ridiculous, and the men's – what there was of them – looked flamboyantly gay. The film followed suit and was an atrocious mess. Many years later I was in Hollywood filming an episode of the comedy TV show, *Murphy Brown*, which starred Candice Bergen. We hadn't met in the intervening forty years and I doubted she'd remember me. She did – albeit reluctantly; she'd done a lot of fine work since that abortion of a film and was embarrassed to be reminded of it, even by somebody as harmless as me. We reminisced briefly about the film and I said I'd bring in my scrapbook the next day, which had lots of photos of Candice and me in our skimpy, silly futuristic costumes. Candice looked stricken.

'Please, Ian – I beg of you – don't. Really. Please not. No, no, I'm serious. Please don't bring them in.'

'Why not?'

We were on the *Murphy Brown* set, surrounded by her TV crew. Candice lowered her head and muttered out of the side of her mouth. 'Because if anybody on this crew got a look at that stuff, my life here wouldn't be worth living. The teasing would be merciless and it wouldn't stop.'

I learned one thing from Cacoyannis. Early in the shooting he commented on the pitch of my voice. 'Talk lower, Ian. You never be leading man if you talk like little girl. Talk more *basso*.'

While I was away in Greece lowering my voice, producer Anatole de Grunwald telephoned Aude Powell, asking my availability for a role in a film. Aude said that I was working abroad and was thus unavailable, so Anatole hired Murray Head to play the part and started shooting *Stranger in the House*. The star of the film was James Mason. For some reason Mason took against Murray Head. He didn't like his acting, he thought he was all wrong for the part, he didn't like working with him – whatever the reason, he pushed hard for Murray to be replaced and Anatole de Grunwald wasn't about to argue with a star like James Mason. So Murray Head – who went on to become the original Judas Iscariot in the Lloyd-Webber/Tim Rice *Jesus Christ Superstar*, and who played a leading role in *Sunday Bloody Sunday* opposite Peter Finch and Glenda Jackson, neither of whom had any problem with him whatsoever – was unfairly dumped, which left Anatole de Grunwald in the difficult position of finding a replacement over the weekend. On Friday – and on the off-chance – he made another call to Aude Powell.

'Is there any chance whatsoever that Ian is back?'

'He gets home tomorrow.'

'Tomorrow? Then I want to see him tomorrow.'

I got off the plane and went straight to a meeting with the famous producer. De Grunwald explained that, yes, I would be replacing an actor and that all the scenes they'd shot with Murray Head would have to be reshot with me – and although this was Saturday afternoon, I would be starting filming first thing on Monday morning, doing the big twenty-first-birth-day-party speech in front of James Mason, all the cast, and a hundred extras – and what was left of the weekend was going to be taken up with costume fittings and make-up tests and learning a longish speech as well – and would I like the part under these slightly rushed circumstances because it was mine if I did? Which was how I found myself making a second very bad film in under six months.

The trouble with *Stranger in the House* wasn't the story, which was adapted from a Georges Simenon novel – and it certainly wasn't James Mason, who managed to garner some very good reviews when the very bad film came out. It was the self-conscious, painfully overdrawn depiction of trendy 1960s youth, which managed to make the film look dated within minutes of its release. Geraldine Chaplin played Mason's daughter, I played one of her friends (and – *spoiler alert* – the murderer) – and along with several other young actors, we cavorted about being bored and hip and swinging. Bobby Darin – who at the time was a top American singing star – appeared as an evil ship's steward. He had a catchphrase – 'Ain't that so?' Darin said it so often and with such a cool and sardonic curl of his lip that quite soon he began to irritate. The same could be said of all the younger members of the cast; much of what we were asked to do was grating in its relentless trendi-ness. Only James Mason was bearable.

Perhaps because he felt a little guilty over the firing of Murray Head, Mason decided to show some small, impersonal interest in the replacement. He decided he quite liked my acting, but that wasn't enough. He needed some sort of additional invest-ment. He found it in my wardrobe. 'I don't like the kid's coat,' he said one day, so filming stopped while I, director Pierre Rouve and Mason himself all went off to a gentlemen's outfitter shop and Mason sat in a chair while I modelled a number of overcoats for his approval. 'That one,' said Mason, pointing at the hideous fuzzy brown thing I was wearing at the moment. I wore that ugly coat for years, just because James Mason had approved it.

James Mason was the only actor I've worked with who would refuse to come out of his trailer until he heard the *clack!* of the clapperboard, signalling that expensive 35mm film stock was churning pointlessly and wastefully through the sprockets at one-and-a-half feet per second. Mason was not a patient man and have spent too many years waiting on set for all those last-minute adjustments that always seem to be needed *after* the actors had been summoned and are standing ready and waiting on their marks. So he stayed in his trailer until he heard that 35mm film was actually being exposed – then he'd stroll casually into place and play the scene to perfection.

Once he invited me and my fuzzy coat to walk with him to the end of Brighton pier. It was a cold day and windy too and there was nobody about. We got to the end of the pier and looked out over the heaving grey sea. 'Well, that's not very interesting, is it?' said Mason. 'Don't know why we bothered.' The same could have been said about the film we were making. *Stranger in the House* – called *The Cop-Out* in the USA – was another film that has sunk, deservedly, with little trace. There were more to come.

The Invincible Six was a film with a similar plot to – but with a slightly smaller cast than – *The Magnificent Seven.* I played a member of a group of resourceful jewel thieves who find themselves rescuing defenceless Iranian villagers from the attacks of a bunch of savage bandits. The title was a good example of false advertising because halfway through the film I disproved *my* invincibility by dying at the feet of Elke Sommer, who was playing, with German efficiency, a Persian hooch dancer. Equally misleading was the tagline of the movie: 'Six thieves and a woman turn a desert into a hotbed of violence, passion, destruction and chaos – they'll do anything to live!' This breathless hype overstates by a long way the entertainment value of the film, which is low. It ended up being just as lousy a film as *Stranger in the House* and *The Day the Fish Came Out*, and like them it's never been seen since; a fate that – for my movie work at least – was becoming familiar and even funny.

The Invincible Six was shot in Iran, with Iranian financing. The producers, Morteza and Mostafa Akhavan, were successful film makers in their native country and were both immensely rich as a result. They had the idea of expanding their loyal Iranian audiences to include the rest of the world, hence the international cast of Stuart Whitman, Curd Jürgens, Elke Sommer, Jim Mitchum, Lon Satton, the wonderfully named Isarco Ravaioli, and me. Behrouz Vossoughi, the great Iranian movie star who couldn't walk down a Tehran street without a crowd gathering, played a minor role.

The Shah of Persia was at the height of his power and the Akhavan brothers were rich and influential, so we actors were invited to several royal parties, including the birthday party of the Queen Mother. It was a glum affair and Diane – who, as always, was with me on location – caused the old lady to blench at the shortness of her miniskirt. Amir Abbas Hoveyda, the prime minister, visited the set. He saw that, like him, I smoked a pipe. The next day a boxed Dunhill, milled from the finest briar, arrived in my hotel room with his compliments. When the revolution came in 1979, Hoveyda – Iran's longest serving prime minister – was one of the first to be shot.

There were a lot of minor princes hanging about, all well-educated in Europe or in the USA, all with too much money and all with nothing to do. Several took a shine to Diane. One prince in particular liked her very much. With Persian courtesy he asked for my permission to escort her, in an entirely brotherly fashion, to interesting places while I was busy filming. Permission given – because you don't want to withhold it from a nephew of the Shah of Iran – he took her for a spin in his new Ferrari. Diane made the social error of saying how nice it was. The prince's face fell. He stopped the car, took the keys out of the ignition, and handed them to Diane with a bow. In Iran, you must never admire an object in the possession of somebody else; custom dictates that they should immediately make you a present of it. Diane told him not to be a silly boy, she didn't want his Ferrari and, having been educated at Eton, surely he'd learned enough bad manners to ignore the etiquette of his native country? The prince was grateful – not because he couldn't afford to give Diane his Ferrari, but because he'd been on a waiting list for months, the car had only just arrived, and he hadn't finished showing it off to all his princely brothers and uncles and cousins.

The Invincible Six was director Jean Negulesco's penultimate film. Up until then he'd had a fine career. Known as a woman's director, he was responsible for hits like *How to Marry a Millionaire*, *The Mask of Demetrios*, *Three Coins in the Fountain*, *Humoresque* and *Boy on a Dolphin*, which introduced Sophia

Loren to British and American audiences. Born in Romania in 1900, Jean claimed to have been employed at the age of twenty-one by the Hotel Negresco in Nice as a professional gigolo. He certainly studied art with his fellow countryman Constantin Brâncuşi in Paris and was friends with Amedeo Modigliani and Maurice Utrillo. He knew everybody in the Hollywood of the 1930s through to the 1960s and, according to him, had made love to most of the female ones. He was a charmer and a delight and he became a good friend to Diane and me and even painted some pictures for us. But he couldn't rescue the turkey that was *The Invincible Six.*

Wuthering Heights and *Waterloo* were a little better.

I played Edgar Linton in *Wuthering Heights.* This was the role that David Niven, playing the character opposite Laurence Olivier and Merle Oberon in the famous William Wyler version of 1939, claimed was one of his least favourite parts. It was mine too.

We filmed in Yorkshire, on the real moors, and in colour, but the fake black and white studio moors in the Olivier version still looked better than ours. Anna Calder-Marshall was a sensitive and truthful Cathy and Timothy Dalton did a lot of terrific smouldering as Heathcliffe. Julian Glover was an excellent Hindley and was the only resident of Wuthering Heights to produce an authentic Yorkshire accent; everybody else from that unfortunate household, including Nelly the maid, spoke – for some unaccountable reason – as if they shopped exclusively at Harrods. Hilary Dwyer was a fine Isabella and it was good to work with her again so soon after *Witchfinder General.* I did my best, but my Edgar Linton still came across as a dreary milksop. The only forceful moment I managed to provide was

The Little Minister, with Helen Mirren. *(© BBC Photo Library)*

The Millionairess, with Penelope Keith *(© Catheine Ashmore/Zoe Dominic)*

In Venice filming *Return of the Saint*, with Cathryn Harrison. *(© Bert Hill/REX/Shutterstock)*

Filming *Return of the Saint* – if a cliff was handy the bad guys always fell off it. *(© ITV/REX/Shutterstock)*

The Saint's horse – his name was Fury and his main job was with Lloyds Bank.
(© REX/Shutterstock)

In Rome with the Saint's Jaguar XJS. *(© REX/Shutterstock)*

One of the more relaxing days on *Return of the Saint*. (© *ITV/REX/Shutterstock*)

This is Your Life – me, Nanny and Eamonn Andrews. (© *FremantleMedia Ltd*)

(left) At Chichester Festival Theatre in *The Devil's Disciple*, with Mel Martin. *(© JOHN TIMBERS/Arenapal)*

(below) Tom, Dick and Harriet, with Lionel Jeffries and Brigit Forsyth. *(© TopFoto/Arenapal)*

(right) The Waltz of the Toreadors, with Trevor Howard. *(© Catherine Ashmore/Zoe Dominic)*

(below) With Roland Curram and Gary Bond in *Design for Living. (© Arenapal)*

(left) The Common Pursuit, with Robert East and Nina Thomas. *(© Arenapal)*

(below) Three Sisters, with Joanne Whalley, Katharine Schlesinger and Sara Kestelman. *(© Arenapal)*

when I accidentally slammed a heavy oak door on Anna's hand, nearly breaking her fingers. She went white as a sheet, uttered not a sound, was very brave and forgave me. The film was competently directed by Robert Fuest and, when it came out in 1970, was received by critics and cinema audiences with indifference.

The legendary Italian producer Dino de Laurentiis – at the request of Franco Zeffirelli – had paid to bring me to Rome to test for the Burton/Taylor film of *The Taming Of The Shrew*. A wasted investment. A few years later, I met him again at a London audition for something or other. The audition was in his hotel suite and was conducted by someone other than Dino, who was busy doing something else in his bedroom. In the middle of my audition, Dino poked his head out of the bedroom and stared at me for a few seconds. Then he said, 'Ian – you come in here.' I went in. Dino closed the door and stared a bit more. Then he said, 'Ian – what you do tomorrow?'

I said I didn't do anything tomorrow.

'What you do next day?'

Again, nothing.

'And day after?'

I admitted my calendar was embarrassingly empty.

Dino nodded in satisfaction. 'OK. So – today, you come with me, we fly to Rome, I test you for part of Prince Something-or-other in big film I make from big Russian book. OK?'

I said it was very OK, but what about the audition that was supposed to be going on in the other room?

Dino waved a dismissive hand. 'No, you no good for that one. But perhaps you are good for Prince Something-or-other.' So I went to Rome and got tested all by myself for the part of

Prince Something-or-other from a big Russian book – and then the project was shelved, forever as it turned out, and Dino had now wasted two round trip airfares on me, and two expensive Roman hotel rooms for at least two weeks – which was why he thought he might as well capitalise on his investment by using me at last in the movie *Waterloo*.

Waterloo was an immense undertaking. An American/Italian/Russian coproduction, it was filmed briefly in Rome, and then mostly in western Ukraine, in the countryside around the town of Uzhgorod. Uzhgorod, which roughly translates as 'Snake City', is close to the borders of Hungary – and Slovakia, which, when we filmed there in 1969, was still incorporated into the larger state of Czechoslovakia. *Waterloo* was shot there for a good reason: much of the Red Army was stationed near Uzhgorod, which lay conveniently close to the borders of those two troublesome satellite states – and it was the Red Army that provided the twenty thousand troops to play the French and English and Prussian armies that clashed on that historic day in 1815.

Many of the young Soviet soldiers were used to dressing up in Napoleonic costumes and going to war in them; they'd done it before, for the same director, when he'd made his monumental eight-hour epic of *War And Peace*. Sergei Bondarchuk had not only directed that enormous project – it took seven years to complete – but he also played Pierre Bezukhov in it. Sergei didn't appear in *Waterloo*, perhaps having learned his lesson about directing and acting in an epic film being too much for one man; instead he set about the task of pulling together an international cast, headed by Rod Steiger as Napoleon Bonaparte and Christopher Plummer as the Duke of

Wellington. The rest of the cast was equally stellar: Jack Hawkins, Virginia McKenna, Michael Wilding, Dan O'Herlihy, Orson Welles and Rupert Davies, whom I knew well from *Witchfinder General*. There were dozens of Russian actors, many famous in their native land, playing minor roles, and a bunch of English supporting actors – Terence Alexander, Richard Heffer, Peter Davies, John Savident, Jeffry Wickham, Donal Donnelly, and me among others – filling in some of the officer and private soldier parts.

My role was Sir William de Lancey, Wellington's quarter-master general. In terms of lines to be learned, it was an undemanding part. During the Duchess of Richmond's famous pre-battle ball scene, which was filmed in Rome, all I had to do was waltz charmingly with my wife, played by the very young and beautiful Veronica de Laurentiis, one of the daughters of Dino de Laurentiis (it is just possible that nepotism might have played a small part in her being awarded the role). When news came of Napoleon's advance, I – along with all the other British actors playing members of Wellington's staff – had to look concerned, but in an unruffled, English sort of way. I had a brief but touching moment saying goodbye to my wife – which might have been an unnerving experience for Veronica de Laurentiis because she immediately retired from acting for a while and designed clothes and wrote books instead. Later, on the battlefield in Russia, I had to stay close to Christopher Plummer because, in essence, I was his amplified echo. 'The army will retreat a hundred paces,' Chris would mutter at me, and my job was to turn in my saddle and bellow, 'THE ARMY WILL RETREAT A HUNDRED PACES!' It took the chore out of learning my lines.

Being in Rome again, if only for a fortnight or so while we filmed the famous ball, was a joy. Going to Russia and staying there for two months while we filmed the battle scenes was not. Just getting there was arduous. Diane had no intention of being left alone in England for so long, and had determined to come with me, bringing Emma who was now six years old, and Titus, newly born, at a mere six weeks old.

The English cast – who, having filmed already in Rome, all now knew each other – met up in Budapest, in still-communist Hungary. From there we were to catch a train that would take us through the night to the Soviet border. It was a train we nearly missed. Jack Hawkins and Michael Wilding presided over a noisy and drunken dinner party in Budapest and we were having so much fun, we almost didn't make it to the station.

The train was making jerking, clanking movements as Diane, Emma and I threw Titus and our luggage for two months into an empty compartment. It smelled of urine and was filthy. The seats were wooden slats and the windows wouldn't open. The train pulled out of the station and, in darkness, chuffed slowly east across the Hungarian plain. Diane and I put the children to bed in the overhead luggage racks, which, being made out of coarse string netting, were a little softer than the seats.

Nobody slept much and we were all exhausted when, at dawn, the train pulled into the ominous-sounding border town of Chop. This was where we first came up against the dour and forbidding Russian officialdom. The Hungarian authorities in Budapest had been all smiles and helpfulness; the immigration and customs officers at Chop looked as if they would enjoy throwing the lot of us down a well. Our suitcases were opened and searched minutely. We'd brought some colouring books for Emma and these were examined page by page for any incriminating Western propaganda. Next to me was Jack Hawkins, also having his baggage searched. Jack had brought a copy of *Playboy* magazine. His customs officer had seized it and was also going through it page by page, but at a very much slower pace than *my* customs officer – who, out of the corner of his eye, suddenly noticed what it was that his colleague was examining, and why it was so much more interesting than a child's colouring book. My guy's eyes drifted off Emma's book and he slowly craned his neck further and further towards his colleague until he was resting his chin on the officer's shoulder; all four of their eyes were now popping at the pictures of naked American ladies. Gradually, and casually, a number of other customs officers strolled over and joined them, until a small crowd of uniformed men was gathered round Jack Hawkins' magazine. Jack looked quite pleased at the attention his light reading matter was attracting. Once all the naked ladies had been checked over, with the magazine being turned this way and that to get all possible alternative views, the rest of the pages were then examined with painstaking thoroughness. Every cartoon was scrutinised and puzzled over, every advertisement examined for possible anti-communist sentiments – not that any of the guards understood a word of English; and why would they? We were probably the first non-Hungarian/Czechoslovak/Russian visitors they'd ever met. Emma's colouring book by this time had been dropped indifferently back into the suitcase and, since our guy seemed to have lost all interest in us, Diane and I unobtrusively packed everything back up again, and crept away, leaving Jack Hawkins to have his magazine confiscated by the border guards who, having grinned happily at much of *Playboy*'s content, now glowered fiercely at Jack while they pocketed it. When Jack politely asked for his magazine back, we heard for the first time the word that came to symbolise Soviet society for us. 'Nyet.' Some wag on the film unit later gave us a name for our surroundings: 'Nyetnam'.

Uzhgorod was a backwater and the townspeople – most of whom had never met anybody from beyond a radius of twenty miles – were initially suspicious of the invading film makers. Later, after they understood we were harmless, we learned that a rumour had been circulated by the local commissars that all English, American and Italian actors were riddled with a particularly virulent strain of syphilis and that any sort of fraternisation could be lethal.

We all stayed in an hotel that was the pride of Uzhgorod. It had been built only recently and was considered thoroughly up to date and luxurious. The place was infested with cockroaches. The temperature, the flow, and the colour of the bathwater were erratic. The beds were lumpy, and the food uneatable. When I saw our room, where the four of us were to spend the next eight weeks, I slumped on the bed and almost cried. Diane was more practical; she busied herself by making a home for us. In effect, she became a Soviet housewife. One day, with an air of triumph about her, she came back to the hotel from shopping in Uzhgorod. She'd seen a queue of excited women forming outside a shop and, without knowing why everybody was lining up, she instinctively joined in too. The object of the anticipation turned out to be a delivery of cheap saucepans. Diane bought one. She also bought a single electric hotplate made of flimsy tin and sometimes cooked for us in our hotel bedroom. Other members of the cast and crew did the same. The Italian crew somehow arranged for regular deliveries of pasta to be sent from home and they held noisy dinner parties in their rooms. Rupert Davies had been an inmate in the infamous Stalag Luft III German prisoner-of-war camp in World War II and was credited with three attempted escapes; these experiences had made him resourceful. He invented a toaster. He bought two of the tin hotplates, and a ball of string. He hung one hotplate, upside down, from the central light fitting in his bedroom ceiling. He'd cut the strings long, so the hotplate dangled about six inches off the floor. The other hotplate sat, right side up, on the floor directly below. Rupert would put a slice of coarse Russian bread into a rack of his own devising and make himself toast.

Accidentally, Rupert also ended up with the only bedroom free from cockroaches. He started to run a bath and then fell asleep on his bed. The bath overflowed. The water spread across the bathroom floor, on into the bedroom, out through the window and eventually cascaded in a lacy waterfall over Rupert's balcony. The hotel employees were very angry and yelled loudly in Russian, but Rupert didn't care. He'd been a POW; he'd made a toaster; and all his cockroaches had drowned.

Jack Hawkins had a top floor room with a balcony. He would hold small parties up there. He liked pointing out the sights of Uzhgorod to his guests but it was difficult for him to speak. He'd had cancer of the larynx, which had forced a laryngectomy on him. With no vocal cords, those famous gruff Hawkinsonian tones were gone. Instead, he'd perfected the only alternative at that time, which was esophageal speech – produced by pumping air from his mouth into his upper esophagus. The air was then released in a kind of regulated belch back through his mouth, while Jack simultaneously articulated the words he wanted to say. Each gulp of ingested air could produce, at the most, three or four single-syllable words, so speaking was a laborious and difficult process. If there was any chattering or music or extraneous noise going on anywhere near him he was hard to understand – so when he wanted to be heard, Jack would bang with his fist on the nearest flat surface and we'd all fall silent. Because it was so difficult for him to say anything, he reserved his voice until he had something pithy to say.

In front of the hotel there was what once had been a flower-bed. Now it was just a sad little wasteland of baked, cracked mud. In the middle stood a solitary leafless twig – dry and dusty and long dead. Jack banged his fist and we all stopped talking and Jack pointed down at the twig, gulped twice, and belched out, 'Blaze of – *gulp* – fucking colour.'

In that moment, he reminded me of my father, dragging a shivering guest around a frostbitten Copford garden.

Hawkins was fascinated by the passing traffic. There was very little of it in Uzhgorod in 1969. He noticed that one truck chugged by with monotonous regularity – the same truck over and over again, a small yellow vehicle with an indefinable air of purpose about it. It hurried this way, it hurried that way – and Jack developed a theory that the truck was empty and that all this toing and froing was entirely for his benefit. '*Gulp, gulp*. Can't fool me. *Gulp*. Bloody thing is – *gulp* – empty. Trying to –*gulp* – convince me that – *gulp* –somebody's busy – *gulp* –in this – *gulp* – godforsaken place. *Gulp*. Bollocks.'

Michael Wilding and Jack Hawkins became close friends. Michael had once been married to Elizabeth Taylor, was now married to Margaret Leighton and, by the time I knew him, looked like the White Knight from *Alice in Wonderland*. He was almost as vague and twice as funny. He claimed to have become a film star by accident. He had been, he said, the best extra in Hollywood and perfectly happy being one. Deliriously so, in fact. Then one day, 'Some fool of a producer came along and made me a movie star. Bastard. The most miserable day of my life.' Having made several dancing films with Anna Neagle, in which he waltzed his co-star elegantly around ballrooms with the camera mostly favouring her, he claimed to have the most famous back-of-the-head in the business. He was a reluctant actor and was the only one I ever met who liked giving his lines away to any colleague who happened to be standing nearby. 'Oh God, I don't want to say that – or that – or that . . . Dear boy, why don't you say all that for me?'

Michael and Jack both liked to drink but I think a greater bond was formed between them on the strength of their mutual incomprehensibility. While Jack's problem was obvious, there was nothing wrong with Michael Wilding's voice at all, other than the volume at which he chose to speak, which was sometimes so low that there were occasions when nobody understood a word he said. He once told me a funny story. It was a very funny story and I laughed immoderately, but in truth the only three words I heard were 'Marlene', and 'Dietrich', and 'Suppositories'.

Sometimes Jack and Michael would include Terence Alexander in their private drinking sessions. After a couple of hours Terence would reappear, reeling drunk and limp with the effort of deciphering what they were talking about. 'For God's sake, somebody say something I can bloody understand,' he would beg us.

By the time the British contingent arrived in Russia, filming of *Waterloo* had already been going on for several months and most of the French scenes, including all those involving Rod Steiger's Napoleon, were finished and in the can and Steiger had gone home. It seemed he'd behaved on the set as imperiously as the character he was playing. One of the Italian crew summed him up. He framed his face with his fingers. 'This is Rod Steiger's long shot,' he said. Then he moved his fingers to frame only his eyes. 'And this – this is Rod Steiger's close-up.'

One of the few actors from the French side still in Uzhgorod – he had yet to complete all his scenes – was the American actor Dan O'Herlihy, who played Marshal Ney. He'd accepted the part mainly (he told us) because of the terrific scene in the script when Marshal Ney confronts Napoleon – just escaped from Elba – on his march up through France. It was a big scene and Marshal Ney had most of the lines. The night before it was due to be shot, Steiger sought him out.

'You know this scene we're doing tomorrow, Dan.'

'Yes. Looking forward to it, Rod. Been working really hard on it.'

'I've done a bit of work on it too.'

'Oh yes?'

'It's much better now. Now it's genius. Here's what happens. I come over this hill, you see, in long shot – and the camera tracks with me as I walk all the way down the hill and gradually, slowly, gradually, slowly, I march up to where you are—'

'Camera is on you all this time, Rod?'

'On me the whole time, Dan. It's gonna be great. Anyway, I

come up to you and I look at you for a bit, and you look at me, and there's this terrific tension – and then I say this.'

Dan O'Herlihy looked at 'this'. It was a two-page speech.

'That's great, Rod. And – er – what do I say?'

'Ah. That's the best part, Dan. You're gonna love it. *You don't say anything!* See how brilliant that is?'

'Me not saying anything is brilliant?'

'Absolutely! The *silence*, you see? The tension! The drama! It's brilliant!'

Dan noted drily that, when it came to tension and drama and brilliance for Rod Steiger, silence had nothing to do with it.

Christopher Plummer thought he'd better see what his co-star had been up to, so he spent several hours watching all of Steiger's daily rushes. We heard that he emerged from the darkened room a shaken man.

'It's the biggest bloody performance I've ever seen!' he muttered. 'He rips down the curtains, he chews up the carpets, he bellows, he screams, he cries – and to top it all, apparently Napoleon's either got the most frightful indigestion, or the worst case of piles the world has ever seen! I can't compete with that! What the hell am I to do when it's my turn?'

That most seasoned of old professionals, Jack Hawkins, came up with a solution. '*Gulp*. Every time they – *gulp* – cut to Wellington – *gulp* – say something droll. *Gulp*. Audience will start – *gulp* – to look forward to – *gulp* – seeing funny Wellington after – *gulp* – five minutes of – *gulp* – hammy old Napoleon.'

Christopher took this excellent advice and went to the history books and rewrote his part to include almost all of Wellington's famous remarks – with the predictable result that he was indeed droll and witty and charming and a relief from the histrionics of Rod Steiger.

Whether working there or just visiting, the battlefield was a remarkable thing to see – and it was all real; there were no computer-generated images in 1969. To recreate the look of Waterloo in 1815, Russian engineers had bulldozed away two hills, laid five miles of roads, transplanted thousands of trees, sowed fields of crops and reconstructed four historic buildings. To create the mud, six miles of underground irrigation piping was laid beneath the ground. The battle scenes were filmed using five Panavision cameras simultaneously – from ground level, from 100-foot towers, from a helicopter, and from an overhead railway built across the location. If you chanced to arrive at the wrong time, which was when the soldiers – all twenty thousand of them, already dressed in their 1815 uniforms – were being marched into the area, you could sit for hours in your car waiting for them to pass you by. Sometimes there would be a small brass band honking away to encourage the troops over the last few hundred yards. The soldiers were very young, many of them from Mongolia – and all probably relieved that they'd been posted here to be extras in an historical movie, rather than to quell riots over the border in Czechoslovakia or Hungary.

Once on the location, they were formed up in their correct squads and then moved about the battlefield by sergeants who bellowed into microphones. The microphones were linked to enormous loudspeakers mounted on trucks, so they too could be moved to different spots. We actors were warned not to stand too close to the backs of these mobile amplifiers; the sound blasting from the speakers could deafen you.

Equally hazardous were the Russian versions of wind machines. These were essentially old Yak fighter aircraft left over from World War II. Their wings had been removed and circular safety cages fitted over the huge propellers. A single Yak, with its back to you – and its unsilenced V12 Klimov engine hammering away at full revs – produced a blast of air that could knock you off your feet. The sound was even more deafening than the loudspeakers, so if you were a spectator that day, you stayed clear of both.

We were also careful to stay upwind of the smoke machines – more trucks, each capable of creating dense clouds of white, grey or black smoke – which were used to enhance the look of the battle or, more practically, to mask in the distance whatever needed to be masked, like passing cars or a too-modern building. These enormous smoke-producing contraptions made life miserable – and probably shortened it too – for Jack Hawkins who, breathing as he did through a hole in his neck, lacked the ability to filter the air he was taking into his lungs. We all came off the battlefield at the end of the day with our faces smudged with soot; Jack's lungs must have been caked in the stuff.

But for all these hazards the spectacle was extraordinary: twenty thousand extras, drilled to perfection, wheeling and advancing and retreating in unison, their bayonets flashing in the sunlight, their uniforms making splashes of colour against the ground – and then a detachment of French cavalry would thunder by, sabres gleaming, plumes flying – followed perhaps by a regiment of the Gordon Highlanders, their broad brown Mongolian faces grinning sheepishly at the shame of wearing tartan skirts – it was no wonder that we preferred being where the filming was taking place, rather than staying in Uzhgorod all day where there was nothing to do and nowhere to go – and if you did try to go anywhere beyond the borders of the town you'd be met by a guard with a submachine gun, who would shake his head at you and say 'Nyet' at you until you turned back.

Most of the English actors were playing officers, so we spent our time on the battlefield astride horses and never had to walk anywhere. Poor Donal Donnelly was an exception. He played a private soldier of the Irish Iniskilling regiment, and spent his entire time on foot with a lot of young Russian actors all of whom wanted to practise their English on him. They liked telling him jokes; as Donal said, wearily and more than once, 'A joke you try to tell – in a language with which you are not fockin' familiar – is never, ever, fockin' funny.'

We officer actors trained with our horses for several days before we were asked to appear on the battlefield. The training consisted of us riding at various paces round and round a ring while an old, bandy-legged Russian cavalry officer threw fireworks at our horses' feet. Quite soon my horse stopped shying; he became used to me and all the loud noises, and we were beginning to form a bond – as were all the mounted English actors with their horses – when he was 'borrowed' by a Yugoslavian stuntman for a scene I wasn't in. The next day I was given a different horse. My original mount was dead. I never found out how the poor animal had died but his corpse was pointed out to me a few days later. His innards had been removed and the space stuffed with straw and now he was nothing but a prop on a battlefield. A prop among others – more than a few horses were lost during the filming and ended up stuffed by the art department. We knew little of this – scenes that were dangerous to animals were shot when the sentimental English were not around, but this was Soviet Russia, there was no RSPCA, and filming a nineteenth-century battle was a dangerous business for everybody concerned. We might even have had a human death. An older soldier, huddling with his fellows inside one the famous British squares formation, had a heart attack at his first sight of the French cavalry charging at him.

The stuntmen, who were mostly Yugoslavs, were not sentimental; if in the course of a stunt a horse died, it died. On the other hand, if it could be saved, they would do everything in their power to save it. A curious mixture of kindness and cruelty. I once saw a dozen or so of these stuntmen jump from their mounts and cluster around an exhausted horse that had fallen and was lying helpless on its side, close to drowning in thick, clinging mud. The men gathered around it and lifted the animal bodily up and out of the bog. They carried it on their shoulders and laid it tenderly on dry ground, and stayed with it while it recovered its breath, stroking and soothing the creature – all the while ignoring the shouts from the Russian assistant directors to come back to work.

The Yugoslav stuntmen reacted unpredictably to intimidation. One morning, in the hotel dining room, one of their number was told 'Nyet' once too often. All the man wanted was an egg, and all he was getting from the surly waiter was, 'Nyet'. The stuntman got up, picked the waiter up by the back of his jacket and, dangling him from one vast hand, he marched with him into the kitchen. A minute later the stuntman came back out – minus the waiter, but with an egg.

My daughter Emma had her own problems. She was a pretty little six-year-old and was soon the darling of the Russian lady concierges. At the head of each flight of stairs, and on every floor, was a landing with a table and chair. On the chair sat one of these woman. They were all heavy, hirsute Russian *babushkas*, with a pungent body odour all their own. Their job was to monitor the comings and goings of the guests and, in effect, they worked for the KGB. With most of us adults they were grim and aloof, but with Emma all their maternal Russian affections for small children came flooding out and they would grab at her and envelop her in their powerful arms and crush her to their huge bosoms and pinch her cheeks and give her wet, smacking kisses and scream Russian endearments in her face – so that just getting past them without attracting their attentions became, for Emma, an Olympic track and field event. She would start to run while still a long way down the corridor, picking up speed as she approached the landing – and then dart, like a determined terrier, past the grabbing hands and the pursed lips, and hurtle down the stairs – but she could rarely evade the *babushka* on the floor below, because that old lady, alerted by the wails of the colleague that Emma had evaded on the floor above, was ready and waiting, arms outstretched, to catch her as she reached her landing.

Alberto De Rossi – the man I secretly blamed for losing me the part of Lucentio in Zeffirelli's *The Taming of the Shrew* to Michael York (although of course Alberto did nothing of the kind because I managed to lose it to Michael York all by myself) – this same Alberto De Rossi was the makeup supervisor on *Waterloo*. I teased him one day by pretending to have been deeply hurt by his naked enthusiasm for my rival for the role. Alberto said, 'Who this pretty girl I see you with alla time?' I told him that her name was Diane and that I'd met her in

Rome because she was there for the same reason I was there. Alberto said, 'You marry her?' I said yes, I did. 'So – if you do the Zeffirelli film and she don't, you maybe *not* marry her?' I admitted the possibility. Alberto spread his hands wide, in that expressive Italian gesture that means *what do you want from me?* 'So, Ian, it's good thing you no do film, because you marry pretty girl, and now you do *this* film – and now you shadduppa your face, OK?'

On 21 July, at 4:56 in the morning, local time, my family and I – along with most of the remaining members of the Waterloo cast – were sitting on the floor in Dan O'Herlihy's hotel room staring at a grainy, black-and-white picture on Dan's television set. Neil Armstrong stepped from the lowest rung of the lunar module's ladder and recited his scripted line and we all cheered, except for Titus who – at six weeks old – could hardly be expected to know what we were so excited about – which wasn't only the wonder at seeing the first human to set foot on the moon, although that was momentous enough; it was also the ingenuity that had brought us the event at all.

The Soviets notoriously never ran any television feeds coming from the West and certainly not anything that demonstrated – in such a spectacular manner – America's superiority in the space race. But Dan O'Herlihy had found a television set from somewhere or other and had installed it in his room – and on this particular night had managed to tune it to a nearby Czechoslovakian television station, which *was* carrying this piece of history. But there was still the problem of the commentary, which was in excited Czech.

The solution was provided by Jack Hawkins, who had brought with him something other than a *Playboy* magazine;

he owned a powerful, long-range radio, which could pick up stations in the USA. So there we were, a bunch of international actors, deep in Ukraine, crowded into a roach-riddled hotel bedroom at five o'clock in the morning, gazing at a Czechoslovakian television programme with the sound turned down, while listening to an American radio commentary detailing the moment when humans first left their home planet and went somewhere else.

The English actors had arrived in a block some two months earlier but we left in dribs and drabs whenever our roles were completed. Several of us finished at the same time so it was a small group of Brits who were driven by bus back to the border town of Chop – where getting out of Russia was easier than getting in – then another long train ride to Budapest and then at last the palpable relief of boarding a BEA flight back to London. I remember sitting tense and watchful in my seat with Diane and the children around me and figuratively holding my breath until the aircraft's wheels left the ground – at which a great cheer went up from me and all the other actors because, for the first time in eight weeks, we felt safe again.

Other film jobs came and went all the way through the 1970s, mostly unmemorable productions. *No Sex Please: We're British* had been a successful stage play in London starring, in the early part of its long run, Michael Crawford and my friend Simon Williams. Crawford was exceptionally funny as the bank clerk Brian Runnicles but he must have been a nightmare to work with because he would reduce the audience to hysterics with a piece of funny business, and would then prolong the business – and the laughter – well beyond the point when the plot stopped being the plot and became a personal playground for Crawford's flights of fancy. Meanwhile his fellow actors – professional to their fingertips – remained mired in the long-lost storyline. Their honest stage reactions to Runnicles' behaviour were soon exhausted by the sheer length of time Crawford took in his quest for laughter, so eventually they were reduced to simply standing mute and expressionless for as long as Crawford wanted the laughter prolonged, which on occasions went on for minutes at a time. I was told he didn't much like his fellow cast members getting any laughs at all and would do everything in his power to stop it happening. When the film of the play was first mooted, the role of Runnicles was naturally offered to Crawford; rumour had it that the offer was withdrawn by the producers because of Crawford's impossible and oddly insecure demands, which apparently included the instruction that all comedy moments not related directly to what Runnicles was either saying or doing were to be removed from the screenplay. This would have been both ridiculous and impossible, so the part was offered to, and accepted by, the ineffable and generous Ronnie Corbett who had spent a lifetime in comedy, knew exactly how it was done and – unlike Michael Crawford – knew precisely when to stop doing it.

Susan Penhaligon and I played the young couple; Arthur Lowe was my bank manager boss; Beryl Reid was Susan's mother – and the bizarre John Bindon played a thug, which was what John Bindon always played because that was what he was in real life.

John's conversation on the set alternated between boasting about how many prisons he'd done time in – mostly for acts of grievous bodily harm inflicted on people who owed money to London hoodlums – and sentimental expressions of gratitude to the film industry for getting him out of his life of petty crime and into travelling the world with people like Richard Harris, who apparently enjoyed Bindon's company enough to arrange small roles for him in several of his films. John had a habit that he thought charming; he would take out his penis, which was enormous – although I only had his word for this – and then walk behind some unsuspecting and seated woman and place the thing on her shoulder. He stopped doing that after a sensibly outraged girl stabbed it with her dinner fork.

Bindon was reputed to have had an affair with Princess Margaret – something the palace denied – but there was no denying the fact that he killed the gangster Johnny Darke in a knife fight. He was found not guilty on the grounds that the *near-decapitation* of his opponent was in self-defence. Bindon's unsavoury reputation grew because when he wasn't shooting films he would go back to his old ways of smashing kneecaps. Producers became wary and this led to fewer and fewer film roles and eventually Bindon died alone and poor, possibly of an AIDS-related illness.

No Sex Please: We're British had been a wildly successful stage farce but not much of its success rubbed off on the film. It was said at the time that some of its failure might have been due to the title itself, which possibly led audiences (who knew nothing of the play) to think they were being asked to watch a porno-graphic movie, which of course it wasn't. Susan Penhaligon and I provided the only sex scene in the film and I was dressed in a three-piece suit at the time. It was during this scene that Susan whispered excitedly in my ear. 'Do you think this is *it*, Ian? The *Big* One? The one that's going to make us stars?'

I whispered back that I thought films like *Lawrence Of Arabia, Saturday Night And Sunday Morning,* or *Blow-Up* were the sort of films that made stars, and that *No Sex Please: We're British* was probably the sort of film that didn't.

I made two films for Amicus, a company often confused with Hammer because of the horror movies they both produced. Amicus was a kinder, gentler and smaller cousin to Hammer and it prided itself on the relative tastefulness of its products. Where Hammer cheerfully injected their Dracula and Frankenstein films with regular doses of naked women, Amicus always drew the line, so the beautiful, talented and stacked Stephanie Beacham kept all her clothes on during *And Now the Screaming Starts,* and the beautiful, talented and not-quite-so-stacked Lesley-Anne Down kept all hers on during *From Beyond the Grave.* Both films starred Peter Cushing, a man so saintly and kindly and wise that being in his presence for only a few minutes could comfort the bereaved and calm the hysteric – both of which categories seemed to be drawn to the man like ants to a picnic. Peter had recently lost his beloved wife Helen and he told me – smiling gently and in a manner both serene and steadfast in its confidence – that life meant nothing to him now and that he was simply waiting to join her. He smoked incessantly and wore a white cotton glove on his right hand to avoid getting nicotine stains on his fingers – or rather on the fingers of Dr Frankenstein, or Professor Van Helsing, or what-ever period character he was playing at the time, none of whom (in Peter's mind at least) would ever have clapped eyes on a packet of Players Navy Cut. He was a dear man and a fine actor.

I have an old poster of *From Beyond the Grave.* Its claims are wonderfully brash:

EVERY ONCE IN A WHILE
A HORROR FILM BECOMES A HORROR CLASSIC.
IN 1931 – FRANKENSTEIN
IN 1932 – DRACULA
IN 1968 – ROSEMARY'S BABY
IN 1974 – THE EXORCIST
THIS YEAR – IT IS –
FROM BEYOND THE GRAVE
. . . WHERE DEATH IS JUST THE BEGINNING.

And then, below – in a smaller and rather less confident font –

<u>*The Film You Will Remember All Your Life*</u>

Actually, no you won't.

It's a sorry fact that almost all the films I ever made are the kinds of movies you'd be hard pressed to remember for five minutes, let alone all your life. *Death Becomes Her* – a fantasy vehicle for Meryl Streep, Goldie Hawn and Bruce Willis – falls somewhere in the you-might-remember-this-for-several-months category. My part was tiny – the sort of role actors like to call a cameo because they don't care to admit to playing any tiny parts at all and 'cameo' sounds as if (A) the part has some meat to it and (B) the actor is actually doing the producers a huge favour by accepting such a snippet – but because Tracey Ullman's character was cut from the film in its entirety, my cameo ended up number five on the credits, just below the beautiful Isabella Rossellini. I played Chagall, a flamboyant Eurotrash beauty consultant with an unidentifiable accent and a tic in his right eyelid. It was a part I would happily have played for the rest of my life – in a long-running TV sitcom perhaps – but all I got were two small scenes and Meryl Streep.

Desperate to look younger – and in a towering rage because she has just encountered Goldie Hawn looking better than she does – Meryl comes to Chagall for something – *anything, money no object* – in order to compete in the youth stakes.

Meryl Streep was kindness itself. I asked if she'd mind if I touched her face? 'It's your scene, Ian. Not mine. I just react. Do whatever you like.' So I did and was very strange and swishy and Miss Rossellini saw the dailies and told me she thought I was 'so *funnee*, Ee-yan.'

I was also in *Puppet Master 5*. I played an evil scientist who gets hacked to pieces by evil puppets. Actually, it wasn't bad.

Chapter 13

Television is, for the most part, regarded by actors as the least artistically rewarding medium. But for me and for my generation of actors it was the most consistently rewarding way of making a living.

The 1960s, 1970s, 1980s and 1990s were the golden age of television for us because, from 6:00 pm until about midnight, most of the shows employed actors. There were very few reality shows during those four decades, probably because the idea of them had yet to occur to anybody. The occasional cooking programme, the odd documentary popped up of course, but on the whole television viewing meant watching actors act – and it was our world for forty years.

I got into television in 1964 and stayed in it until 2001, when the golden age stopped and the reality age began, so I had the best of it, for which I'm grateful. I did a lot of television in forty years, some of which was destroyed shortly after a single broadcast. This loss of perfectly good material was due to the TV companies' habit of reusing expensive video tape by recording over the top of a previous show – producers at that time entertaining no notion that audiences in later years might like to watch a few of them. And then there are television productions I was in that I've forgotten I made – probably because there were so many over the years that getting a job in the medium became commonplace; when one skips easily from job to job, the individual details become blurred.

From the start of my career in the mid 1960s I was getting the occasional small part on television – usually playing the hero's best friend, or the murder victim in the first few minutes of an episode in a detective series. Then my agent Aude Powell sent me on an audition for a Granada television show called *The Liars*. I got the job and moved to Manchester.

The Liars was my first television series. I was one of the leads. I assumed it followed that I was on the verge of stardom. It turned out that I wasn't. The show lasted nine episodes and then was abruptly cancelled through lack of interest on the part of the viewing audience.

The premise behind *The Liars* was that a group of four rich, witty, intelligent and related idlers should compete with each other in telling the tallest of tall stories to gullible listeners. It starred William Mervyn, Nyree Dawn Porter, Isla Blair and me. The show was elitist and highbrow and a little smug – and therefore perhaps irritating. The scripts were excellent, adapted from stories by authors like Guy de Maupassant, Oscar Wilde, Michael Arlen, Anatole France and Saki. Apart from introducing our stories to the credulous, we four also acted out all the parts, which gave us opportunities to show off our versatility.

My versatility was limited – I was, after all, a juvenile lead, and couldn't really be expected to play anything else – at least not on sixty pounds per week, which is what I was paid for starring in an English television series in the early 1960s. William

Mervyn was a popular television character actor, specialising in avuncular clubmen, and he wasn't about to change much either. Nyree Dawn Porter had been tagged with an insulting and thoroughly inaccurate soubriquet by some insensitive wag, who had dubbed her, 'the three worst actresses in England'. Nyree was blonde and beautiful and cool and from New Zealand and she didn't deserve the tag at all. The last of the foursome was Isla Blair, an exceptionally pretty RADA friend of mine. Isla and I became inseparable. I saw us as potential lovers but Isla saw us as brother and sister, so I had to be content with squiring her to Manchester nightclubs and dancing the twist with her and trying, with no success at all, to persuade her that we should go to bed together.

William and Nyree and Isla all stayed with the infamous Manchester landlady, Alma McKay. I spent one night there, listening to Alma holding forth about something or other. She hardly drew breath. The next day I fled and found myself a small flat where I didn't have to listen to anybody and where, if Isla wouldn't come and sleep with me, perhaps somebody else might.

A word of warning about acting with Isla Blair: after *The Liars* finished, some fool of a theatre producer thought it might be a good idea to team Isla Blair and Ian Ogilvy in a production of Noël Coward's *Hay Fever* and put it on in a vast theatre in Hull. This naive fellow had dreams of riding to riches on the coat-tails of two new TV megastars – but he failed to check whether Isla and I were actually megastars, or whether he merely *assumed* we were. It turned out that we weren't. However, the production went ahead and that's when the producer discovered that he'd backed the wrong horses; at one matinee, there were only eight old ladies scattered round the echoing auditorium. The producer discovered his mistake and I discovered the hazards of acting with Isla Blair – at least on the stage. At the end of the play, after the mistreated house guests of the Bliss family have all slunk away, there is the sound of a car starting up outside. For some reason our director had thought it might be rather amusing to insert a funny, period car horn klaxon sound into the offstage effects – and not warn the cast that he'd done so.

When the unexpected *BAAAARP!* sound came, we actors suppressed our hysteria and forged on to the end of the play – all except Isla who, for some unaccountable reason, stopped talking entirely and stopped moving too, apart from a noticeable tremor in the area of her knees. She stood there, mute and immobile, in the middle of the stage and the rest of us had to improvise our way around her until the end. Once the curtain was down, we all clustered round Isla, demanding to know what had happened to her. Isla – with tears of either shame or laughter (or perhaps both) streaming down her face – stepped to one side and pointed at the floor. There was a large puddle on the spot where she'd been standing. So be warned – excessive laughter, if sufficiently stifled, can cause Isla Blair's bladder to throw in the towel.

Television was still in black-and-white and everything that took place indoors was shot in studio by massive, pedestal-mounted video cameras. There were no zoom lenses. Instead, a circular turret at the front of the camera held four lenses of different focal lengths. The turret was rotated manually by the camera operator and as the selected lens slotted into place there was an audible thump. Our sets were monochromatic, uniformly painted a dark terracotta, a colour that apparently worked well for black and white pictures. We would rehearse for a week, then record the episode over a couple of days.

Philip Mackie was our producer, a genial teddy bear of a man with a colossal capacity for alcohol. He came close to firing me. I was often late to rehearsals, usually by five minutes or less. Philip let this go for a while and then one day he took me into a corner and, smiling all the while like a friendly tiger, whispered 'Ian, if you're ever late again, please believe me when I tell you that I shall sack you and replace you with an actor with a sense of punctuality more highly developed than yours.' He scared me badly and I've never been late since. In fact, the best and simplest advice I ever heard given to young actors was from the artistic director of the Mark Taper Theater in Los Angeles. When asked by a student from The American Academy of Dramatic Arts for a couple of pointers about going into the profession, the director said – (succinctly and with a tone of sourness that led me to believe he'd suffered his fair share of difficult and unpunctual actors) – 'Don't be late and don't be an asshole.'

Regularly gathered outside the main entrance to the Granada studios was a small bunch of Mancunian children. When you went in or came out – and until they recognised you for the nonentity you were – they would ask you if you were anybody important? If you said you were, they would shove an autograph book under your nose. Mostly they were waiting for the stars of *Coronation Street*.

Coronation Street was then only about four years old but already it was one of the UK's most popular television shows and its cast were household names. I met most of them at one time or another, often in Granada's canteen. Jack Howarth, who played Albert Tatlock from 1960 until his death in 1984, told me about appearing in the original 1924 stage production of Bram Stoker's *Dracula*. Doris Speed, who played the snooty landlady of The Rovers Return, gave me well-meaning but snooty advice on how to arrange my career. Patricia Phoenix, who played the notorious Elsie Tanner, had me round for drinks at her wonderfully vulgar house, which had its own fully functioning bar, festooned with reproduction horse brasses and pictures of Patricia Phoenix. Jennifer Moss, who played the troubled teenager Lucille, let me take her out to dinner.

I remember *The Liars*, because it was the first series I appeared in, and one of the most enjoyable to make, mainly because of the high quality of the scripts – but the very first television play I was cast in, soon after leaving RADA, was called *Celebration Dinner* and that had been written by somebody less distinguished than a Balzac or a de Maupassant or a Saki, although since it was my first television experience, I went into the first rehearsal thinking it was wonderful. A senior character actor called Geoffrey Keen put me right. In the middle of the read-through he raised his eyes from the script and muttered, 'Christ, this is bloody awful stuff, isn't it?'

I worked for Rudolph Cartier, an Austrian director of great reputation at the BBC, when he made *Ironhand* – an expensive production about the adventures of a sixteenth-century German knight. I played a messenger on a horse. The scene was set inside a BBC TV studio. Mr Cartier insisted that I *gallop* the horse across the limited floor space – I had all of twenty feet to get my mount running flat out, and then stop the animal dead on a small chalk mark on the other side of the studio floor, where Ironhand himself was waiting for my message. This tricky bit of action took many takes and was only successful on the last one because the horse I was riding finally understood what it was supposed to do and did it without any help from me.

Rudolph Cartier had one eccentricity I remember, apart from demanding that horses gallop indoors: he never called 'Action!' and he never yelled 'Cut!' For Mr Cartier it was 'Act!' and 'Stop!' in a precise Austrian accent.

I worked with Marianne Faithfull, on an adaptation of a Somerset Maugham short story. Set on a plantation in Malaya, Marianne and I played an unhappily married couple of rubber planters. The exteriors were shot at Virginia Water – which was transformed from a thoroughly English tourist spot near Windsor castle to the jungles of Malaya by putting a small tropical house plant in front of the camera lens and hoping for the best.

Marianne was beautiful, affecting but fragile. Turning chalk-white, she would sometimes interrupt rehearsals to run to the lavatory and the director was understandably nervous about her ability to recover herself by the time we were to record the show. He brought in a doctor to watch her and tell us what he thought might be wrong. The doctor mingled discreetly with the crew for a day and then reported that it looked to him as if Marianne was suffering from symptoms of drug withdrawal and that, if she stuck to the withdrawing, she'd be fine. She did stick to it and was fine but it was an interesting week.

I worked several times with Herbert Wise, another Austrian director but a man with considerably more charm than Rudolph Cartier, who could be autocratic. Herbie Wise was never autocratic. He was one of those rare directors who – once he liked you – went on using you. In effect, he ran a sort of repertory company of actors and I was lucky enough to be a minor member. I played a small part in a BBC classical series called *Man of Straw*, which starred a relatively unknown Derek Jacobi.

Some time later, Herbie mentioned a brand-new series he was to be involved in – and a role in it that he'd like me to play. He was to direct the last two episodes of the current series – but my character was set to appear in an earlier episode that he *wouldn't* be directing and therein lay the problem – a problem Herbie solved himself by putting in some wonderful words on my behalf with the director Raymond Menmuir, who was so impressed by Herbie's enthusiastic recommendation of me for the part that he gave it to me after the briefest of auditions. The show was *Upstairs Downstairs*.

Upstairs Downstairs became one of those iconic pieces of English entertainment that everybody has at least heard of, if not actually seen – but when we were making it we had no idea that it was anything other than a fairly run-of-the-mill, period soap opera. I played Lawrence Kirbridge, a vaguely Rupert Brooke-ish young poet operating on the fringes of the Bloomsbury set. It was a showy role until Lawrence got into the bedroom; then he turned into a cold, nervous and asexual twerp – which was difficult for me because the person he was in the bedroom with was an old love of mine, Nicola Pagett, who played Elizabeth Bellamy, the daughter of the house.

Nicola was, as always, exceptionally alluring and, because we'd once been brief lovers in real life, we happily flirted all through rehearsals – behaviour that Gordon Jackson, who played Hudson the butler with Calvinistic rigidity, found shocking. His outraged Scottish glare at our silly shenanigans made us laugh uncontrollably. Our giggles added sniffs of Caledonian disapproval to the glare, which only served to make us laugh harder. But poor Gordon only had to bear with our misbehaviour for five episodes; having exhausted the dramatic possibilities of a character so pathetic that he refused to sleep with the glorious Nicola Pagett, the writers got rid of Lawrence Kirbridge by sending him off to the USA with his useless tail between his legs – America being the early favourite dumping ground for terminated *Upstairs Downstairs* characters. Rachel Gurney, who played Nicola's mother, died on the *Titanic* on her way there; and when Nicola decided she'd had enough of her part and withdrew from the series, the writers dispatched her there too.

I once told an American television producer about my short engagement in one of the UK's most celebrated exports. When I detailed my character's storyline, his jaw dropped. '*Five* episodes? Shit – if that had been an American show you'd have been employed for five *years*.'

In those early and middle years of working in British television I often was asked to play weak, ineffectual and spineless characters. Perhaps I was good at them – or perhaps I just looked like one. Whatever the reasons, I played weak and ineffectual and spineless opposite my old RADA friend Gemma Jones in a BBC Classic series called *The Spoils of Poynton*, adapted from the book by Henry James. I played weak and ineffectual and spineless in a BBC Play Of The Week, Pinero's *Trelawny of the Wells*. I played weak and ineffectual and spineless (and dull) in Oscar Wilde's *Lady Windermere's Fan*. I played *staggeringly* weak and ineffectual and spineless and dull in a J. M. Barrie bit of mawkishness called *The Little Minister*, opposite the great Helen

Mirren. She was very good in the play. I was very bad. I was so bad in it, and so conscious that I was bad, that I begged for help from Peter Barkworth, who had stopped teaching technique at RADA and was now acting again – and becoming what he always should have been, which was a television star. Even Peter, who played Helen Mirren's father in this mushy play, was at a loss as to how I should approach the mimsy little priest. On the rare occasions I've met Helen Mirren since then, I've avoided reminding her of the time we worked together – I have a strong suspicion that her estimation of my acting chops were justifiably even lower than mine.

I heard that the BBC were going to make *I, Claudius*, adapted from Robert Graves's great historical novel about the stuttering Roman emperor. Derek Jacobi was already cast to play him. I also heard that Herbie Wise was to direct. By this time I knew Herbie well enough to give him a call.

Me: I hear you're going to do *I, Claudius*.

Herbie: Yes.

Me: Can I be in it?

Herbie: Yes.

Me: Can I play Caligula?

Herbie: No.

Me: Oh. What can I play?

Herbie: Caligula's grandfather, Drusus. He's Claudius's dad. And Tiberius's brother. You're married to Mark Antony's daughter. You're Augustus's stepson. It's a very nice part. He's the only sane person in the entire story.

Me: Yes, but is he weak and ineffectual and spineless?

Herbie: Not at all. He's a great general. You get to wear one of those cool leather breastplate things.

Me: What – the ones with the moulded-on muscles?

Herbie: We'll get you a really nice one.

Me: Oh, good. Thanks. One last question. Who's playing Caligula?

Herbie: John Hurt.

Me: Oh. Right. OK. One more last question. This Drusus – does he live a long time?

Herbie: Not beyond episode three. Sorry.

It seemed my fate to be cast in iconic British television series – but not to survive much beyond three episodes. Drusus would die on the battlefield from a terrible compound fracture to one of his legs.

During rehearsals at the BBC rehearsal tower in Acton – fondly referred to by actors as the Acton Hilton – Drusus was to be carried into his tent, writhing in agony, on a stretcher borne by four strong Roman centurions. The centurions were there at rehearsal, waiting and willing to be strong – and I was there, waiting and willing to writhe – but for some reason the stretcher never appeared. This meant that if we were to rehearse this short but necessary piece of action at all, the four centurions had to *mime* carrying the stretcher – but obviously I couldn't mime lying down on it. So in the absence of a real stretcher I simply walked alongside the centurions and into my tent, and left out the writhing entirely. My point being that you can't act agony from a horribly smashed and mutilated leg when you're *walking* on the thing.

Once inside the tent, I lay down on the bed and only then started to writhe. Herbie stood this for several days and then he said, 'Ian – aren't you ever going to act being in pain on the *stretcher?*' I explained that of course I would, *when a stretcher arrived*, but that it was pretty hard to act agony from a broken leg when one was actually using said leg to get to where one was supposed to be . . . but when a stretcher could be supplied – and I could lie down on it – then, and only then, could I (convincingly, I hoped) act a chap who was in mortal pain from a wound so appalling that it precluded any and all ambulatory movement—

Herbie said, 'OK, OK – fine. So . . . am I to understand you can only act horizontally?'

I said that, under the current circumstances, that seemed a reasonable assumption.

'You should put that on your résumé,' said Herbie.

To this day Derek Jacobi calls me Dad.

Herbie put me in *The Gathering Storm*, a biopic that covered the few years before Winston Churchill took over the reins of government from Neville Chamberlain. It boasted a star-studded cast – Virginia McKenna was Clemmie Churchill, Robert Beatty was Lord Beaverbrook, Patrick Stewart was Atlee, Ian Bannen was Adolf Hitler, Angharad Rees was Sarah Churchill, Clive Francis was Randolph Churchill, and I was Edward VIII.

Our star (and a great coup for the BBC for getting him to do the part at all) was Richard Burton as Winston Churchill who, after rehearsing at the Acton Hilton for several days with Herbie Wise and the assembled cast, suddenly discovered that he was a Welshman and that therefore – since Winston Churchill had sent British troops to quell (with extreme prejudice) the Welsh coal miners' strikes of 1910 and 1911 – it followed that he should despise Churchill as thoroughly as the miners of the Tonypandy riots did. This attitude coloured his behaviour and that, along with alcohol, made him a difficult man to be

251

around. Apparently he'd stopped drinking for some time before this engagement and only started again because some fatuous BBC producer pressed a glass of neat whisky into his hands at the celebratory party the Corporation threw for Burton to welcome him to the production. After that, and all the way through rehearsals, Richard was erratic and unpredictable. One morning he would be all smiles and friendly greetings; the next he would studiously ignore everybody except the pretty girls and the actors he'd heard of.

On a couple of mornings he never turned up at all. Herbie called us together and said, with ill-concealed anger, 'I could tell you that Richard is ill but I won't. I refuse to. The fact is, he got blind drunk last night and now he's grotesquely hungover and won't be in today at all and quite possibly not tomorrow either.'

My scenes with Burton – when Churchill tries in vain to persuade Edward to give up Mrs Simpson – were the first to be filmed. Richard seemed nervous. Shortly before the cameras started to roll, he approached me – pretty much for the first time; I was one of the actors of whom he'd never heard. 'Look here – what happens if I dry?' he asked, and I heard for the first time a trace of humility in his famous voice. It seemed he'd never done television before.

I said, 'You just stop. They'll do another take. It's like film.' He looked relieved, wandered off and never spoke to me again.

The most fun an actor can have is to work on a show written by and starring Michael Palin and Terry Jones. These two Monty Python alumni wrote a spoof of the Victorian novel *Tom Brown's Schooldays*. They called it *Tomkinson's Schooldays* and it became the first of their renowned *Ripping Yarns*, a series of Pythonesque, Boys' Own adventure stories, with titles like *Across the Andes by Frog, Roger of the Raj* and *Murder at Moorstones Manor*.

Tomkinson's Schooldays was the pilot episode of the series and I was lucky enough to be cast as Grayson, The School Bully (the character was *always* addressed as 'School Bully', even by the over-obsequious headmaster, played to creepy perfection by Michael Palin who shared most of the rest of the roles 50/50 with Terry Jones). Grayson was of course based on the character of Flashman in the original story, but Palin and Jones expanded the concept of him to the point where my Grayson ruled over the entire school and the staff like a feared and well-dressed despot; he also smoked, drank and enjoyed the favours of unmarried Filipina women.

It was inspired lunacy, taken very seriously. Palin's schoolboy character was nailed high up on the chapel wall, along with all the other new boys on Saint Tadger's Day; he was seriously hurt by the school grizzly bear, he was caught running away by the school leopard, and he was shot in the stomach during French translation. Recuperating in the school sanatorium, he is visited by his mother, Gwen Watford who, in a chilly and unmaternal attempt to console him, gives him a pair of shoe trees.

I was carried around the school grounds in an open-topped palanquin, borne on the shoulders of four strong boys, and I got to call Michael, 'You dismally untalented little creep' – one of the most patently untrue lines I've ever had to speak. The experience was such a happy one I wanted it to go on forever.

At the end of the 1970s I became, briefly, Simon Templar, in the TV series, *Return of the Saint*. When the series was suddenly and unexpectedly cancelled, I found myself well known but out of work – at least in the genre that had paid the bills since I'd started in the business seventeen years before. Television producers would have none of me. I was Simon Templar, The Saint – and I wasn't anything else and that was that.

But I did appear on television – and quite frequently – during the 1980s, except not often as an actor. I appeared as myself. I was in demand as a celebrity for shows like *Call My Bluff* and *Give Us A Clue* – the first being a clever guess-the-definition word game at the BBC with Frank Muir and Arthur Mitchell, the second being an enjoyable charade lark at Thames Television with Una Stubbs and Lionel Blair. I was a frequent guest on these shows and made just enough to cover my milk bill, but at least they kept me in the public eye whether it wanted me there or not.

Once, on *Call My Bluff*, I actually knew the correct definition of the word our team had been presented with. The word was 'machicoulis'. I don't remember the two false definitions we were given but the moment the member from the opposing team started telling us the right one, I knew I'd heard it before – 'machicoulis' are the openings in the floors of castle battlements, through which defenders can drop rocks on their attackers' heads – and the reason I knew what 'machicoulis' were was because my uncle David Ogilvy had lots of them in the towers of his French château and once I'd nearly fallen through one of them. I whispered to my team leader that C was the correct definition.

'Are you sure?' hissed Frank Muir, sounding doubtful – after all, I was only an actor.

'Absolutely sure,' I hissed back. We won that round – and the next one, because by chance I also knew the definition of the word 'chitting' (which, for those who are interested in these things, means forcing new potatoes to sprout). For a while – at least until I was asked back to *Call My Bluff* and got everything wrong – I had a reputation (with Frank Muir if not with anybody else) of knowing more than I really did.

I got my comeuppance on *Give Us A Clue*. Being a charade game, actors usually excelled at it. I must have been good because they kept asking me back. Then, after appearing on the show at least four or five times, the producers decided that it was all a bit too easy for me and it was time for a challenge. Michael Parkinson was the host of the show and it was his job to give you your piece of paper on which was written the title of the book, film or television show you were to mime. Michael was grinning evilly as he handed it over. 'Good luck with this one, Ian,' he said with a nasty chuckle.

It was a film, a very obscure film, starring Yul Brynner and Marlon Brando. It was called *Saboteur – Code Name Morituri*.

It was the only time I ever lost at *Give Us A Clue*.

I was a guest on *The Morecambe & Wise Show*. Twice. Once was considered something of a coup – an indication that you had arrived and were now famous enough to be included in a select group of guests worthy of Eric and Ernie's attentions. The first appearance consisted of little more than me walking through a door onto the set and being greeted by rapturous applause. This was at the height of the Saint series' popularity when, for a short period, my every appearance in public was greeted by squeals.

On the strength of that one brief walk-on, Eric and Ernie had me back for one of their Christmas specials. I played Mark Antony opposite Susannah York's Cleopatra and Eric

Morecambe's Julius Caesar. Eric wore a wreath of laurel leaves on his head; every time he looked at Susannah the leaves sprang erect. A third guest for this show was Sir Ralph Richardson, there to talk to Ernie about the 'play what he wrote'. After a few days of rehearsals, Eric took me to one side. I thought for a moment he was going to complain about my Mark Antony.

He didn't – he wanted to know why Sir Ralph kept asking him why he was saying that line.

'He keeps asking me, Ian. He keeps saying, "Why am I saying that line?"'

'And what do you say, Eric?'

'Well, I say, "Because it's funny, Sir Ralph".'

'And what does he say, Eric?'

'He says, "Oh, is it?" What's all that about then?'

I said I thought Sir Ralph was most probably pulling somebody's leg. Eric fiddled with his horn–rims for a moment. 'Oh – is that what he's doing? Hah! The old bugger.'

I've never seen two men enjoy each other's company as much as Eric and Ernie enjoyed Ernie and Eric. Eric Morecombe was patience personified. Ernie Wise was a twinkly delight, crammed with energy and ideas, not all of them very good. He'd make a suggestion and Eric would always say that it was a very good idea and that they'd try it out. After a few attempts at making the unfunny funny, Ernie would come to his senses and say, 'It doesn't really work, does it?' And Eric (who'd known from the start that the idea was a stinker) would say that it didn't really but it was worth a try. They say that comedians are an unhappy breed; Eric Morecambe and Ernie Wise must have been the exceptions.

This newfound celebrity led me inevitably to Eamonn Andrews and his big red book. I was a victim of *This Is Your Life*. One day a chauffeured limousine came to pick me up and drive me to an appointment with Columbia studios' publicity chief. Halfway there the driver asked if he could make a brief detour – he had a script he had to drop off. We ended up somewhere in suburbia. Ahead of us – and blocking our way – was a large white tent and a small film unit. Somebody waved us to a stop. My driver helpfully switched off his engine. I sat grumpily in the back seat and cursed under my breath at the delay. I was going to be late for my meeting with the publicity chief . . .

Then suddenly the flaps of the tent flew open and my familiar white Jaguar XJS roared out towards us. Ten feet away it slithered to a stop and Eamonn Andrews got out. He was carrying a big red book under one arm – which was when I realised that there was no Columbia publicity chief, or if there *was* one, I wasn't going to meet him.

For the next few hours I was a prisoner. There was no going home to change clothes (now I understood why Diane had insisted I wear my best suit), no calling agents or friends (in case you cried out to be rescued) – I was driven straight to the New London Theatre and put into a room and left alone with lots of fruit and sandwiches and soft drinks but no alcohol and somebody was posted outside to make sure I didn't escape. Not that I wanted to escape; I'd been a guest on several *This Is Your Life* shows – with old friends like Peter Barkworth, Christopher Cazenove and Simon Williams – and I was curious to know how it worked for the victim. I was also, rather obviously, flattered to be one.

The show included all the available (and presumably willing to put themselves out for the occasion) *Saint* girls who crowded one by one onto the stage and made a fuss of me, which was nice. Then Diane and both my children, who'd been given time off from school. A number of childhood friends and elderly school-teachers trooped on next, including old Mr Tupholme from Sunningdale, who seemed bemused by the whole affair. There were professional friends and contemporaries – Michael York was at the height of his fame and said nice recorded things about me from the back of a car on his way to the airport, and Nicky Henson did the same thing from the back of his motorbike on Waterloo Bridge; Simon Williams and his wife Belinda Carroll came and so did Christopher Cazenove and his wife Angharad Rees. Christopher read aloud the fairly flattering review I'd received from the *Eton Chronicle* when, aged fifteen, I'd played Edgar in *King Lear*. My sister Kerry was flown in from Marrakech; my mother Aileen came on dressed to the nines and effectively took the opportunity to perform an over-the-top audition piece – years later, long after she'd died, I found an entry about the show in one of her diaries. She wrote, 'The Great Day! I was too articulated & loud & theatrical.' At the back of the diary, in which she summed up the year 1979 as being 'A dull, horrible, boring, boring year!' she wrote 'Ian triumphing as the Saint! The best day of the year – *This Is Your Life*.'

The last guest was my dear old nanny, the ex-Miss Aime Domberg. She had married a delightful Polish man called Kasimir, and was now Mrs Aime Misliwiec. The name Aime Misliwiec – which is pronounced something like 'I'm A Miss-Lay-Vitz' – was obviously going to give Eamonn Andrews a problem. Sweating profusely at the prospect of having to pronounce the unpronounceable, he introduced her as 'Amy Mizzlewick, an old friend of the family.' Nanny didn't mind being called Amy Mizzlewick, but she had insisted on 'an old friend of the family' because she thought that being described as 'the Saint's nanny' might embarrass me. That's the kind of nanny Nanny was.

After a couple of plays in London – and after a couple of years during which interest in me as Simon Templar died down a little – I was offered a proper acting job on television again. It was a new TV situation comedy called *Tom, Dick and Harriet,* a Thames Television production, written by the fine and famous comedy team of Johnnie Mortimer and Brian Cooke. (Johnnie Mortimer's real name was apparently Clare Suffolk, so he must have had a grand time at school). Both he and Brian had started out as cartoonists – they met at a cartoonists convention – but they had greater success as writers, with shows like *Man about the House, George & Mildred, Robin's Nest, Keep it in the Family* and *Father Dear Father.* They had written the screenplay of *No Sex Please: We're British,* so I knew them both and admired them unreservedly. Lionel Jeffries was the star, with Brigit Forsyth and me in close support.

Michael Mills produced and directed. A friendly, multi-talented man, with a mouth full of some of the rottenest teeth I've ever seen. His wife was tall and beautiful. Her name was Valerie Leon and, like our writers, she had a connection with *No Sex Please: We're British.* She'd played a role in the film.

Tom, Dick and Harriet taught me to love doing half-hour television comedy. Rehearsals were fun and not terribly taxing, and performing the show live to a studio audience was exhilarating. The writing was excellent, with Lionel getting the lion's share of the jokes, which, given his long pedigree in comedy, was right and proper. Brigit's pedigree was only a little shorter than Lionel's, and mine was shorter still, but we made a good team and the show was well received and went immediately into a second series.

Lionel was inventive and clever and a naturally funny man. One day he found a naked plastic shop mannequin in the prop department at Thames Television. He carried it to my dressing room, laid it out flat on the sofa and told me to take all my clothes off and pretend to be screwing it – and then he'd bring Brigit into the room without knocking, and wouldn't that be funny? I said I thought it would be very funny but I drew the line at taking anything off. I could lower the trousers a bit and I could manage the simulated screwing reasonably well and he'd have to be satisfied with that. Lionel thought me a wimp for not wanting to take the joke to its broadest level but he left me to it – and a couple of minutes later I heard his artificially raised voice outside my room.

'Brigit – Brigit! Diane's here, visiting Ian – come and say hello!'

I started pretend-pumping away at the mannequin, and then the door was flung open and I heard Brigit's stifled scream and I shouted over my shoulder, 'Fuck off, Lionel! Just fuck off out of it!' Lionel started babbling about how terribly sorry he was, and I went on shouting and humping and Brigit, mortified beyond belief, dragged Lionel out into the corridor and closed the door and I heard her whisper, 'Omigod, I'll never be able to look Diane in the face again . . .'

Lionel liked to tinker with his lines. He tried injecting the word 'king' into his sentences, adding a fractional pause in front of the word – 'I don't *want* to go to the –king shops, I want to go to the –king pub!' Michael Mills said he couldn't do that, four-letter words were not allowed in British sitcoms and would he please stop? Lionel said he wasn't *saying* a four-letter word – well, he was, but it wasn't a rude one, it was merely a respectful reference to the royal family. Michael said references to the royal family in the middle of sentences that weren't about the royal family made no sense whatsoever, and anyway that wasn't really the point, was it? Lionel said it was to *him*. Michael said that the point surely was the fractional pause Lionel was making in front of the word 'king' that made it *sound* like he was saying a rude word. Lionel said that was of course the *idea* – but surely, if he wasn't actually *saying* a rude word at all, then it should pass muster? Michael said, no it wouldn't.

The argument became circular and silly and Michael eventually prevailed but it was the start of Lionel's misgivings about the show and his part in it. Then, towards the end of the second series, we heard that Mortimer and Cooke were leaving us to write other things and that their places would be taken by new writers. A speculative script was produced and it wasn't good, which gave Brigit and me fodder for our own misgivings.

Then Lionel decided he didn't like playing to a live audience and why couldn't we do it without them and simply add a laugh track later? While that argument simmered, the crunch that effectively put an end to the series arrived – with an accident.

We were filming a scene on location. Dick (me) is trying to teach his awful old father Tom (Lionel) how to drive a car. The road on which we're practising passes by a lake – and Tom drives straight into it. A nicely comic visual and an unusually action-packed one for a studio-based situation comedy.

Lionel and I were briefed by Michael Mills. 'We've tested it and the water's only two and a half – maybe three – feet deep maximum. So just drive a good way out and then stop and play the scene. We've got three cameras covering you, so just keep going for as long as you can – you can improv a lot of shouting for help if you like.'

Lionel and I looked dubiously at the expanse of dark water. Lionel asked that a boat might be provided in case anything went wrong and I wondered aloud about the availability of some scuba gear. The production team rolled their eyes at these impossible demands from impossible actors and said there really wasn't time for any of this, and anyway it was perfectly safe because the lake's depth had been thoroughly measured and could we please get on?

It occurred to me that it might make a better scene if, once stranded in the lake, one of us could climb out of a window and crouch on the car roof for the shouting-for-help part. My suggestion was welcomed and, since I was marginally slimmer and fitter and younger than Lionel, I was the obvious one to do it. Still on dry land I practised climbing in and out of the side window and then pulling myself onto the roof. It worked fine. Then we got into the car, Lionel driving and I in the passenger seat and, with all three cameras rolling, we drove into the lake at twenty miles an hour.

When a car hits water it's immediately buoyant. It doesn't stay buoyant for long. There are too many holes where the water can get in – but we stayed afloat long enough for the car to bob its way smoothly out into the middle of the lake. The water was pouring in through the bottom of the doors, slowly rising past our feet – but that was all right because it was going to settle on the lake bottom in a minute, in the mere two to three feet of water that we'd been promised.

I muttered to Lionel that I was going to do my climbing-out-of-the-car-and-jumping-about-on-the-roof bit now, and he nodded, a little abstractedly I thought. I pulled myself though the open window and slithered my way up onto the top of the car and started acting Panicky Man – and then Lionel started screaming in what sounded like real panic, so I stopped acting and slid on my stomach toward his side of the car, which immediately listed heavily as my weight shifted in that direction. Lionel screamed even louder.

'We're sinking! We're fucking sinking!'

I said I didn't think that was possible as the water was only two to three feet deep and Lionel shrieked that he thought it was a lot deeper than that – because we're *FUCKING SINKING, IAN!*

Every time I moved, the car tilted under me, which made Lionel scream louder, so I decided to get off. I slipped into the water and dragged myself round to Lionel's window. One look inside the car told me that he was screaming for good reason. It was filling with water. Already the level was at Lionel's waist. The car was undoubtedly sinking – and sinking fast. The rear end began to rise out of the water as the weight of the engine dragged down the front. It was starting to look like the death throes of the *Titanic*.

'You've got to get out, Lionel,' I said, in what I hoped was a helpfully calm voice.

Lionel heaved frantically at the door but the pressure of the water against it made it immovable. 'I can't get out! The door won't open!' Lionel squealed, and there was abject terror in his voice.

'You have to come out through the window,' I said. 'It's the only way.'

'I can't! I can't! I'm too big! I *bloody can't!*'

'You can. Well actually you have to. Now, Lionel.'

I think it was the rapidly rising water rather than my superfluous advice that helped Lionel escape drowning. The pressure from the current squirting powerfully through the door seams washed his legs out from under the steering wheel and then sideways up onto the passenger seat. On his back now, and with a very little help from me, Lionel dragged himself out through the window and flopped next to me in the water. The moment he was clear, the car sank silently and smoothly and out of sight into what we discovered later was forty-five feet of murky water.

If Lionel Jeffries had been a fatter actor – along the lines of Orson Welles or Robert Morley, say – he would have gone down with his Ford and drowned.

We splashed back to shore, where the makeup department were waiting helpfully with two fluffy pink towels (a slightly inadequate gesture I felt, given that Lionel was gasping and sobbing in terror and spent the next few days in a hospital bed being treated for profound shock). I, who had never been in any danger at all once I'd got clear of the car, was struggling to contain laughter – laughter brought on by relief that neither Lionel nor I had drowned – and by the thought of all the interesting *post factum* ramifications Thames Television would be facing. I even found it funny when Michael Mills waded a few feet into the lake and held out his arms in a sort of 'welcome home' gesture, showing that he was at least concerned enough about Lionel and me to get his shoes wet.

It took divers two days to find the car. A stuntman I knew said that driving a closed vehicle into deep water was one of the most dangerous things you could do. Thames Television changed their policies towards involving professional stunt advisers in action scenes. The story was the number one report on the six o'clock ITV news – after all, the accident had been professionally filmed from three angles and made a perfect piece of newsworthy entertainment.

Not surprisingly, the third series of *Tom, Dick and Harriet* was never made.

Anna Karenina might be said to have been *over*-made. There have been at least ten adaptations of Tolstoy's masterwork, for both film and television, and in 1985 I was cast in one of them. I played Stiva, Anna's brother – a charming, feckless fellow who bounces in and out of the story in a minor way. Jacqueline Bisset was Anna, Paul Scofield was Karenin and Christopher Reeve was Vronsky. The director was Simon Langton, the son of my old friend David Langton, who'd played the father of the house in *Upstairs Downstairs*. We filmed in Hungary, by Lake Balaton and then later in Budapest.

It was a happy company. Joanna David played my wife Dolly. Joanna was the quintessential upper-class Englishwoman, with all the attendant graces and manners and reticence of a woman in her position – or so our American producers thought. Over time, Joanna lulled them into a false sense of security; she served them tea and biscuits in the afternoon and was so solicitous about their health and talked so often of the weather and was so utterly sweet and dainty with everybody that they became desperately anxious to please this shy English rose in any way they could. Joanna picked a day on which she might appear a little out of sorts. Our Americans were distraught – what on earth could they do to make her happy? Was there anything – *anything* – she wanted and, if there was, why then they would get it for her –

'Oh, but you're too, too kind. Well actually, there is just one thing I would rather love – that is if you could possibly manage it?'

'What, Joanna? Name it! You shall have it!'

'No . . . it's nothing really. I'm just being silly.'

'No, you're not. Come on – out with it! What do you need?'

'It's too much trouble. I couldn't ask.'

'You can! You can!'

'Oh, you're all so lovely. Well – if you really want to know . . . the thing is . . . I'm absolutely dying for a fuck from somebody presentable as long as he's got an enormous cock. Do you have such a thing?'

Paul Scofield played Karenin – probably because he needed the money. It was said of him in his later years that he preferred the quiet of a country life and only came out to do an acting job when his accountant told him he was running short of cash. He was a delightful genius and we were in awe of him, with the result that we were inclined to leave the great man alone. Too much alone, it transpired. One evening while we were bustling about in the hotel lobby preparing to go out to dinner he asked, sadly, where we were all going. We mentioned a local restaurant. 'Can I come too?' said Paul, in a small and timid voice. After that we included him in everything; a pedestal can be a lonely place.

Christopher Reeve was an odd man. Charming, handsome and a very good actor but – during the shooting of our film at least – he could sometimes be a small nuisance. He questioned every shot, every set-up, every piece of direction that Simon Langton tried to give him, making it obvious to all of us watching him that what he really wanted to be was the director. There was an overgrown-puppy quality to him, a sort of bouncy enthusiasm for everything under the Hungarian sun, which wore some of us down. I sometimes got the impression that Jacqueline found him a bore – at dinner in the hotel, she would try to get somebody other than her leading man to sit next to her.

He and I had a riding scene and, from the moment we got on our horses, it was apparent that Christopher was a novice – and a nervous – rider. I touched my heels to my horse's flanks and reined him in at the same time, just to see if I could make him a little livelier than he first appeared. Predictably, my horse gathered his muscles and lifted his head and did a little exploratory shuffle with his hooves – and Christopher screamed and clutched at his mount's mane because his horse began making some slight sympathetic movements of its own; and yet it was on this film that Christopher developed his love of horses and riding although – from the panic-stricken pleas that I stop doing whatever I was doing to my horse because it was making his horse uncontrollably twitchy – I might have hoped that I'd put him off riding entirely. Obviously I didn't; it was a fall from a horse that paralysed him and eventually killed him.

In the late 1980s a small television phenomenon occurred. For about three years, a lot of American television producers came to the UK to make pilot episodes for projected US network series. I think the producers were under the impression that American audiences wanted to see what the rest of the world looked like; it turned out they didn't, not really. They preferred their own back yards. But for a short while there were mobs of Los Angeles and New York TV bigwigs staying at the Athenaeum Hotel on Park Lane and holding auditions for pilot episodes for the US television networks.

I managed to bag three of them, playing the kinds of parts I'd never played before. *Return of the Saint* had been given only a cursory (and very late at night) outing in America, and I was almost unknown there, so the parts that I auditioned for, and then played, were a long way from Simon Templar. It was encouraging to be cast, by an American casting director, as a character that no English casting director would ever have considered me for and, even if he had, no English producer would ever have allowed me to play. I was Stephanie Powers' tax inspector – later to become her love interest – in one. I played a disgruntled businessman opposite Richard Harris in another – it was a remake of the old *Maigret* detective series, which had once starred my old friend Rupert Davies. And I was an Italian CIA operative, masquerading as a pasta chef, opposite Beau Bridges, in a third.

The Stephanie Powers vehicle was called *Maggie* and it featured Ava Gardner in a supporting role. Anthony Andrews had worked with her in the past and asked me to give her a kiss from him. I relayed the message to Ava who, even in late middle age and with an ocean of booze inside her, was still one of the most alluring women I've ever seen. She pushed her glorious face forward for the Andrews kiss and I obliged with a peck on her cheek. She withdrew, looking a little disappointed. 'I don't think he meant it like that,' she murmured.

The *Maigret* pilot was filmed almost entirely on board a working cruise ship, sailing round the Canary Islands. The ship was nothing like the gleaming white palaces that cruise round the world – and occasionally sink – today; this was a converted car ferry and it was full of cheery British holidaymakers, intrigued by our film-making and determined to make the best of the fact that they were on a converted car ferry with Richard Harris and not on a gleaming white palace with nobody in particular.

Richard Harris had given up drinking a long time before we made this pilot episode but he still enjoyed the *proximity* of alcohol, if not its consumption. Every evening he would ask me what I'd be drinking for dinner. I, who know nothing about wine, said I thought a bottle of this colour or that colour would be nice. Richard would scan the wine list and pick something out for me. When it was brought to the table, he would wave away the wine waiter and open the bottle himself. In Richard's hands it was a slow and loving ceremony. One the cork had been pulled, he would sniff it appreciatively. He would take my wine glass and carefully pour, dribbling the wine gently down the sides as if frightened to wake it up. Then, under his supervision, I had to have a sniff myself and then do a little swirl before I could take a gulp. Richard watched every move. 'Fockin' lovely, eh?'

It was as if he was drinking, vicariously, through me.

Herbie Wise, my old and loyal friend and director, cast me in the Beau Bridges vehicle, a CIA caper called *Three of a Kind*. We shot it in Ireland and the south of France. My Italian pasta chef was cheerfully voluble and I had fun putting 'a' at the ends of my words – which is, of course, how you play Italian pasta chefs.

The fee for playing – in an American television pilot – what would be a leading role should the pilot ever develop into a series was, at least in the late 1980s, very good – and it occurred to me that, since American producers seemed to be employing me a lot more than English ones, it might be an idea to go to Los Angeles and see if I could get them to go on doing it. Shelagh McLeod, who had played Beau Bridges' girlfriend in *Three of a Kind*, and who lived in Los Angeles with her American husband, invited me to stay.

So in 1989 I did.

A little later I met an American called Kitty and moved in with her. We got married. I've been there ever since. Which is another story.

Chapter 14

I n about 1974 my agent telephoned to tell me that a man
called Bob Baker wanted to buy me lunch.

Bob turned out to be a small, compact man with silver hair
and a pencil moustache. He seemed a little shy, manifested by
a reluctance to look me in the eye for longer than two or three
seconds at a time. We had a nice lunch, during which he
explained that he'd produced the original *Saint* television series
with Roger Moore and that he was hoping to revive the show
and would I like to take over the character? Apparently Bob's
wife had seen me in *Upstairs Downstairs* and thought I might
be good for the part – which struck me as odd because it would
be hard to think of two more disparate personalities than
Lawrence Kirbridge and Simon Templar. Of course the truth
was that I looked a little like Roger Moore and Bob Baker's wife
had perhaps suggested that it might be best to play safe and cast
the new Saint with an actor who resembled the old one.

Whatever the reason though, here was Robert S. Baker, the
producer/director of early, low budget British horror films with
titles like *Blood of the Vampire* and *The Flesh and the Fiends* –
but who later found his true calling in turning the works of

Leslie Charteris into a vehicle for Roger Moore – offering me, *without an audition*, the part that, more than any other role he'd had before, had elevated Roger's name into a household one. Obviously I said I'd be delighted. Bob Baker, who sometimes stammered a little when he was nervous, admitted that he hadn't actually got any *immediate* plans to make the series because his old boss Lord Lew Grade hadn't yet been told of Bob's intentions – but as soon as he got the green light from Grade, we'd be up and running.

Six years later, in early 1978 – by which time I'd forgotten all about Bob Baker and the nice lunch – my agent called to say that *Return of the Saint* – or *The Son of the Saint* – or *The Something of the Saint* (the 'something' yet to be decided) – was mine if I wanted it. I said I did, with more enthusiasm than perhaps I should have shown, with the result that I cheerfully accepted a lousy deal, in which I was to be paid about £2,400 per episode – with no residual payments for repeat showings, and no foreign sales payments whatsoever – in effect, a complete buy-out for evermore. There was a small rising pay scale for each new projected series but even if it ran for ten seasons I was never going to get rich from this show. I was paid about sixty thousand pounds for the entire, 25-episode series of *Return of the Saint* ('*Son of*' and '*Something of*' having been sensibly discarded) and the last money I saw from the show was in the summer of 1979. So much for the myth that fame and fortune belong together.

If the money side of the thing was bad, the rest of it wasn't. For the eighteen months it took to shoot the show, I was in a sort of Shangri-La where life was perfect and, thanks to makeup and hairspray, I didn't get any older. I travelled to exotic places,

I kissed exotic girls, I drove exotic cars and planes and boats – when I socked the bad guy he always fell unconscious, when I pointed my little pistol at a group of villains armed with submachine guns they always dropped them with a clatter.

For eighteen months I was the centre of attention, the core around which the small world of a film unit revolved. Within a couple of weeks of starting shooting the crew found me pleasant and professional enough to allow them to call me 'Guv'nor'. The directors listened to my suggestions and sometimes incorporated them. Even my stunt double, the charming but certifiably mad Les Crawford, showed me deference – until one day, fairly early on, when I insisted on doing a bit of rough stuff that Les felt should have been done by one of his stuntmen.

'I've got to tell you, Ian – you're being a bit of an arsehole.'

'What? Me an arsehole? Why? What did I do, Les?'

'You don't have to show off, you know. You don't have to prove you're macho. You're *playing* the hero, you don't have to *be* one. You're the Guv'nor. That should be enough.'

'Look, all I did wa—'

'What you did was take a job away from one of my boys. That's being an arsehole. Not only that – but he'd have done it better than you. The audience won't know the difference – they'll *think* it's you, and they'll go, "Ooh look at that Ian Ogilvy – isn't he a tough son of a bitch!" You keep doing stuff that stuntmen should be doing, you could get hurt. If you get hurt, the filming's shut down and we all lose money. Thanks, arsehole. If a stuntman gets hurt, they get another one in. So next time you feel the urge to be butch, for fuck's sake just sit down and let somebody else do the work.'

Good advice. Whenever I hear an actor boasting that he does his own stunts, I seethe. Stunts are, by definition, too dangerous for an actor to perform. They include being set on fire, or being involved in car crashes, or falling from great heights onto cardboard boxes. The insurance firms that cover the actors' health during the shooting of a film prohibit them from doing anything like that – and, if the actor still insists, the company will withdraw its coverage, something no producer dares to risk. What an actor really means when he claims the stunts for himself is that he performs his own *action*, which can include stuff like fight scenes and riding horses and tripping over his bulging wallet, although it has to be said that I never tripped over mine.

There was a lot of action in *Return of the Saint* – and, if it was action, then I did most of it. If it was a stunt, I didn't. That wasn't me flying the helicopter, that wasn't me jumping off the ten-foot wall, that wasn't me spinning the Jaguar 180 degrees and roaring off in the opposite direction. That *was* me hitting a man who looked like André the Giant and who obligingly fell over with no further argument. That *was* me driving the Jaguar at a sedate pace along an empty highway. That *was* me riding a white horse in the marshes of the Camargue. Anything riskier, I pretty much did as I was told and sat down and let a more qualified person do it for me.

Les Crawford was very pleased with a practical joke he played on Malcolm Christopher, our overworked and supremely efficient production manager. He breezed into Malcolm's office and announced that he'd bought all the cars and vans needed for the scenes on the following day. 'What do you mean you've *bought* them?' said Malcolm, going a sickly shade of grey.

'The cars – a Mini, another Jag and the Cortina – I've bought 'em. Bought 'em all. And a van, of course. Gotta have a van.'

'But – but – you can't just go out and buy—'

'No, it's OK, Malcolm – the budget can handle it, no problem. And we've got to have the cars, don't we? And the van – gotta have the van.'

'But – but – it's not your *place* to – and how much – and we've already got – Jesus Christ, Les – what were you *thinking?*'

And here Les reached into his pocket and pulled out four little Matchbox toy models and scattered them across Malcolm's desk.

The first four or five episodes of *Return of the Saint* were set in the south of France. In contrast to Roger's show, which rarely went beyond the bounds of the Elstree studios backlot, we went on location. Nice, Monte Carlo, Cap Ferrat and the area south of the town of Arles, in the vast reed-covered wetlands of the Camargue. The night before shooting began, Bob Baker invited me to have a drink with him in the hotel bar in Nice.

'Um – about tomorrow, Ian – with this character of Simon Templar – just remember – um – well – just don't be too *English.*'

I had no idea what he meant. Not until about three weeks later – during which time I suspected that Bob was thinking I was being far too English – when I finally understood what he wanted. I was playing a scene with the beautiful Gayle Hunnicutt, who came from Texas. Her character gets herself bogged down in the clinging mud of the Camargue and the Saint offers her a bath. Gayle sat in the muddy bathwater while

I hovered in attendance. She had a seductive line – 'You know, Simon, you're a very attractive man.'

My reply was the sort of line that should really have been delivered by Cary Grant, so that's how I delivered it, in a vague Cary Grant impression – a vague Cary Grant impression being the only impression I'm vaguely good at. 'And you're a very dirty girl,' I said, through gritted teeth and a wry Cary Grant-ish grin.

Bob saw the dailies that evening and came running. 'That's *it*, Ian! That's *exactly* how to play him!'

So that's what I did. And twenty months later, when the series first began to air, one of the kinder reviews in one of the least critical of newspapers read: 'Ian Ogilvy, in the name role, either accidentally or deliberately, gave a passable impersonation of Cary Grant but without his charm.'

Some time during the shooting of that early episode, Gayle and I were having drinks in the bar of the Voile d'Or, a fabulously elegant and fabulously expensive hotel in Cap Ferrat. The episode director Cyril Frankel was there too, and so was Bob Baker – and a rare but honoured visitor to our shoots, the creator of *The Saint* himself, the then septuagenarian Leslie Charteris. A group whose good opinion of me was – for me at least – a priority.

Gayle seemed nervous. She leaned over and whispered in my ear. 'Ian – do me a favour and go to the window and look down at the harbour and tell me if there's a Chinese junk there?'

An odd request, I thought, and a 'yes' answer a bit unlikely – but I looked out of the window anyway and there in the harbour, its gleaming teak hull incongruous among the sleek white plastic yachts of the millionaires, was a full-sized Chinese junk. I reported back to Gayle. 'Oh, God,' she moaned, burying her face in her hands. 'He's here.'

A moment later he was. There was a hearty bellow from the bar's entrance and a beer barrel dressed in a striped rugby shirt advanced into the room. 'Hunny-cunt!' it roared, its arms stretched wide. 'Give me a kiss, you fucking lovely Texan whore!'

The barrel staggered over to our table, resolving itself on the way into the unmistakable figure of a well-oiled Oliver Reed. Bob Baker tried to make the introductions.

'Oliver – lovely to see you again . . . we're filming the new *Saint* series . . . I think you know our director Cyril Frankel . . . and Gayle of course . . . this is Leslie Charteris . . . and last but not least, our Saint himself, Ian Ogilvy.'

Reed glared at me balefully and silently for five seconds. Then – '*You?* The *Saint?* You're a poof! You're a fucking *poofter!*'

Elegant French heads turned and stared. Gayle and Bob and Cyril and Leslie all looked at me. There was only one thing I could do.

'Right, Reed. Come on. You and me. Outside.'

I'm not a brave man and have never been in a real fight in my life, but the shame of yielding to Oliver Reed – without even a token resistance, and under the gaze of so many people, some of whom needed to think I was at least a little bit like the hero I was portraying – overcame any fears of French hospitals and French orthopaedic surgeons and French nurses, all of whom were probably very good of course, but all the same.

I found myself marching towards the exit, with Reed at my side. Suddenly he grabbed my head and tucked it under his arm in a vague sort of wrestling hold. I got myself out of that with surprising ease and took up what I hoped looked like a professional boxing stance. So did Reed. We danced around each other, our arms windmilling away, and I found myself thinking, *This is like being back at school pretending to fight Ranulph Fiennes . . . and Reed is not nearly as tall as Ranulph Fiennes . . . and his arms are not nearly as long as Ranulph Fiennes' . . . and to the best of my knowledge Ranulph Fiennes wasn't drunk . . . and omigod, I might even have a chance of landing something here . . .*

I never got the chance to land anything because Reed suddenly lost interest in having a fight and decided to be my best friend instead. 'You're not a poof! You're all *right!* Come and have a fucking drink!'

Arm in arm, we returned to the group but, before I got my fucking drink, Reed appeared to experience a sort of epiphany when – through his drunken stupor – he realised he'd just been introduced to the creator of the *Saint* himself, the legendary Leslie Charteris. Abandoning me, he stared owlishly at Leslie and screamed, 'You're Leslie *Charteris?* I can't *believe* it! You are Leslie-fuckin-*Charteris!* Fucking *fantastic!* An honour! Jesus-fucking-*Christ!* Leslie *Charteris!* Fuck!'

Then a wonderful thought occurred to him. He lurched to the bar, shoved aside the bartender, reached over and picked up a very small, slightly serrated fruit knife – the sort barmen use to shave off a slice of lemon peel or spear a maraschino cherry. Brandishing the tiny knife, Reed advanced on Leslie. 'We're gonna be blood brothers!' he howled. He grabbed the old man's hand and was about to press the sharp edge down on his wrist when it occurred to him that, since it was his idea, perhaps as a matter of form he ought to go first. He dropped Leslie's hand and then made a tiny, bloodless scratch on his own wrist and held it up for all to see.

'Blood brothers!' he bellowed and once again grabbed Leslie's hand.

Nobody moved. A sort of general paralysis gripped all of us and, anyway, I felt I'd done my bit. Then, to everybody's relief, before Reed could get round to slicing Leslie open, the captain of his junk arrived – an enormous German, who took Reed firmly by the arm and escorted him, now meek as a lamb, out of the bar.

Les Crawford heard about it and became theatrically outraged. 'He did *what?* He insulted my Guv'nor? I'll fucking *have* him.' He stormed off down to the harbour and marched up the junk's gangplank, bawling, 'Come out here, Reed – I want a fucking word with you!'

Oliver Reed knew Les Crawford – and also knew him well enough to avoid having the sort of word with Les that Les wanted to have with him, so he invited him down below decks where there was less room for punching – and where the booze was – and offered him a drink. Les accepted. He went on accepting for the next two days. When at last he returned to the set a good fifty-eight hours later, he was promptly fired.

Another Les – Leslie Norman – was an altogether different creature. Leslie Norman was the father of the well-known film critic Barry Norman. He'd been a director of many of Roger Moore's *Saint* episodes but had since retired, mainly because he'd contracted the same illness – and undergone the same operation for it – that Jack Hawkins had suffered. Without a voice – other than the short, belched-out phrases that he could manage only with enormous effort – Leslie Norman had decided to pack in film directing altogether and not say anything very much for the rest of his life. Bob Baker had other ideas and dragged him out of retirement, promising him an assistant director with a good strong voice who could do all his noisy talking for him. Reluctantly, Les allowed himself to be dragged. In the end, he directed five episodes – the most of any director hired for the job, matched only by Hungarian director Peter Sasdy.

I first met Les Norman on the set, the morning we were to start shooting a fresh episode. I'd been given a new set of pages – rewrites of the script I'd already looked at – and I thought them even worse than the originals. I'd been told by the crew – most of whom had worked with Les before – that he was a martinet, a tyrant, a man of explosive temperament, a man who could and did make strong men cry – so I decided that if I wanted to incorporate *my* script changes, rather than the truly dreadful ones I'd just been given – and which had obviously been scribbled hurriedly and at the last minute by some untalented hack – then I should approach the martinet like Crazy Horse approached General Custer – in force and with no quarter given.

'Hi, hello, I'm Ian, how do you do, lovely to meet you, heard so much about you, so excited to be working together, these new pages are complete crap, aren't they – what untalented idiot wrote them, that's what I want to know?'

Les's round fishy eyes glared. 'I – *gulp* – did.'

I suddenly felt like Custer – but resolutely (because there was nothing else I could really do) I went on acting like Crazy

Horse. 'Well, that's something I can't take back, can I?' I said, cheerily. 'I do apologise – but I have to say I still think they're crap. Now, I've had a go at them myself, if you'd like to have a look?'

Silently, Les held out his hand. Silently, I proffered my own typed pages. He skimmed my rewrites and then thrust them back at me contemptuously. 'This – *gulp* – is fucking crap – *gulp* – too.'

For a moment we stared at each other, like a coupe of feral cats meeting in an alley. Then I saw the funny side of this and started to laugh and – miracle of miracles – Les started to laugh too, and on that day and on all subsequent days I said *my* crap and not *his* crap and ever afterwards we were the best of friends and he never played the martinet with me at all. I discovered how to cheer him up if he was having a difficult day. I would ask him how his son Barry was? Les was wonderfully proud of his son's success and he would beam with delight and tell me all about him.

His fury was reserved for those whom he thought incompetent; there was a scene where some unfortunate bit-part player had to take a hypodermic syringe out of its case and, in extreme close-up, inject the needle through the rubber stopper of a clear glass vial and extract the contents. He had no dialogue; all he had to have were steady hands. The poor man was already nervous. Les was in one of his more aggressive moods and had given the poor fellow a belched-out third degree as to whether he thought he'd be up to the job – with the result that the poor player's hands had developed a slight but visible tremor in the close-up.

'Cut! Do it – *gulp* – again!'

Take two was worse. The tremor was now even more obvious than it had been in take one. 'Cut! Stop fucking – *gulp* – shaking! Again!'

Take three looked as if a small earthquake was taking place just outside camera range.

'*Cut!* Again! What's the fucking – *gulp* – matter with you?'

Several agonising takes later – by which time the poor actor appeared to be in the final stages of Parkinson's disease – I thought I might step in and see if I could help. I put my mouth close to Les's ear. 'You're just making it worse, Les,' I whispered. 'He's terrified of you now.'

'And so he – *gulp* – fucking should be – *gulp* ... Get me somebody else! I haven't – *gulp* – got fucking time for this!'

The sweating, trembling, white-faced actor was sent away and a member of the crew, who knew Les's ways and wasn't impressed by any of them, took over the task and did it with no shaking at all.

In fact, for all his ferocity, Les was a much loved and much admired director because, while he detested people who came on his set unprepared, or unable to do the job at all, when he came across somebody with talent – and somebody who had obviously given the job thought and who then brought it off with imagination and flair – then he admired unreservedly, and showed it too. In one of the episodes we filmed in Italy, there was an elderly Italian actress who spoke no English. She had learned her lines phonetically and delivered them with such a moving theatrical intensity that she made the old tyrant cry. Afterwards, with tears glistening on his cheeks, Leslie pressed her hand and belched 'Grazie! – *gulp* – grazie! – *gulp* – *grazie!* –' in the old lady's face. She looked disconcerted but she smiled and nodded and then, thinking perhaps that Les needed comfort of some kind, she placed her own wrinkled old hand tenderly against Les's damp old cheek.

It was a moving moment.

'Fuck's sake, get a room,' muttered Mike the focus puller.

While shooting an episode in Venice, Leslie revealed his more playful side. Diane and Emma and Titus were visiting me and they often spent time on the set. Diane was constantly concerned that one or both of the children might do something to disrupt filming – a justified fear because Titus had once got his knee stuck in some iron railings at the Barbican in London while shooting an English episode and, since the railings were to be featured in the next shot and having a small boy stuck in them would only have complicated the plot, he had to be quickly removed. Filming stopped and a mortified Diane watched as four strong men tried to bend the railings enough for Titus to be freed.

Ever since that embarrassment, Diane had been extra careful to keep him out of the way. Les noticed this almost obsessive concern of hers and, when Diane wasn't looking, he drew ten-year-old Titus aside and whispered in his ear.

The scene was a dialogue between myself and an older actor – a close-up on him, while I delivered my lines to him from behind the camera. Everything was ready to go; but when 'Action!' was called it didn't come as a bellowed roar from assistant director Gino Marotta; it came as a piping little squeak from my small son Titus.

The poor actor, already nervous about pleasing the hard-to-please Leslie Norman, immediately dried and started to babble apologies. I babbled apologies back at him, saying it was all my son's fault and not his in the least. Titus, with all the outrage a ten-year-old boy can muster when he feels unfairly accused, pointed a finger at Les and howled, 'It wasn't me! It was *him!* He *told* me to do it!'

Les shook with silent laughter. When he recovered, he said he was terribly sorry to Diane, and that it was all his fault to the actor, and it was all quite inexcusably unprofessional of him and it would never – *gulp* – *never* be repeated. Then he got Titus to do it again.

This early introduction to the power of a film director has stayed with Titus; he and his wife Candida Brady now make award-winning movies.

Another fine old director that Bob Baker yanked out of semi-retirement was Charles Crichton, who had directed so many of the great Ealing comedies of the 1950s. Ten years after directing two episodes of *Return of the Saint*, Charles was pulled out of retirement again by John Cleese to direct *A Fish Called Wanda*. It was his last film – and a triumphantly funny coda at the very end of his life.

We were shooting an episode in the French countryside, in an area famous for the great granite rock eruptions that towered over the scenery. Charles, who had terrible teeth, muttered, 'Place reminds me of the inside of my mouth.'

Roy Ward Baker, who had directed me in *And Now the Screaming Starts*, came on board for two of the English episodes. Roy was one of the most outwardly lugubrious men I've ever met. His face seemed to droop with some kind of deep, internal sorrow. When I got to know him a little better I discovered that – while maintaining this woeful air for the world to see – this was in fact a cover for the laughter that bubbled permanently inside him.

Peter Sasdy had directed me and Gemma Jones in the BBC classical serial *The Spoils of Poynton* and he'd done a magnificent job on it – so when I heard he was to be one of the *Saint* directors I was delighted. By the time we completed his first episode, I was less delighted. Peter's expert handling of in-studio BBC video cameras made him a one-of-a-kind director, and a fine one at that. But Peter let loose among foreign locations, fast cars and large crowd scenes did not go so smoothly, although he didn't seem to notice.

He did a tremendous amount of homework on the script and came to the set fully prepared. Every shot had been meticulously worked out – but it seemed like it had been done in his hotel room, and not on the actual location itself. He brooked no argument and would listen to no suggestion – not from me, not from our director of photography Frankie Watts, not from anybody. His ideas were set in concrete. The shot had been worked out and decided upon and that was that. The result was an unhappy crew and an uneasy leading man – but an initially happy Bob Baker, who saw just how efficient Peter Sasdy was because he managed to bring in most of his five episodes on time and under budget.

Later, when the individual episodes were being edited, some vital shots were missing, which was probably due to the rigidity in the shooting schedule. Precious days had to be set aside during filming the next episode in order to pick them up. Bob Baker himself became a little restless at this, and he became more than restless when Peter filmed a scene in one of the Italian episodes in such a nonsensical manner that I finally lost my patience and went to Bob to complain.

The scene was a car chase – me in the Jaguar XJS in pursuit of a bad guy in a much slower car. A narrow street, with a

Y-shaped junction towards its end. The idea was that the villain would drive at full speed down the street – appear to be taking the left-hand fork of the Y – and then, at the last minute, jerk his steering wheel to the side and squeal off down the road on the right. The Saint, hard on his tail, doesn't react in time and shoots off down the wrong road.

All very fine if Peter hadn't decided to shoot the sequence with me and the bad guy driving the *other way*. Instead of approaching the branch in the road from the *bottom* of the Y, he insisted we come at it from the opposite direction. Now, in order to make the turn (which became for both of us an impossibly tight, U-shaped one) the driver of the wicked car was forced to slow down to a crawl – and I, right on his tail, had to slow down too – with the ridiculous result that the Saint himself – a fellow with the eyesight of an eagle, the reflexes of a mongoose and the driving abilities of a Mario Andretti – failed to notice in time that the man he was tailgating *at five miles an hour* had suddenly – and miraculously – turned right . . .

I suggested to Peter that this was absurd. He said it would work out fine in the editing. I suggested we shoot the scene going in the opposite, and *logical* direction, which we could do going cheetah speed, rather than going the other way at sloth speed. Peter said we couldn't do that because it was a one way street. I said we owned the street for the day, that we had the road blocked off with policemen at either end who were there to stop anybody from interfering with our filming and that, anyway, this was Italy where everybody drove the wrong way as a matter of course, particularly down one-way streets during car-chase scenes – which was sort of the *point* of one-way streets in car-chase scenes, surely? Peter said he'd worked it all out the night before and this was the way it would be. I went to Frankie Watts and asked him if I was mad. Frankie said I wasn't in the least bit mad but the way Peter wanted the scene shot was lunacy. I told Peter I was unhappy but we did as we were told – and later that evening I managed to tell the story to Bob Baker.

'Oh, my God! But Ian – you should have *stopped* him! You should have refused to do it like that!'

Bob hadn't thought this through at all. I said, with some enjoyment, 'You mean to tell me, Bob, that I now have autonomy on the film set? You mean that I have the authority from you to countermand any direction I'm given if I feel it's not the right one? That I have full control on how we shoot the show from now on?'

Bob let this sink in. Then his slight stammer came into effect. 'N-no! N-no, of course n-not. No. Not at all. Ah. Right. I see what you mean. Oh, b-bloody hell.'

That was Peter's last episode. It was a pity. I'd admired him unreservedly during *The Spoils of Poynton* and we'd become friendly too. By the end of his five episodes of *The Saint* the crew and I were happy to see him go.

Another Hungarian *Saint* director was Peter Medak, a much more easy-going man and one whom we all liked a lot. Peter cast his wife, Carolyn Seymour, in the part of a scheming murderess, a part she played to its slinky hilt. We were shooting at night in Wardour Street and Carolyn decided this was the moment to give her husband a bad time. She created a few minor difficulties for him, in a sort of flexing of her conjugal muscles. A couple walking down the street saw her sitting grumpily in the back seat of a car, while her ever-patient husband and his crew waited for her to emerge. 'Is that Carolyn Seymour?' asked the woman, excited at spotting a celebrity.

'No,' drawled Peter. 'It's just some stupid extra. A very bad one too. I don't like her at all. She is so ugly. In fact I think I fire her now. Excuse me, please. Hey you! Ugly girl in the car! You are fired!'

Carolyn wound down her window. 'Fuck off, Peter.'

Gino Marotta was the first assistant director on half the episodes in the series, in particular those we filmed in Italy. With a name like Gino Marotta it might be reasonable to think the man had a smattering of Italian. He didn't. Gino had two words only, 'Si!' and 'No!', both bellowed with supreme confidence even if he hadn't understood the question. Gino was the voice Bob Baker hired to do Leslie Norman's shouting for him, and it was a big voice. He like practical jokes. 'Phone call for you, Ian.'

'Thanks, Gino – where is it?'

'On the wall, Guv'nor. Just round the corner.'

It took me a while to remember that telephones hanging on fake walls, in film sets, on sound stages, inside a film studio were likely, more often than not, not to be connected to anything.

Once we were filming a skiing episode high in the Dolomite mountains of northern Italy. It was directed by Peter Sasdy at his most earnest, which might explain why Gino decided to disrupt the proceedings, probably in order to lighten the general gloom that had, by now, descended on all of Peter's shoots. Gino's job was to signal to a small party of expert skiers to come swooping down the mountainside and fly past me and the camera. He had a small silver whistle to blow as the cue for the skiers to start their run. Two hundred yards up the mountain, the skiers were ready and waiting. Down below, the camera and the sound and I were up and running. Everything was primed to go—

'Hang on, sir,' called Gino. 'Little problem.'

'What?' said Peter. 'What's the matter?'

'Lost the pea, haven't I?'

'The *pea*? What pea?'

'The pea in my whistle, sir. It's not there any more. Must have fallen out.'

'But . . . but – it works without the pea, doesn't it?'

Gino looked shocked. 'Without the *pea*, sir?' He sucked air in through his teeth, like a plumber being asked to do something about a blocked lavatory. 'No, sorry, sir – can't be done, sir. Have to have the pea.'

'Well – where is it?'

'Must've dropped out somewhere in the snow, sir. If we all look for it very hard indeed it might turn up.'

'All right! All right!' screamed Peter, oblivious to the suppressed grins that surrounded him. 'Everybody – look for the pea!'

Studiously the crew started to search the snow for Gino's pea. Some of the more waggish members got down on all fours and started looking underneath individual snowflakes. I had to turn away and stare fixedly at the horizon and try to stop my shoulders from shaking. Eventually – seconds before Peter Sasdy's patience shrank to a singularity – it was found, this metaphysical pea, and returned to Gino, who looked mightily relieved. 'Thank goodness for that. Don't know where we would have been without my pea.'

The glamour of shooting episodes in Rome and Monte Carlo, in Florence and Cap Ferrat, in Cortina and Venice, was offset by the episodes shot in England, where we spent time at places like the Southall gas works, the London docks and the backlot at Elstree Studios. I got to know Elstree Studios very well. Diane and I were then living in an Edwardian house in Raynes Park, next to Wimbledon in south London, and Elstree was (and still is) situated in north London, on the opposite side of the city. Every morning my driver Billy would arrive outside my house, always exactly on time and with a perfect selection of serious and not-so-serious newspapers stacked in the back seat.

We hardly ever spoke because Billy understood that we didn't need to. We drove in companionable silence. I slept, or read the *Sun* or *The Times*, and arrived at the studio in as good a mood as it's possible to achieve when dragged out of bed at five o'clock in the morning to face pages of mostly trite dialogue with which I endlessly tinkered, if only to reduce their triteness. Leslie Norman's opinion of my efforts was probably right – my stuff was just as crappy as the original – but at least it was *my* crap and I felt comfortable with it. I always warned my fellow actors that there could be minor changes to our dialogue scenes but that they would always get the same cue and that my rewrites were going to be the same length – and impart the same information – as before; and it all worked fairly well, until one day a script was delivered that was so bizarre that not even my crap rewrites could help the crap original.

A third of the way into shooting the series, a new producer had been brought on board – an American called Anthony

Spinner, who had an excellent track record in the USA, having produced, or executive produced, spy and cop series like *The Man From U.N.C.L.E., Baretta, The Mod Squad* and *Cannon*. I was told that Anthony was being brought in to help us sell the show in America.

His first move was to reduce significantly the violence in our stories and take away all our guns. This was apparently in response to a general toning-down of ferocity in American television shows – a short-lived movement that lasted, as far as I could see, about as long as it took us to complete our series. The moment we finished was the moment when everybody else returned to cheerful screen mayhem, which left us with a sort of nanny-knows-best series where nobody got hurt, there was never any blood and the villains gave up their weapons merely on my say-so. A giant would approach with intent to kill. I, half the giant's size, would chop him delicately on the side of his neck and the giant would fall over and obligingly go to sleep. It was all rather ridiculous.

The bizarre script turned out to have been written by Anthony Spinner. It had the Saint fighting vampires. There might have been werewolves too. Given the extreme improbabilities that riddled all our previous scripts, it seemed that Spinner thought there was nothing wrong with introducing a few more, even if it did involve the world of the supernatural. It was too much for me. I didn't go to Bob Baker about this because the screenplay must have been approved by him already; instead I called Leslie Charteris. 'Leslie, it's Ian Ogilvy—'

'I was wondering when I'd hear from you. I assume it's about this vampire aberration?'

'It's awful, Leslie.'

'Of course it is. But so were lots of the others too and you never called me about any of them.'

'I thought I might be able to improve them a bit. I rewrite some of the dialogue, take out some of the clichés.'

'I noticed. I have to say yours aren't much better.'

'But I can't do anything with this – it's the *concept* that's awful and I can't change the concept, can I?'

'No, you can't. But I can. Leave it with me. I'll kill this one if it's the last thing I do.'

And he did. Without comment, the offending script was dropped and a new one substituted. The new one was no better than Spinner's but at least it didn't have vampires in it. Anthony approached me a couple of weeks later. 'It was you, wasn't it? You got my script scrapped.' I said that we couldn't have vampires, not in a *Saint* story. Spinner took it in good part but I never got the feeling that he liked the show at all and was happy when he finally left us in Italy, after a rumoured minor run-in with a local Mafia boss, who didn't like the way Anthony was looking at his girlfriend, who happened to be my leading lady that week. Anthony – perhaps wisely – decided to go home.

One of the many rewards for being Simon Templar was the succession of beautiful and talented women and men who came and acted the supporting roles. Every week there was a new girlfriend for Simon Templar, twenty-five in all, one for each episode. Occasionally two. It seemed the Saint was fickle. Judy Geeson, Gayle Hunnicutt, Susan Penhaligon, Kathryn Leigh Scott, Mary Tamm, Britt Ekland, Elsa Martinelli, Catherine Schell, Prunella Gee, Kate O'Mara, Annette André, Sarah Douglas, Tessa Wyatt, Catherine Harrison, Sharon Maughan,

Carolyn Seymour, Zienia Merton, Fiona Curzon, Jenny Hanley, Anouska Hempel, Diane Keen, Ciaran Madden, Muriel Odunton, Linda Thorson, Lynn Dalby – and Rula Lenska, who was voted the crew's favourite *Saint* lady. She got the Lobster Award – an uncoveted prize since only the crew and I knew that it existed. We certainly never told Rula she'd won it. That would have involved an explanation and the explanation would have revealed what a lot of silly schoolboys we were.

There was an actual lobster – it was a life-size plastic one, picked up in some tourist shop and fastened with baling wire to the radiator grille of one of our trucks. The award was based on the filthy and probably drunken sketch that Peter Cook and Dudley Moore improvised on their *Derek and Clive* recordings, in which Peter Cooke described 'the worst job I ever had', which was pulling lobsters out of Jayne Mansfield's bottom. Hence our Lobster Award, the high scorers being girls from whose bottoms we would gladly pull lobsters. Britt Ekland, who was a bit too starry for us, only got three lobster points out of 10; the points were not just for looks, they were also awarded for being an all-round good egg. Rula Lenska was beautiful – and also an exceptionally good egg.

A side note.

Peter Cook came to my fortieth birthday party and at midnight telephoned the police to complain about the noise. When they arrived, a small and puzzled crowd gathered in the hallway to protest that we really weren't being all that noisy. 'Well, we've had a complaint,' said one of the policemen. 'Somebody called to complain.'

'That would be me,' said Peter, pushing his way to the front of the crowd.

'Ah – Mr Cook. It was you that called, was it, sir?'

'It was indeed.'

'But – you're at the party, sir.'

'You noticed that, did you? Astonishingly perceptive of you, officer. I expect you're a detective, aren't you?'

'Why did you telephone us, Mr Cook, if you yourself are a guest at the party?'

'Because it's too bloody noisy in here. Can hardly hear myself think. Frightful state of affairs. Can't you do anything about it?'

'Goodnight, Mr Cook. And not more silly phone calls, please. We've got quite enough to do without you wasting police time.'

The Saint was plagued by villains, but he had some friends as well. Joss Ackland was a villain. He played a demented assassin who, in Joss's view (if not in anybody else's) enjoyed his kills so much that they gave him orgasms. These post-mortem shudders of pleasure that Joss insisted were part of his character were cut out of the finished product because this was a family show and, besides, they looked silly. Other than the orgasms, and a strange wig they gave him to wear, Joss was wonderful.

Sam Wanamaker, my old friend from the horrible *The Day the Fish Came Out*, appeared in one episode as a friend-of-the-hero, and was so much liked that he was given another episode to direct.

Stuart Wilson, a terrific villain, was kindness itself when he saw how irritably tense I was getting with our director Peter Sasdy.

The Austrian star Helmut Berger played another villain. Helmut was one of the most beautiful men I've ever met. He'd been the Italian film director Luchino Visconti's lover for many years – but it was said that he'd also had affairs with Bianca

Jagger and the model Marisa Berenson among others. Helmut showed me how to buy shirts in Rome – but only if you're Helmut Berger. It doesn't work if you're somebody else. Here's how it's done: walk into the most expensive shirt shop in Rome. Gaze with contempt at the wares and dismiss with a wave of the hand anybody who offers to help you. Pull a shirt from the stack on the shelf, drag it from its wrapper and undo it, scattering pins with abandon. Savagely crumple the material to see if it wrinkles. Hold wrinkled shirt up against oneself and gaze critically into a mirror for ten seconds, then throw shirt on the floor and shout, 'No! Horrible! *Disgusting!* Not to be seen *dead* in!' Repeat until pile of discarded shirts on the shop floor reaches a satisfactory height, then throw up hands in horror at the shoddiness of the merchandise and storm out of shop without having bought a thing.

Mel Ferrer appeared in an Italian episode with the extraordinarily beautiful Elsa Martinelli. Mel had been married to Audrey Hepburn and he lived in Hollywood. Elsa was married to Count Franco Mancinelli Scotti di San Vito and she lived in a palazzo. I was married to Diane and we lived in Raynes Park, SW20.

Esmond Knight was a friend in a wheelchair. Esmond had been badly injured during the naval encounter between the HMS *Prince of Wales* and the stupendously powerful German battleship, *Bismarck*. Esmond was blind for two years, regained limited sight in one eye and then, for the rest of his life, suffered from fluctuations of near-blindness to no sight at all. I'd worked with him once before, rehearsing with him at the BBC rehearsal rooms in Acton. Esmond would learn the floor plan of the set by counting the number of steps needed to get to his position

– all he wanted from you was to be pointed in the right direction. Once he knew where he was going and how long it would take to get there, Esmond *acted* being able to see. It was remarkable. To audiences it appeared that there was nothing wrong with him at all.

Roger Moore didn't make an appearance in our series but he did turn up unexpectedly at our hotel somewhere in Italy. He was driving through the country on his way to someplace else, heard where we were and decided to pay us all a visit. He knew most of our crew already, having worked with many of them on his own series – Bob Baker was nothing if not loyal and had succeeded in getting many of his old team together for our remake. A small crowd of us gathered in the hotel bar and we started drinking with Roger. Diane was visiting me in Italy and we had a dinner date, so I excused us and we left for our restaurant.

When we got back to the hotel several hours later we found a small disconsolate group still sitting in the bar – but now they were sitting in semi-darkness. The bar was closed but nobody, least of all Roger, wanted to go to bed. I had a case of wine in the back of my car; somebody found a corkscrew. Diane retired, but the rest of us stayed in the dark bar, getting steadily drunker while we listened to Roger telling stories. The drunker we became, the better the stories sounded.

Eventually I staggered off to bed, leaving Roger and director of photography Frankie Watts alone in the darkness. The next morning I had a blinding headache and a mouth full of dead moths. I stumbled down to the hotel lobby. Frankie was there. He looked worse than I did. 'Bastard kept me up all night,' he muttered. 'Wouldn't let me go to bed. I feel awful.'

We shuffled our way outside to our waiting cars. The bright Italian sun seared our bloodshot eyeballs. Even our hair hurt. There was a cheery shout from the parking lot. 'Good morning, chaps! Lovely day, isn't it? I feel terrific!' It was Roger Moore, looking like a healthy teenager – a teenager who, no later than 9.00 pm the night before, had gone to bed with a glass of warm milk and a teddy bear. At that moment, and until we felt better, Frankie and I pretty much loathed Roger Moore.

Frankie liked being in Italy because he loved all things Gucci, as long as they had the famous red and green Gucci stripes on them. He wore Gucci loafers and Gucci jackets with a Gucci wallet in the breast pocket. On his birthday the crew gave him a present – a big Gucci box wrapped in red-and-green Gucci paper. The box contained another box decorated with the Gucci stripes. Frankie was excited. He opened the Gucci box – and inside was another, slightly smaller Gucci box. Inside that was a smaller Gucci box and inside that another, even smaller Gucci box. The final Gucci box was very small, but perhaps big enough for a nice Gucci watch. Frankie prepared his face to look overwhelmed with gratitude. Slowly, he opened the little box. Inside was a sheaf of Italian lire notes – Frankie's per diem expenses money for the week.

Halfway through making the series we had a break. It was long enough for Diane and me to take a holiday in the Seychelles and – on our return – for me to do a BBC television production of the restoration play, *The Beaux' Stratagem*. Tom Conti and I were the two leads, Sam Wanamaker's daughter Zoë was my love interest – and the rest of the cast was made up mostly of highly regarded members of the Royal Shakespeare Company. I was in awe of all of them – these were seriously classy actors who would most likely look down their talented noses at something as cheerily cheesy as *The Saint* – so I kept my mouth shut about what I was doing and hoped nobody would find out until after we'd finished. I hoped in vain – somebody discovered I was the new Simon Templar and word got round the rehearsal room quickly. Their reaction was the opposite of what I'd feared. The cry went up – and it wasn't an ironic one – 'Please, please, *please* can I be in one?' I suppose when you work almost exclusively on the classics, the idea of romping around doing fight scenes and car chases and saying lines like, 'Cross me one more time, Templar and I'll put you in the morgue!' can be attractive.

Return of the Saint never really ended for me – at least not in any official way – because there was no saying goodbye to the crew, no farewell party, no tears that it was all coming to a halt. The sorry fact was that nobody entertained any idea other than the one in which we'd all be regrouping shortly to start work on the second series. The show was undoubtedly successful. It was popular at home and was selling briskly all around the world. A second series would be cheaper – no more south of France, no more Italy – we'd content ourselves this time round with Elstree Studios and the Southall gas works. Everybody was happy and confident that we would all start up again very soon.

But our boss, Lord Lew Grade, wasn't happy. I got the impression that he wasn't entirely behind our show, a feeling that stemmed from the fact that we never met. The man paying the bills never visited, he never called – the closest I came to him was when Lady Grade asked me to MC a charity raffle she was involved in.

Lord Lew hated the early clothes I'd been put into – he was right about them because they were relentlessly trendy and, within a year, even laughable. When I got into the classical suits Lord Grade demanded I felt more comfortable. He also hated the cost of *Return of the Saint* and couldn't understand why we had to go on location at all when Roger Moore had rarely left Elstree – and the fact that he never said hello to me leads me to believe that he also pretty much hated my portrayal of Simon Templar – in which opinion he wasn't entirely alone.

Most of the English television critics ripped the show to shreds. One or two were kind to me but others weren't. The television watching public, on the other hand, appeared to love it – except for the ones that didn't. Once, when we were shoot-ing in a London street, we attracted the usual crowd of sightseers. I overheard a teenage girl – in a voice dripping with disdain – commenting about me to her teenage companion. 'Yeah, I suppose he's *quite* good-looking . . . in that way my *mother* likes.'

And on another occasion, with a similar crowd of onlookers, a small boy came up to me, peered suspiciously into my face and said, 'Hey, mister – when's the *real* Roger Moore coming, then?'

I met the great Broadway star Elaine Stritch, who was living in England at the time. She had a suite at the Savoy hotel, paying a reduced rate for her rooms on condition that she mentioned that she lived there every time she appeared on a chat show, which was frequently. Miss Stritch, gravel-voiced and belligerent, laid into me about *The Saint*. 'Jesus, kid – at the beginning I thought the show was *godawful*! And you were godawful in it! I swear to God, it was fucking *unwatchable!* But you know what? I stuck with it! I *did* – I stuck with it! And you know what, kid? It got *better!* And by Christ, so did *you!* By the end of the show I thought you were *terrific!* I *did!* Whaddaya say to *that*, huh?'

I said that the episodes she'd watched so adhesively once a week hadn't been shown in the order they'd been filmed – for example, the first one that had aired – an Italian episode with Judy Geeson – had been filmed close to last.

'No – fuckin' impossible!' snarled Miss Stritch. 'I tell ya, kid – ya got better and better!'

I suggested, tactfully, that the inevitable conclusion must be that, rather than the show and I getting steadily better, what had actually happened was that Miss Stritch's critical faculties regarding the show and me had been getting steadily worse.

She seemed nonplussed, which was rare for Elaine Stritch.

While Elaine Stritch's opinion of us changed over time, Lord Grade's didn't. It was also apparent to everybody who dealt with him that his interest in being a television mogul was waning in favour of being a *movie* mogul, perhaps along the lines of a Louis B. Mayer or a Harry Cohn. The effect of this change of heart was that Lord Grade took the profits from all his successful and wildly popular television shows, including mine, and put them into making unsuccessful big budget films with no audience appeal whatsoever. One of them was a movie called *Raise the Titanic*. It was said that when Lord Grade saw the final budget for this horrendously expensive flop he was heard to mutter, 'Raise the *Titanic*? It would have been cheaper to lower the ocean.'

This and other missteps sent his company into financial free-fall and in 1982 it was bought by a South African entrepreneur called Robert Holmes à Court, who promptly fired Grade and the entire staff.

When I heard this I will admit to enjoying a frisson of *schadenfreude*. I was sad and disappointed that it had come to an end. We all were – perhaps no one more so than Bob Baker, who had worked harder than anybody at getting it off the ground. Simon Templar – the Saint – is an extraordinary creation. As a boy, I read all the *Saint* books I could lay my hands on. We all did. Later, when James Bond appeared, we dropped Simon Templar in favour of 007 for one simple reason: Simon Templar didn't do sex; James Bond did, all the time.

But Templar has nothing if not longevity. I made only twenty-five episodes of my series, in comparison to Roger Moore's approximate a hundred and twenty-five of his. But before Roger there had been something like twenty-seven previous Saints in film and radio since the 1930s, including Vincent Price, Tom Conway and George Sanders. The character had been portrayed many times before Roger Moore and I came along and there would be several more Saints after us, including Simon Dutton, Val Kilmer and Adam Rayner.

Because of the extraordinarily iconic nature of the part whoever plays him finds himself, whether he likes it or not, living with the character for the rest of his life. And on the whole, and taking into account all the pros and cons of the thing – I'm glad I was a Saint.

Chapter 15

I've had a marvellous time.

It occurred to me the other day that when I find myself on my death bed (assuming there'll be a bed and not, perhaps, a ten-car pile-up with me at the bottom of it – and, if there is an actual bed, that there'll be enough mental faculties left to me to be able to think about things a bit) I could look back on my life and regret absolutely nothing about it at all.

One hears of poor souls who mutter how they wished they'd done a bit of this, and a lot more of that – and hadn't wasted so much of their lives doing *any* of the other. I won't be muttering any such thing. I've done everything I ever wanted to do, and have avoided doing everything I never wanted anything to do with.

I never wanted to climb mountains or breed cats, so I didn't. I tried being a stand-up comedian once – something I *thought* I wanted to be but then discovered I didn't. It was a charity evening at the Albert Hall and I was the MC. A week before the gala night the organisers asked me if I could possibly see my way to filling in for a couple of minutes while the next act got itself ready? I could use material of my own choosing . . . and I thought, Ahah! Here's my chance to have a go at something I always wanted to try.

I wrote a fabulously funny two minutes and rehearsed them repeatedly in front of the bathroom mirror. I made myself cry with laughter every time. On the actual night I was nervous, but not debilitatingly so. I walked on, found my spotlight and delivered my first excruciatingly witty joke to a packed Albert Hall and three people in the front row tittered politely. After that nobody tittered at all. I performed the rest of my two minutes of gut-busting comedy to a stony silence and then stumbled off, hot with embarrassment. A couple of months later, when the shame had subsided, I started telling the story at dinner parties – as a funny one against myself. At one of these events, Robert Powell was among my audience. When I finished the story – having garnered at least one more laugh than I'd got from a packed Albert Hall – Robert said, 'I was there, that night, you know.'

I said, 'Ah well – then you saw me die a serious death up there, didn't you?' Of course I was expecting Robert to say something along the lines of 'No, no, Ian – you were fine. No, honestly, you were *terrific*.'

Instead Robert, with a degree of glee that I've since found hard to forgive, said, '*I'll* say you did. In fact, you died such a death that I've never seen *anybody* die before.'

So I never tried that again.

But I've tried everything else. I've been what I always wanted to be – an actor for most of my life, with some degree of success; when acting partially dried up for me, I turned my hand to something else I'd always hankered after: I became an author and a playwright. I've written ten books and five plays and had most of them published. I directed some of those plays, and directed others as well, written by better playwrights than me. I've even passed on some of my theatrical experience to American drama students.

I've avoided sports that involved a ball or a puck or a shuttle-cock, while enjoying sports that don't, like skiing and riding and scuba diving – all three of which I did to my heart's content, only stopping doing them when I thought my heart might not be so content any more on account of the coronary it was inviting.

Something else I always wanted to do: I learned to fly a plane.

A big day in my flying course was when I was given a test – to fly solo in an aerial triangle from Denham to Coventry, then on to Southend, and finally back to Denham.

On the first leg all went well for a while until I began to think about how all English fields look the same and where, exactly, was I? Then, mercifully, a big airfield appeared right in front of me, which was obviously Coventry. I radioed their control tower and said I was coming in for a landing and the Coventry traffic controller said, 'Really? Because we can't see you,' – which was just silly of him, because there it was, Coventry Airport, right in front of me. Besides, by this time it was too late to argue because I was on my final approach. I touched down on the runway, light as a feather, and was slow-ing down in anticipation of being complimented on my landing and then being given instructions about where to taxi, when I noticed that the control tower was covered over – top to bottom, windows included – by a thick growth of ivy. Also, there were no other aeroplanes in sight. Also, the Coventry traffic controller didn't reply when I asked him what the hell was going on? I pulled to one side of the runway and taxied to a stop. Then I got out of the cockpit and stood on the wing and stared around me and tried to cover the anxiety I was starting to feel by shading my eyes in the manner of Biggles after a successful sortie against the Huns. A lorry roared up the runway towards me. It stopped twenty feet away and six uniformed men jumped out.

'What the fuck do you think you're doing?' shouted one of them.

'Um . . .' I said, nervously, because there were six of them and uniforms have always impressed me – 'Um – I suppose this isn't Coventry, is it?'

'Coventry? *Coventry?* That's twenty-five miles away! This is Gaydon, mate. Hasn't been an airfield for gawd knows how many years. We test Land Rovers here.'

Then they recognised me, which was both an embarrassment and a relief.

'Oh, blimey – look, it's the fuckin' Saint! And he thinks this is fuckin' Coventry!'

Howls of laughter. They had to cling to one another to stop themselves falling to the tarmac.

I said, 'Am I in trouble?'

'Not with us, mate. We couldn't give a toss. I daresay your flight instructor might be a bit pissed off with you, though.'

I asked what they thought I should do and they suggested I take off and pretend nothing had happened. I said I'd have a hard time explaining why I'd disappeared for a bit. One of them said I could claim I'd been forced to make an emergency landing at a disused airfield because of a bird strike. I said I didn't think that would work at all.

'Course it will! Yeah – start her up, mate, get the prop going round nice and fast and we'll chuck a pigeon at you.'

I took off, explained what had happened to the Coventry control – 'Yes, we wondered what had become of you. *So* glad you didn't crash' – and flew back to Denham – failing that particular test in a spectacular fashion not seen by the Denham flight school before and probably not since either.

I made a parachute jump with the Red Devils, the British Army's parachute regiment display team. Jumping alongside me was the Doctor Who of the day, Colin Baker.

I flew in Concorde. Twice.

In the early 1960s, I travelled in that grand old ship the *Queen Mary*, now permanently docked at Long Beach in California. On the return trip, I travelled in her slightly larger sister ship, the *Queen Elizabeth*, now permanently sunk in Hong Kong harbour.

Thanks to a friendly underground driver called Henry, I rode with my grandson in the driver's cabin of a Northern Line train.

I've been all over the world, except to Australia. And South America. I haven't been there either. Or Japan.

I've had a few very close friends, which are the best kind to have. Nicky Henson and Simon Williams and Julian Holloway have been the closest. And I've loved some remarkable women and some of them have loved me back.

One of the problems associated with writing a memoir is the question about who to include in the story and who to leave out. One of my agents wrote a book about his life and left me – his longest-serving client – out of the thing entirely. I never even got a mention. This was perhaps because, of all his clients,

I was one of the least interesting – to him anyway. So I understood and took only slight umbrage and have left him out of my story too.

Simon Gray included lots of references to me in his published diary, *Unnatural Pursuits*. He sent messages to all of those he'd written about, asking us to read the proofs and let him know if there was anything at all we objected to, or thought was simply untrue – in which case he promised to change it. I felt I came over as a pleasant but slightly fatuous ex-public schoolboy but I had no objection to that. I was more excited about being able to look myself up in his index to worry about the portrayal. (In fact, looking oneself up in the indexes of books that mention you is one of the pleasures of being an actor.) I called Simon up and got his wife Beryl instead. I asked her to pass on the message to Simon that I was perfectly happy with what he'd written about me.

'You mean you *like* the book?' Beryl asked, sounding slightly incredulous.

'Yes – I thought it was fascinating. Why? Don't you?'

'I *hate* it! Or at least I hate the way he's written about himself – he comes over as a whiny, boozed-up incompetent, and he's not that at all. Ugh!'

Objections can come even from people who don't like the way you've written about *yourself*.

I'm inclined to like anything written about me because it means somebody out there has given me a passing thought – friendly or not – and then taken the trouble to write it down; but loving friendships can be lost because of hurt feelings and I don't want to lose any friends. There is equal danger in omitting people from the story as there is in including them – and the greatest risk of enraging your subjects lies in the thorny thickets of love.

I've written briefly about my first marriage and nothing at all about my second because that story belongs in another book set in the USA. But before the first, and between the two, I had love affairs. Some lasted a long time; some were over in a flash. All of them were joyful episodes as far as I was concerned. I behaved badly at the end of some, and was myself hurt at the end of others. A few affairs just atrophied naturally. I've remained good friends with almost all of the women – which is why I won't write about them. I would rather incur their wrath for leaving them out, than incur it for putting them in.

The Queen on the other hand . . .

I worked briefly for the Dunhill company and, in a friendly gesture, they invited me to their tent at Windsor, where they were one of the sponsors of the polo matches held there. I watched a bit of the polo but soon tired of it because all the action seemed to take place on the far side of the field and, at that distance, it just looked like people on horseback searching for their car keys. One of the riders was Prince Charles but he was always so far away it could have been anybody. I wandered back into the tent, where there were about twelve fellow polo-phobes, all clutching champagne stems and all obviously as disenchanted with the match as I was.

Then the Queen came in. Tweeds, headscarf, muddy welling-ton boots. Accompanied by what I assumed was an equerry. I turned away and looked purposely in the other direction – I thought, The poor woman must be so sick of being stared at. Five minutes later I felt a tap on my shoulder. It was the equerry.

'It's Mister Ogilvy, isn't it? Would you like to meet Her Majesty?' he murmured.

I imagined that she'd probably met quite enough people today to want to be bothered with one more so I murmured back, 'No, no – that's perfectly all right, I'm sure she's had enough . . .'

The equerry bent his head a little closer, narrowed his eyes and said, through now-gritted teeth, 'No. I will say it again. Would you like to meet Her Majesty?'

Realising that this was a summons and not an invitation – (and that a summons meant that the Queen must have spotted me across the tent and either recognised me, or thought I might be nice to talk to, or just thought I looked lonely) – I said I'd be delighted. I followed the equerry to the middle of the tent, where the Queen stood alone.

'May I present Mr Ian Ogilvy, ma'am.'

The equerry drifted away. The Queen, who was smaller than I'd imagined her to be, smiled and said how nice it was to meet me. There was a slight pause – and I thought how this poor woman had spent her entire public life hearing of the experiences of others and never having the opportunity to relate any of her own; which is why I did what you're told not to do, which was to ask the Queen a question.

For some reason I remembered the name of the horse she used to ride on ceremonial occasions, and I thought, If there's one thing the Queen likes, it's horses.

'I was wondering, ma'am – whatever happened to Bombardier?'

The porcelain china face lit up and the Wedgwood blue eyes sparkled. 'Oh – my goodness! Well, it's funny you should ask!

Because I've just been to see him! He's very old of course, but he lives here at Windsor, in his own field just half a mile away. I visit him every time I'm here and today was no different. So I went into his field you see, and he came trotting over, as always, because we know each other terribly well, of course – great old friends, in fact – and I always take him a carrot or an apple or something – and I was just giving it to him you see, when I heard this awful snorting and thumping noise and I looked up and there was this huge stallion charging at me! At full gallop! I had no idea what he was doing in Bombardier's field, but here he was, pounding towards me, and his eyes were all red and his ears were laid back and his enormous teeth were bared – just like *this!*' – (and here I claim to be one of the few commoners for whom the Queen has performed her homicidal horse routine) – 'and I knew without a shadow of doubt that he was going to *kill* me so I ran, quite literally *ran*, as fast as I could to the gate and got out just seconds before he attacked me and – well, the fact is – you very nearly lost your sovereign.'

The equerry returned and hovered. He'd probably been watching us and been appalled to see his employer actually talking animatedly to the nobody, rather than listening passively but with feigned fascination while the nobody told her of his adventures in the train on his way to Windsor – and that would never do. I was gently manoeuvred away and the Queen was introduced to somebody else – but I like to think that, for all of a minute and a bit, she got to do something she rarely did and that was to tell an amusing story to a total stranger.

Which is what I hope I've been doing to you.